P9-BVH-386

TREATMENT OF OBSESSIVE-COMPULSIVE DISORDER

CLINICAL APPLICATION OF EVIDENCE-BASED PSYCHOTHERAPY

ꞔ

A Series of Books Edited By

William C. Sanderson

In response to the demands of the new health care environment, there is a movement in psychology (and in all of health care) toward defining empirically supported treatment approaches (i.e., treatments that have been shown to be effective in controlled research studies). The future demands of psychotherapy are becoming clear. In response to pressures from managed care organizations and various practice guidelines, clinicians will be required to implement evidence-based, symptom-focused treatments.

Fortunately, such treatments exist for a variety of the most commonly encountered disorders. However, it has been extremely difficult to disseminate these treatments from clinical research centers, where the treatments are typically developed, to practitioners. More often than not, the level of detail in treatment protocols used in research studies is insufficient to teach a clinician to implement the treatment.

This series, *Clinical Application of Evidence-Based Psychotherapy*, will address this issue. For each disorder covered, empirically supported psychological procedures will be identified. Then, an intensive, step-by-step, session-by-session treatment application will be provided. A detailed clinical vignette will be woven throughout, including session transcripts.

All books in this series are written by experienced clinicians who have applied the treatments to a wide variety of patients, and have supervised and taught other clinicians how to apply them.

Social Phobia:
Clinical Application of Evidence-Based Psychotherapy
Ronald Rapee and William C. Sanderson

Overcoming Shyness and Social Phobia:
A Step-by-Step Guide
Ronald Rapee

Specific Phobias:
Clinical Applications of Evidence-Based Psychotherapy
Timothy J. Bruce and William C. Sanderson

Cognitive-Behavioral Treatment of Depression
Janet S. Klosko and William C. Sanderson

Marital Distress:
Cognitive Behavioral Interventions for Couples
Jill H. Rathus and William C. Sanderson

Treatment of Obsessive-Compulsive Disorder
Lata K. McGinn and William C. Sanderson

ꞔ

TREATMENT OF OBSESSIVE-COMPULSIVE DISORDER

Lata K. McGinn, Ph.D.

William C. Sanderson, Ph.D.

JASON ARONSON INC.
Northvale, New Jersey
London

This book was set in 12 pt. Fairfield Light by Alpha Graphics of Pittsfield, New Hampshire, and printed and bound by Book-mart Press, Inc. of North Bergen, NJ.

Copyright © 1999 by Jason Aronson Inc.

10 9 8 7 6 5 4 3 2 1

Library of Congress Cataloging-in-Publication Data
McGinn, Lata K.
     Treatment of obsessive-compulsive disorder / Lata K. McGinn,
William C. Sanderson.
          p.   cm.
     Includes bibliographical references and index.
     ISBN 0-7657-0211-8
     1. Obsessive-compulsive disorder—Treatment. I. Sanderson,
William C. II. Title.
     RC533.M425 1999
     616.85'22706—dc21   98-54404

Printed in the United States of America on acid-free paper. For information and catalog write to Jason Aronson Inc., 230 Livingston Street, Northvale, NJ 07647-1726, or visit our website: www.aronson.com

To my parents, for everything.
—Lata K. McGinn

This book is dedicated to my wife and children: Lynn, Kristen, and Billy, who have provided me with life's ultimate reward.
—William C. Sanderson

৵ Contents ৵

Foreword		ix
Preface		xi
Acknowledgments		xiii
1	A Cognitive-Behavioral Model of Obsessive-Compulsive Disorder	1
2	Session 1: Assessment	15
3	Session 2: Psychoeducation	47
4	Session 3: Cognitive Restructuring (Phase I)	77
5	Session 4: Cognitive Restructuring (Phase II)	109
6	Session 5: Exposure and Response Prevention (Phase I)	153
7	Session 6: Exposure and Response Prevention (Phase II)	203
8	Session 7: Exposure and Response Prevention (Phase III)	233
9	Session 8: Maintaining Gains and Preventing Relapse	257
	References	273
	Index	289

✌ Foreword ✌

There has been an explosion in the interest in the interest in literature on cognitive and behavior therapy during the past two decades. To a large degree, the increasing interest in cognitive behavior therapy (CBT) is due to the accumulation of a substantial body of research demonstrating the efficacy of these treatments for a wide range of disorders. In addition, the demands of managed care have increased practitioners' interest in short-term treatments.

Although research on cognitive behavior therapy continues to accumulate at a rapid rate, training in and dissemination of these approaches has lagged behind. For example, despite being the only empirically supported psychotherapeutic approach for OCD (see Chambless et al. 1997), at present only 41 percent of graduate psychology programs have training available in this approach (Crits-Christoph et al. 1996). As a result, many practitioners seek out books on cognitive behavior therapy in an effort to fill this gap in their training. However, despite the growth of books available, many do not provide the detail necessary to implement treatment effectively, especially for those with no prior training in the general CBT philosophy. Although no book can substitute for supervision and must ultimately be supplemented by it, there is clearly a need for dissemination of "how-to" treatment manuals, and Drs. Lata McGinn and Bill Sanderson have provided it with utmost skill and mastery.

The strength in this book lies in its ability to provide the clinician with session-by-session details allowing for the successful implementation of treatment. Richly detailed transcripts woven throughout the book will leave the clinician with a precise sense of what to say, what to do, what to assess, and so forth. In addition, Drs. McGinn and Sanderson tackle difficult situations that are likely to come up during treatment, thereby allowing for a full appreciation of the complexity of treatment. The case illustrations throughout provide an excellent depiction of what takes place during treatment, allowing the reader to "watch" the implementation of the various strategies.

A unique contribution of this book is its integration of the recent advances in utilizing cognitive restructuring with the traditional behavioral strategies for the treatment of obsessive-compulsive disorder. A growing body of research now supports the use of cognitive therapy as an effective treatment for OCD, and I am delighted to see these techniques recognized and applied successfully to this very difficult clinical problem. Drs. McGinn and Sanderson have succeeded admirably in their goal to educate and train clinicians in the cognitive behavioral treatment of obsessive-compulsive disorder.

Aaron T. Beck, M.D.
University Professor Emeritus
Department of Psychiatry
University of Pennsylvania
July 1999

✎ Preface ✎

Innovations in cognitive-behavioral therapies and the advent of serotonergic antidepressants have dramatically improved the chances of successful treatment for individuals with obsessive-compulsive disorder. Although many articles and books have been written on behavior therapy, no book or manual has yet emphasized a treatment combining cognitive and behavior therapies. This book is the first to describe a complete cognitive behavior treatment and as such combines psychoeducation and cognitive restructuring with traditional exposure and response prevention techniques. The techniques described were primarily developed by Aaron Beck, Edna Foa, Paul Salkovskis, and Gail Steketee; thus we have drawn on their previous work. However, since clinical applications of these techniques form the bulk of this book, we have also added and modified some features when needed. For example, we begin with psychoeducation, a component of many cognitive behavior therapies. Additionally, in later chapters, we outline specific strategies to help patients engage in response prevention.

This book encompasses a detailed session-by-session guide that will provide clinicians with a template for treatments they administer, from the assessment phase to the conclusion of treatment. Not only do clinicians learn how to assess and treat obsessive-compulsive disorder using cognitive behavior therapy (e.g., How is cognitive restructuring conducted?) but they actually witness the decision-making process that therapists face in each session (What should I say now? Should I restructure the thought now or merely trace the automatic thought? How do I decide whether I should do imaginal exposure?). Other books have gone as far as to describe components of treatment and have even provided a clinical snapshot of what occurs in therapy. We believe that this book is akin to a videotape of a complete therapy, illustrating exactly how it takes place in a clinician's office.

We feel that there is an immense need for a book like this, particularly in light of the changes occurring in managed care that require clinicians to offer short-term, effective treatments more often than they ever have before. We hope that this book fills in the gaps in the current literature and provides clinicians with a glimpse of treatment as it is conducted in our office.

Some facts require explanation before we begin. The case example depicted in the book is not based on any one patient but instead represents a composite of several individuals and patients with obsessive-compulsive disorder. Second, although the case example and the therapist woven throughout the book are both designated as female, no bias is intended by this fact. The case was written from the perspective of the first author, who is female, and the case example was designated as such entirely by the result of an unfolding creative process. To present some balance, all general case examples have been designated as male. Finally, the term *patient* is used instead of *client*, since that is the term used within our work settings.

✐ Acknowledgment ✐

I am deeply indebted to everyone who has been directly or indirectly involved with the writing of this book. I would like to acknowledge Martin P. Seligman, whose work first piqued my interest in psychology, Aaron T. Beck, who has been and continues to be my ultimate source of inspiration, and Dianne Chambless, for giving me my first glimpse of cognitive behavior therapy. I would also like to acknowledge Edna Foa, Gail Steketee, and Paul Salkovskis, whose pioneering work on cognitive-behavioral treatments of obsessive-compulsive disorder have been described in this book, as well as my patients, who, in triumphing over their symptoms, have enabled me to become a better psychotherapist.

I would like to thank T. Byram Karasu, Chairman of the Psychiatry Department at Albert Einstein College of Medicine, for providing me with the academic freedom to write this book, and all my colleagues at Montefiore Medical Center for supporting me through all my academic endeavors: Gregory Asnis, Judy Berenson, George Como, Estelle Herschfeld, Margaret Kaplan, Alec Miller, Nancy Ruiz, Bruce Schwartz, and Scott Wetzler. I would like to especially acknowledge William Sanderson, who has been an invaluable mentor, colleague, and friend over the years, and add a special note of thanks to Scott Parker, Warren Tryon, and Jeffrey Young, from whom I have learned a great deal.

I would like to give my deepest thanks to my parents and sisters, whose influence on my life has been immeasurable, and to my friends and in-laws, who understood that the book came first. Finally, I would like to thank my husband, Tom, for being endlessly patient, understanding and flexible when yet another weekend was spent writing, and my daughter, Ariana, born in the midst of writing, for giving me the time I needed to finish this book.

Lata K. McGinn
Albert Einstein College of Medicine
Bronx, New York

First, I would like to acknowledge the individuals who have been directly involved and have had the most significant influence in my professional development: David H. Barlow, Aaron T. Beck, Susan G. O'Leary, and Jeffrey Young. I would also like to acknowledge T. Byram Karasu, Chairman of the Psychiatry Department at Albert Einstein College of Medicine, who has provided me with the opportunity to be productive in my academic endeavors. Numerous colleagues have served as collaborators, advisers, and friends over the years, including Greg Asnis, Tim Bruce, Janet Klosko, Alec Miller, Lata McGinn, Ron Rapee, Jill Rathus, and Scott Wetzler. Finally, I would also like to acknowledge the many patients I have treated who have provided me with the motivation and challenge to evolve as a psychotherapist.

William C. Sanderson
Rutgers University
Piscataway, New Jersey

CHAPTER

1

A Cognitive-Behavioral
Model of Obsessive-
Compulsive Disorder

INTRODUCTION

The *DSM-IV* (APA 1994) defines obsessions as "persistent and recurrent thoughts, ideas, images, or impulses that are experienced as intrusive and inappropriate, that are not simply excessive worries about real-life problems, and that cause marked anxiety or distress (e.g., thoughts of killing a child, becoming contaminated). The person recognizes that they are a product of his own mind and attempts to suppress or ignore the obsessions or to neutralize them with some other thought or action" (p. 422). Compulsions are defined as "repetitive behaviors (e.g., checking the stove, handwashing) or mental acts (e.g., praying silently, counting numbers) that the person feels driven to perform in response to an obsession or according to rigid rules. The compulsion is aimed at preventing or reducing distress or preventing some dreaded situation; however, the compulsions are either unrealistic or clearly excessive" (p. 423) (see Table 1–1 for complete *DSM-IV* criteria).

Three major differences are noted between the *DSM-III-R* (APA 1987) and the *DSM-IV* (Riggs and Foa 1993). First, insight into illness is no longer necessary for the diagnosis so long as the excessiveness or senselessness of obsessions and compulsions is recognized at some point during the course of the disorder. Second, compulsions are now recognized as behavioral *or* mental events, whereas previously compulsions were noted as only behavioral events and obsessions were considered to be mental events. Finally, the functional relationship between obsessions and compulsions is now further elaborated in the *DSM-IV*. Originally proposed by Foa and Tillmans (1980), the functional model of obsessive-compulsive disorder (OCD) suggests that obsessions increase anxiety while compulsions are performed in order to reduce the anxiety generated by the obsessions. Hence, mental events that increase anxiety (e.g., images of mother dying) would be classified as obsessions while mental events (repeating "I love mother") or behavioral events (check-

Table 1–1. *DSM-IV* Definition

A. Requires the presence of either obsessions or compulsions:

Obsessions (as defined by 1, 2, 3, and 4)

1. Recurrent and persistent thoughts, ideas, impulses, or images that are experienced at some time during the disturbance as intrusive and inappropriate and that cause marked anxiety or distress.
2. The thoughts, impulses, or images are not simply excessive worries about real-life problems.
3. The person attempts to ignore or suppress the obsessions or to neutralize them with some other thought or action.
4. The person recognizes that the obsessional thoughts, impulses, or images are a product of his or her own mind (*not imposed from without as in thought insertion*).

Compulsions (as defined by 1 and 2):

1. Repetitive behaviors (*e.g., handwashing*) or mental acts (*e.g., praying silently*) that the person feels driven to perform in response to an obsession or according to rigid rules.
2. Behaviors or mental acts are aimed at preventing or reducing distress or preventing some dreaded situation; however, these behaviors or mental acts are not connected in a realistic way with what they are designed to neutralize or prevent or are clearly excessive.

B. At some point during the course of the disorder, the person has recognized that the obsessions are excessive or unreasonable Note: this does not apply to children.

C. Obsessions or compulsions are severe enough to cause marked distress, are time-consuming (*i.e., take more than one hour a day*), or significantly interfere with the person's normal routine, occupational (or academic) functioning, or usual social activities or relationships.

D. If another Axis I disorder is present, the obsessions and compulsions cannot be restricted to the content of that disorder (*e.g., preoccupation with food in the presence of Eating Disorders; hair pulling in the presence of Trichotillomania; concern with appearance in the presence of Body Dysmorphic Disorder; preoccupation with having a serious illness in the presence of Hypochondriasis; preoccupation with sexual urges in the presence of a Paraphilia; or guilty ruminations in the presence of Major Depressive Disorder*).

Table 1–1. (*Continued*)

E. The disturbance is not due to the direct physiological effects of a substance (*e.g., a drug of abuse, a medication*), or a general medical condition.

Specify if:

With Poor Insight: If, for most of the time during the current episode, the person does not recognize that the obsessions and compulsions are excessive or unreasonable.

Reprinted with permission from the *Diagnostic and Statistical Manual of Mental Disorders, Fourth Edition*. Washington, DC: American Psychiatric Association, 1994.

ing the gas stove) that reduce anxiety would now be classified as compulsions.

Confirmation for the functional model of OCD comes from several sources. Studies have demonstrated that obsessions are associated with increased anxiety and discomfort. For example, obsessions have been found to increase heart rate and alter skin conductance to a greater degree than do neutral thoughts (Boulougouris et al. 1977, Rabavilas and Boulougouris 1974). In addition, touching contaminated objects has been found to increase heart rate, the subjective experience of anxiety (Hodgson and Rachman 1972), and skin conductance (Hornsveld et al. 1979). Conversely, studies have demonstrated that performing handwashing and checking rituals in response to an urge to ritualize leads to decreases in anxiety (Hodgson and Rachman 1972, Hornsveld et al. 1979, Roper and Rachman 1976, Roper et al. 1973).

COGNITIVE-BEHAVIORAL MODELS OF OBSESSIVE-COMPULSIVE DISORDER

In order to understand what symptoms become the focus of cognitive-behavioral treatment and why certain treatment components are used to remediate these symptoms, an understanding of the theoretical assumptions behind the cognitive-behavioral treatment (CBT) model is necessary.

Behavioral Models

Two-Stage Theory: A Classical/Operant Conditioning Model

Mowrer's two-stage theoretical model of the acquisition and maintenance of fear and avoidance behaviors (Mowrer 1939, 1960) has been further elaborated to explain the onset and maintenance of symptoms in anxiety disorders and OCD (Dollard and Miller 1950). This model proposes that a stimulus that does not automatically elicit anxiety or fear (*a neutral stimulus*) becomes associated with a stimulus (*an unconditioned stimulus* or *UCS*) that naturally elicits anxiety or fear (*an unconditioned response* or *UCR*) by being paired with it. Through this pairing, the previously neutral stimulus (*the conditioned stimulus* or *CS*) now becomes conditioned or capable of eliciting fear or anxiety on its own (*the conditioned response* or *CR*). For example, John may become anxious if he smells gas after he receives third-degree burns in a fire at a gas station. Because the smell of gas becomes associated with being burned (UCS), it now becomes capable of eliciting fear on its own (CS).

In explaining how fear or anxiety maintains itself, the model proposes the following. The individual develops avoidance and escape behaviors (e.g., retreats when he smells gas) in order to reduce the anxiety elicited by the conditioned stimulus (gas), and by doing so is negatively reinforced by the cessation of anxiety which follows. In other words, despite the fact that the CS (gas) is no longer paired with the initial traumatic stimulus or UCS (being burned), the conditioned fear response continues because the individual is negatively reinforced by the experience of reduced anxiety that follows the escape or avoidance behaviors. As a result, the individual never learns that the CS is not dangerous in and of itself. The fear response does not extinguish because the individual does not learn that the CS is no longer being paired with the UCS.

In specifically explaining the onset of OCD, the two-stage model suggests that obsessive fears, which take the form of recurrent and intrusive thoughts, images, ideas, or impulses, also develop via this conditioning process. For example, neutral objects such as toilet seats or knives may begin to create discomfort because they are initially paired with an anxiety-provoking event. However, because obsessions are intrusive, passive avoidance and escape behaviors are usually insufficient to alleviate the anxiety associated with their arousal. Hence, compulsive or ritualized behaviors are developed by individuals in order to reduce the anxiety created by the conditioned stimulus (in this case, the obsessions), and are maintained by their success in doing so.

Evidence for Mowrer's two-stage theory of the development of fear is insufficient. Not only do a majority of patients with anxiety disorders, including OCD, deny a link between symptom onset and specific traumatic events (Rachman and Wilson 1980), but also this model does not take into account other modes of onset reported by patients such as *informational learning* (e.g., becoming fearful of germs after hearing about a news report on the breakout of *E.coli* among schoolchildren) or *observational learning* (growing up with a parent who is constantly afraid of catching a disease) (Foa and Kozak 1986).

By contrast, there is far more support for Mowrer's two-stage conceptualization of the maintenance of fear. Studies have demonstrated that environmental cues trigger anxiety (Hodgson and Rachman 1972, Hornsveld et al. 1979) and that obsessions increase distress (Boulougouris et al. 1977, Rabavilas and Boulougouris 1974). Research has also demonstrated that performing handwashing and checking rituals following an urge to ritualize leads to decreases in anxiety (Hodgson and Rachman 1972, Hornsveld et al. 1979, Roper and Rachman 1976, Roper et al. 1973).

Cognitive Theories

Although several cognitive theories have been used to explain OCD symptoms (A. Beck 1976, Beech and Liddell 1974, Carr 1974, Foa and Kozak 1985, Guidano and Liotti 1983, McFall and Wollershein 1979, Pitman 1987, Reed 1985, Salkovskis 1985, Warren and Zgourides 1991, Wegner 1989), the two most comprehensive cognitive theories are described here in some detail (Foa and Kozak 1985, Salkovskis 1985). For a summary account of other cognitive theories, interested readers are invited to read Jakes 1996, Riggs and Foa 1993, or Steketee 1993.

Foa and Kozak's Information Processing Model

Based on Lang's model (1979), Foa and Kozak conceive of fear as an "information network" that exists in memory (Foa and Kozak 1985). This memory network contains representations about fear cues, fear responses, and their meaning. According to them, all anxiety disorders have the following impairments in these networks: (1) faulty estimate of threat (e.g., perceiving danger or threat when there is objectively none); (2) excessive negative "valence" for the feared event (excessive degree of affective response); (3) extreme response to danger or threat (physiological reactivity); and (4) persistence of fears (continuing to perceive danger despite evidence to the contrary).

Foa and Kozak (1985) suggest that although all anxiety disorders involve specific impairments in the memory network, OCD differs from other anxiety disorders in that inferential judgments about harm appear to be impaired. Accordingly, an individual suffering from OCD will conclude that an event or situation is dangerous unless it is proven safe without a doubt. Furthermore, even if information suggests that a situation is not dangerous, or even if harm does not occur after exposure to a certain event or situation, individuals with OCD still fail to learn from direct experience and will not conclude that the particular event or situation is safe. As a result, rituals designed to reduce the occurrence of harm do not provide ultimate safety and must be performed repeatedly.

Foa and Kozak also indicate that specific types of fears are unique to obsessive-compulsive disorder (Riggs and Foa 1993). Some individuals with OCD develop excessive connections between anxiety and a particular stimulus (e.g., a garbage can), and overestimate the threat of harm related to the feared stimulus (I will catch a disease if I take out the garbage). Other individuals fear the meaning of certain situations (books should always be lined up in order of height) and not the stimulus itself (a book). In other words, in this case it is the asymmetry that induces the anxiety and not the books themselves.

While there is some support for the notion that individuals with OCD tend to overestimate threat, no clear evidence yet exists to suggest that they exhibit a stronger negative valence for feared situations (Steketee 1993), and preliminary research disproves the observation that individuals with OCD have higher physiological reactivity than normals (Foa et al. 1991). Other theoretical propositions espoused by Foa and Kozak (1985), such as persistence of fear, have yet to be tested.

Salkovskis's Cognitive Model

According to this model (Salkovskis 1985, 1989), intrusive obsessional thoughts by themselves do not lead to increased anxiety or distress. However, in individuals with OCD whose belief systems are characterized by responsibility and self-blame, such thoughts trigger (secondary) negative automatic thoughts, and it is these negative automatic thoughts that lead to increased anxiety or distress. For example, an individual who has intrusive thoughts about his mother getting stabbed will experience increased anxiety or distress only if he has underlying beliefs such as "only bad people have aggressive impulses toward their parents," or "my mother will die if I have obsessions about her death." Such beliefs may be more likely to give rise to negative evaluative thoughts such as "I am a terrible person for imagining that my mother will be stabbed to death" when the intrusive thoughts occur. In other words, obsessive thoughts lead to anxiety because they are appraised negatively. In this model, ritualized or compulsive behaviors are performed in order to reduce this sense of responsibility and self-blame, and in doing so reduce the distress associated with the obsessions.

According to Salkovskis (1985), the OCD patient's exaggerated sense of responsibility and self-blame is characterized by the following dysfunctional assumptions:

(1) having a thought about an action is like performing the action; (2) failing to prevent (or failing to try to prevent) harm to self or others is the same as having caused the harm in the first place; (3) responsibility is not attenuated by other factors (such as low probability of occurrence); (4) not neutralizing when an intrusion has occurred is similar or equivalent to seeking or wanting the harm involved in that intrusion to happen; and (5) one should (and can) exercise control over one's thoughts. [p. 579]

Preliminary research supports Salkovskis's (1989) contention that individuals with OCD have an increased sense of responsibility and self-blame regarding harm. However, critics argue that appraisals and neutralizing behaviors do not, in and of themselves, explain why obsessions become abnormal; they further contend that the proposed themes of responsibility and self-blame explain some obsessive-compulsive themes (such as aggressive, sexual, or blasphemous thoughts) better than others (contamination fears and cleaning rituals) (Jakes 1996). Finally, critics also note that a successful intervention (reducing the sense of responsibility and self-blame) does not imply causation (that an increased sense of responsibility caused the obsessions to occur in the first place) (Jakes 1996).

TREATMENT RATIONALE AND COMPONENTS

Symptoms treated within a cognitive-behavioral framework include the obsessive thoughts, images, impulses, or urges, as well as the compulsions, which may take the form of ritualized thoughts or behaviors. Also targeted in treatment are the secondary automatic thoughts that develop among patients with obsessive-compulsive disorder (e.g., I am a bad person for having such thoughts). Essentially, the two primary goals of cognitive-behavioral strategies (psychoeducation, cognitive restructuring, exposure, and response prevention) are (1) to alleviate the anxiety associated with obsessions, thereby reducing the frequency and persistence of these thoughts, images, impulses, or urges, and (2) to break the association between compulsions and the subsequent feelings of relief or reduced anxiety.

Psychoeducation and cognitive restructuring are used to normalize the obsessions and compulsions. In *psychoeducation*, the patient is directly educated about the disorder, including the definition, demographics, etiology, treatment, and so on, in order to alleviate the sense of shame that most patients carry around with them. It enables them to learn that they are suffering from a psychiatric illness and that there are many other individuals with the same problem.

Cognitive restructuring (A. Beck 1976, J. Beck 1995, Salkovskis and Kirk 1997) attempts to restructure the secondary dysfunctional automatic thoughts (e.g., I am a bad person for having such thoughts) that individuals with OCD have following their obsessional images, thoughts, urges, or impulses (images of mother being stabbed). As dysfunctional assumptions and beliefs are challenged and substituted with more rational ones (Having a thought about my mother being stabbed does not mean I am a bad person, I love my mother, and I cannot control all the thoughts that pass through my head), the anxiety regarding the obsessions themselves is believed to decline. Ultimately, this leads to a decline in the occurrence of obsessions because the resulting anxiety that fuels the obsessions has declined. In other words, as more rational beliefs and assumptions become internalized, the anxiety regarding the obsessions declines, and the obsessions themselves occur less frequently.

Exposure techniques (Riggs and Foa 1993, Steketee 1993) attempt to break the association between obsessions and anxiety by directly exposing patients to the anxiety triggers rather than by challenging the dysfunctional automatic thoughts that follow obsessions (cognitive restructuring). In systematic exposure, individuals are exposed over a prolonged period of time to specific phobic stimuli (e.g., taking garbage out) that trigger their anxiety about their obsessions (I will get germs and die from salmonella poisoning if I take the garbage out), until their anxiety reaction is eliminated (habituation). Eventually, because the phobic stimulus is not followed by the feared consequence (the individual is not covered with germs, does not get salmonella poisoning and die), patients become habituated (or nonreactive) to the previously feared stimuli (can take the garbage out with reduced or no anxiety). Because this exposure is done in a systematic, hierarchical fashion, patients learn to tolerate manageable levels of anxiety as they confront low-grade phobic situations and then ultimately face more anxiety-provoking stimuli. The success of exposure is attributed to the fact that as patients tolerate prolonged confrontation with these anxiety triggers without trying to escape or to neutralize the thought with some other thought or action, they learn that their catastrophic fears do not occur and, as a result, their anxiety associated with these obsessions ultimately dissipates. As they become habituated to these obsessions, patients experience a reduction in obsessive thoughts.

Response prevention techniques (Riggs and Foa 1993, Steketee 1993) attempt to block ritualized behaviors or thoughts, with the goal of breaking the association between ritualized behaviors and thoughts and the subsequent feelings of relief or reduced anxiety. This technique involves the blocking of compulsions (e.g., leaving the kitchen without allowing the compulsive behavior of checking the stove).

Patients are given a rationale for response prevention, presented with specific rules, and are generally assisted by family members to comply. If possible, response prevention begins in the first treatment session. By the end of treatment, patients are presented with guidelines for "normal behavior" because many do not know what constitutes normal behavior (what amount of handwashing is appropriate).

Data from *DSM-IV* field trials indicate that compulsive thoughts or behaviors do not occur without obsessive thoughts (Riggs and Foa 1993). Hence, for patients who present with ritualized thoughts or behaviors, treatment strategies used to reduce ritualized thoughts or behaviors should be used in conjunction with strategies designed to address obsessive thoughts.

Session 1: Assessment

| | *Check* |
Session Goals	*When Done*

1. The Session ☐
   - Formulate agenda for the current session
   - Build therapeutic alliance
   - Establish the diagnosis
     - ( ) Principal
     - ( ) Comorbid
   - Collect following information
     - ( ) Diagnosis and severity of illness
     - ( ) Anxiety triggers (external and internal)
     - ( ) Feared consequences
     - ( ) Avoidance behaviors
     - ( ) Ritualized thoughts and behaviors
     - ( ) Degree of insight
     - ( ) Mood
     - ( ) Onset and course of disorder
     - ( ) Prior treatments
     - ( ) Patient motivations and expectations of treatment
     - ( ) Determining treatment eligibility
   - Present findings

2. Next Week (5 minutes) ☐
   - Discuss homework to be completed (self-report questionnaires and forms)
   - Anticipate potential stressors that may occur during the week

CASE EXAMPLE

Allison is a 24-year-old woman who presented to our anxiety clinic for treatment after her husband threatened to leave her if she did not obtain psychiatric treatment. Upon evaluation, it became evident that Allison had become stricken with what she called her "mind fever" as a teenager. At 16, she had become so preoccupied with becoming "diseased" from "ticks and bacteria," that she not only stopped attending high school but avoided leaving her house. She had also begun washing her hands multiple times a day and had begun wearing gloves to attend to the simplest of household chores. She remembers a few years where her symptoms became less severe and more under her control, allowing her to socialize and conduct her activities of daily living. She met her husband around this time, and within a year they were married. Allison remembers a resurgence of symptoms two years following her marriage when she was getting ready to attend her first semester in college. In addition to her obsessions about ticks and bacteria, she now began having violent, horrific images of her husband dying or becoming maimed. Her handwashing behaviors increased but, most significantly, Allison now began to ritualistically repeat a series of numbers (e.g., "6, 6, 6, 6, 6, 6") and phrases ("God is mighty," "mercy, mercy") fairly continuously throughout the day. Her husband, Michael, reported that she seemed to be in a fantasy world pretty much all day. She dropped out of college during her first semester, could not leave the house without Michael, stopped cooking ("I can't touch knives") and cleaning ("I feel the ticks will latch onto my skin and I won't even know it"). A few months before she presented to our clinic for treatment, she had become increasingly depressed and reliant on her husband. She would become hysterical if Michael did not come home exactly on time, if he went to the gym after work, or traveled out of town on business. She called him multiple times a day at work to check if he was all right, to the point that Michael began avoiding her calls at work. Things came to a head when Michael was required to attend a work-related conference in Philadelphia but could not go because Allison became tearful, agitated, and out of control. She locked herself in her bedroom weeping hysterically until Michael promised that he would not leave town. A few weeks later, Allison was brought to our Anxiety Clinic by her husband, and was diagnosed with obsessive-compulsive disorder.

SESSION OVERVIEW

During the first session, the therapist confirms the principal diagnosis, rules out other diagnoses, and ascertains if the patient has additional problems or comorbid conditions that may need to become the focus of treatment. The rest of the time is spent in collecting the necessary information that will help the therapist design the treatment sessions. Although this phase is described as occurring over one session for purposes of illustration, information gathering may take up to two to three sessions to complete. Much of the information is obtained via clinical interview, during which the therapist asks the patient a series of structured questions about the patient's symptomatology, onset, family history, level of functioning, and so on. However, the clinical interview is supplemented by self-report questionnaires and forms that the patient is asked to complete.

As the therapist gathers the necessary content, she also focuses on building a therapeutic alliance with the patient. The interaction between the therapist and patient during this session is particularly critical since it will help the patient make a decision about whether or not to begin therapy and will set a tone for future sessions.

THE SESSION:
BUILDING A THERAPEUTIC ALLIANCE

Although a tremendous quantity of information needs to be gathered prior to treatment, it is imperative to note that building a therapeutic alliance in the first session is just as crucial. This session lays the groundwork for all future sessions. Patients with OCD want to know that you care, listen, understand, accept them without judgment, and, above all, that you are qualified to treat them and their disorder. Although most patients with anxiety disorders feel anxious when they first come in for therapy, patients with OCD, because of the nature of their illness, are far more likely to feel a deep sense of shame, guilt, or embarrassment regarding their symptoms. In the first session, Allison expressed her shame at having images of her husband being killed or maimed: "I know I love him, so why do I think such terrible things about him? A therapist once told me that this meant that I was angry at him, that I unconsciously wanted him to die. If that's true, I'm a bad person and I deserve to go to hell."

Due to the bizarre nature of many symptoms, OCD patients are often initially fearful that the therapist will perceive them to be crazy. As Allison put it, "I was afraid that you would lock me up in a nuthouse, and throw away the key. How many people do you know that go around counting numbers all day?" In fact, it is important that therapists react with composure no matter how bizarre or strange the symptoms appear (e.g., feeling that one might accidentally strangle a child); otherwise the patient may begin to withhold crucial information and reduce the efficacy of treatment. Toward that goal, therapists must familiarize themselves with the range of obsessive-compulsive symptoms before they begin OCD treatment (Yale-Brown Obsessive-Compulsive Scale [Y-BOCS]; Goodman et al. 1989c).

OCD patients are likely to be secretive of their symptoms: consequently, careful questioning without judgment is crucial in obtaining the information. For example, although Allison told her therapist about her obsessive images of her husband being killed or maimed, it was not until the third session that she finally revealed that, in many of her images, she pictured herself inflicting the harm. Her shame and fear of being perceived as immoral or of having others perceive her obsessive thoughts as unconscious wishes kept her silent until she felt she could trust her therapist. Allison's thoughts were normalized, and she was assured that many patients with OCD presented with similar symptoms.

ESTABLISHING THE DIAGNOSIS

Principal Diagnosis

The first session should be used to establish the diagnosis of OCD. Differential diagnoses are ruled out before a principal Axis I diagnosis of OCD is given (see Table 2–1 for ways to differentiate OCD from other Axis I disorders). The essential features of obsessive-compulsive disorder are *obsessions* (recurrent and persistent thoughts, ideas, impulses, or images that are experienced at some time during the disturbance as intrusive and inappropriate, and that cause marked anxiety or distress), and *compulsions* (repetitive behaviors or mental acts that the person feels driven to perform in response to an obsession or according to rigid rules). To warrant the diagnosis of OCD in accordance with the *DSM-IV*, the individual (1) may have either obsessions or compulsions, (2) must recognize at some point during the course of the disorder that the symptoms are senseless or excessive, and (3) must have symptoms severe enough to cause marked distress or impairment in functioning or must be time consuming (take more than one hour a day).

Based on the Structured Interview for the DSM-III-R (SCID-P) (Spitzer et al. 1992), Allison was given a principal Axis I diagnosis of Obsessive Compulsive Disorder. To assess for the severity and content of her symptoms, the Y-BOCS (Goodman et al. 1989b, Goodman et al. 1989c) was administered (she received a score of

Table 2–1. Differentiating Obsessive-Compulsive Disorder from Other Axis I Diagnoses

Differential diagnoses	What needs to be distinguished	How to tell the difference
Depression	Depressive ruminations versus obsessions	Patients with OCD try to suppress obsessions while depressed patients do not suppress their ruminations.
Specific Phobia	Phobic avoidance exhibited by both	Although both may fear and avoid similar things (e.g., needles), they perceive danger in different ways. Essentially, the danger perceived in OCD is far more intrusive (fear that they will get contaminated by a needle) than in specific phobia (pain of injection). As a result, escape or avoidance works to reduce the fear experienced in specific phobia (e.g., escaping from the doctor's office), although it is not as effective in OCD (What if the contaminant on the needles is still on my hands?). Hence, ritualized acts develop to reduce the anxiety where escape and avoidance failed.
Generalized Anxiety Disorder	Worries versus obsessions	Worries are usually more reality based and appropriate in content (What if my son is mugged on the way back home?), while obsessions are usually more unrealistic and inappropriate (What if I accidentally poison my son if I cook for him?), or are far more greatly exaggerated. In the event that obsessions are about real-life circumstances, the distinction may be made by presence or absence of compulsions.

Table 2–1. (*Continued*)

Differential diagnoses	What needs to be distinguished	How to tell the difference
	Checking rituals occasionally present in GAD	If checking rituals are present in GAD, they are usually related to safety or illness. In addition, GAD rituals are usually cognitive in nature and tend not to involve the washing, checking, and counting rituals typically observed in OCD.
Hypochondriasis	Illness-related concerns versus obsessive concerns with somatic content	The distinction is best made by determining the presence or absence of compulsions since compulsions are more commonly present in OCD. The differential may also be made by determining the presence of *other* obsessions or compulsions.
	Somatic checking rituals and repeated requests for reassurance exhibited by both	If the patient presents with somatic obsessions only and has somatic checking rituals, including repeated requests for reassurance that are designed to alleviate the anxiety associated with these somatic concerns, the differential is difficult.
Body Dysmorphic Disorder	Obsessive preoccupation with an imagined physical defect versus obsessions about physical blemishes	The distinction may be made by determining the presence or absence of compulsions since compulsions occur more commonly in OCD. The differential may also be made by determining the presence of *other* obsessions or compulsions.
	Compulsive checking behavior exhibited by both	If the patient only has obsessive fears about physical defects and has checking rituals, including repeated requests for reassurance that are designed to alleviate the anxiety associated with these concerns, the differential is difficult.

Tourette's and Tic Disorders	Stereotyped motor behaviors versus compulsive rituals	Stereotyped motor behaviors that characterize tics and Tourette's are involuntary and are not designed to alleviate anxiety associated with obsessions.
Delusional Disorder	Nonbizarre delusions involving real-life situations versus obsessions that have delusional intensity	The distinction is best made by determining the presence or absence of compulsions since a majority of people with OCD experience both obsessions and compulsions, while most with delusional disorder do not exhibit compulsive rituals.
Schizophrenia	Schizophrenic delusions versus obsessions with particularly bizarre content (e.g., I will be infected by the the city of Atlanta just by reading about it in the paper)	The distinction is best made by determining if the patient has other symptoms of schizophrenia such as loose associations, hallucinations, flat or inappropriate affect, thought insertion, or projection. In addition, intrusive thoughts experienced by patients with schizophrenia are usually attributed to external forces while the ones experienced by individuals with OCD are usually attributed to internal ones.
		If patients present with enough symptoms of both disorders, the clinician may have to consider a dual diagnosis.

25, suggesting moderate impairment). Her obsessions included thoughts about becoming contaminated by ticks and bacteria, and recent images about her husband being maimed and killed. Despite the fact that Allison was well aware that these obsessions were a product of her own mind, she feared that she was going crazy. At the time she presented for treatment, these obsessions were recurrent, persistent, and extremely intrusive, occurring six to eight hours a day. In order to alleviate the anxiety she experienced when these obsessions occurred, Allison felt driven to perform several compulsive rituals. She washed her hands up to forty-two times a day. During each handwashing, Allison thoroughly scrubbed her hands six times. When she presented for treatment, her hands were severely chapped and reddened from the continual washing. To alleviate her anxiety, induced by the images of her husband, Allison had more recently developed a series of mental rituals. She repeated certain numbers (e.g., 6, 6, 6, 6, 6, 6, or not 3, 3, 3) and phrases (God is mighty; I challenge you not) six times each, innumerable times a day. In fact, Allison had begun repeating these words and numbers automatically to ward off future obsessions or harmful consequences that might arise from these obsessions. Often, she repeated these numbers and phrases when she experienced any increase in stress. As a result, she spent so much time ritualizing that she was unable to complete any life tasks (making the bed, cooking, shopping) and spent the majority of the day in bed.

Other measures to assess for general severity of illness include the Beck Anxiety Inventory (BAI) (Beck et al. 1988a) and the Beck Depression Inventory (BDI) (Beck et al. 1988b). The BAI and the BDI are excellent self-report measures of general severity and may be given to patients at the beginning, middle, and end of treatment to see if they are improving over the course of treatment or not.[1]

---

1. Both questionnaires may be obtained from Psychcorp (1-800-228-0752, Psychological Corporation, San Antonio, Texas).

Patients may also be given general measures of disability such as the Sheehan Disability Scale (SDS) (Leon et al. 1992) to assess the degree to which the symptoms are interfering with the patient's functioning.

Comorbidity

Comorbidity refers to the presence of independent psychiatric disorders in which the patient meets diagnostic criteria for more than one syndrome, and is therefore assigned multiple diagnoses. These multiple diagnoses, taken together, account for the patient's entire clinical presentation, symptomatology, and course of illness. More often than not, OCD occurs with other symptoms and complaints such as depression, anxiety, phobic avoidance, and excessive worry (Tynes et al. 1990). Previous research has demonstrated that the presence of comorbid disorders may have a negative impact on treatment (see Wetzler and Sanderson 1997) and specifically within OCD, the presence of severe depression may negatively impact on the effectiveness of behavioral treatment of OCD (Foa et al. 1982, Foa et al. 1983b, Marks 1977, Rachman and Hodgson 1980) (see Table 2–2 for a complete list of psychiatric disorders that tend to co-occur with obsessive-compulsive disorder).

Allison met criteria for a secondary Axis I diagnosis of Major Depressive Disorder. For the last few months, she had been feeling "low" almost all the time. She would weep at the slightest provocation and berate herself for being so "sick" that she could not be a "normal" wife for her husband. She had lost six pounds over the last three months, had begun having difficulty falling and staying asleep, and although she made sure she was clean, had lost interest in looking presentable and fashionable the way she previously did. Since the OCD was more severe, we decided that it would become the focus of treatment, and that we would later reevaluate the depression to see if it needed an independent course of cognitive-behavioral therapy.

Table 2–2. Comorbidity of Obsessive Compulsive Disorder with Other Psychiatric Disorders

Comorbid Axis I Disorders	Percent of Individuals with OCD Meeting Criteria for a Comorbid Disorder	
	Range	Studies
At least one other Axis I disorder (current)	43–83%	56% Moras et al. (1994), 48% Rasmussen and Tsuang (1986), 83% Sanderson et al. (1990), 42% Yaryura-Tobias et al. (1996)
Major depressive disorder (current)	29–33%	31% Rasmussen and Eisen (1992), 33% Sanderson et al. (1990), 29% Yaryura-Tobias et al. (1996)
Major depressive disorder (lifetime)	12–67%	12% Moras et al. (1994), 28% Karno et al. (1988), 50% Crino and Andrews (1996), 67% Rasmussen and Eisen (1992), 67% Sasson et al. (1997), 12–60% Weissman et al. (1994)
Anxiety disorder (current)	24%	24% Rasmussen and Eisen (1992)
Anxiety disorder (lifetime)	25–70%	49% Karno et al. (1988), 54% Rasmussen and Eisen (1992), 25–70% Weissman et al. (1994)
Specific phobia (current)	4–28%	4% Moras et al. (1994), 25% Sanderson et al. (1990), 28% Yaryura-Tobias et al. (1996)
Specific phobia (lifetime)	24–48%	48% Karno et al. (1988), 22% Sasson et al. (1997)
Social phobia (current)	5–24%	24% Moras et al. (1994), 8% Sanderson et al. (1990), 5% Yaryura-Tobias et al. (1996)

Social phobia (lifetime)	16–42%	42% Crino and Andrews (1996), 16% Karno et al. (1988), 18% Sasson et al. (1997)
Panic disorder (current)	8–12%	12% Moras et al. (1994), 8% Sanderson et al. (1990)
Panic disorder (lifetime)	12–54%	54% Crino and Andrews (1996), 12% Karno et al. (1988), 12% Sasson et al. (1997)
Alcohol disorder (current)	8%	8% Rasmussen and Eisen (1992)
Alcohol disorder (lifetime)	14–24%	24% Karno et al. (1988), 14% Sasson et al. (1997)
Drug abuse or dependence (lifetime)	16%	16% Karno et al. (1988)
Hypochondriasis (current)	10%	10% Yaryura-Tobias et al. (1996)
Body dysmorphic disorder (current)	10%	10% Yaryura-Tobias et al. (1996)
Eating disorder (lifetime)	17%	17% Sasson et al. (1997)
Tourette's syndrome (current)	7%	7% Yaryura-Tobias et al. (1996)
Tourette's syndrome (lifetime)	5–7%	5% Rasmussen and Eisen (1992), 7% Sasson et al. (1997)
Schizophrenia (current)	11%	11% Yaryura-Tobias et al. (1996)
Schizophrenia (lifetime)	12%	12% Karno et al. (1988)

COLLECTING INFORMATION

Once the diagnosis is established, further information regarding OCD symptomatology is still necessary before treatment can begin. In order to generate an effective treatment plan, clinicians need to obtain detailed, written information regarding the obsessive-compulsive symptoms and assess their effect on the patient's life. This may take up to three or four hours to complete. Most therapists blanch at the idea of spending so much time asking questions and feel pressured to begin treatment as soon as possible. Often, a sense of urgency is communicated by patients themselves ("When do I actually start to feel better?"). It is necessary to remind patients that collecting pertinent information is an important part of the treatment, and that obtaining this information helps the therapist devise an effective, targeted treatment plan that will help them improve. One way to hasten the process is by splitting the assessment sessions into two long sessions instead of three or four forty-five minute sessions (see Table 2–3 for a sample summary table and see Table 2–4 for a summary table of information gathered during Allison's assessment session).

Anxiety Triggers

What makes the patient feel more anxious?

Although the clinician is already familiar with the patient's obsessions by this stage, obtaining detailed information about the exact stimuli that have become associated with the obsessions, thereby triggering anxiety or the urge to ritualize, is crucial in mapping a specific plan for treatment. For example, it is not enough to know that Allison has contamination obsessions, or even that her contamination fears have to do with ticks and germs. In order to generate an effective treatment plan, it is important to know that Allison's contamination fears about becoming infested with germs or ticks are triggered when she takes out the garbage or handles soiled clothes.

**Table 2–3. Assessment and Information Gathering:
Sample Summary Table**

Information to Gather	*Summary Description*
Diagnosis	Principal: Secondary:
Severity of illness and mood state	Principal: Secondary:
Onset and course of disorder	Onset: Course of Illness:
Prior treatments	Medication: Psychotherapy:
Treatment motivation and expectations	
External anxiety triggers	
Internal anxiety triggers	
Degree of insight	
Feared consequences	
Avoidance maneuvers	
Ritualized thoughts and behaviors	Behavioral Rituals: Mental Rituals:
Treatment eligibility	

Knowing specific triggers allows the cognitive-behavioral therapist to make a change in specific situations. In fact, as will be evident later, the CBT process involves conducting a series of such changes in specific situations until treatment effects culminate, thereby generalizing to all areas of the patient's life.

Table 2–4. Assessment and Information Gathering: Allison's Summary Table

Information to Gather	Summary Description
Diagnosis	Principal: Obsessive Compulsive Disorder Secondary: Major Depressive Disorder
Severity of illness and mood state	OCD: Severe MDD: Moderate
Onset and course of disorder	Onset: Age 16 Course of Illness: Waxes and wanes, with two major spurts to date
Prior treatments	Medication: Luvox, Prozac, Anafranil, moderate response. Currently started on Anafranil Psychotherapy: None
Treatment motivation and expectations	Motivation fluctuates. Volunteers feelings of hopelessness about ever getting better but can be reassured, and occasionally feels somewhat hopeful
External anxiety triggers	Garbage, soiled laundry, toilets, entering toilets, knives, sister-in-law, garbage cans, newspapers
Internal anxiety triggers	Images of Michael getting injured, dying of a heart attack, getting strangled, getting stabbed, hearing the words of the song "Devil in a Blue Dress," which would play in her mind every now and then, seeing the color blue in her mind, heart skipping a beat, feeling hot or tingly
Degree of insight	Fluctuates during and in between sessions; is occasionally able to acknowledge that her symptoms "make no sense"
Feared consequences	Fears that she will become infested with bacteria, ticks Fears that Michael's face will get mutilated and that he will die
Avoidance maneuvers	Does not glance at or use knives; does not allow Michael to use knives; does not use public toilets; does not take the garbage out; does not handle soiled clothes; cleans the house with gloves only; will

Table 2–4. (*Continued*)

	enter public restrooms to freshen up only with gloves; will wash her hands using her own bar of soap and bottled water in public bathrooms; cannot visit with her sister-in-law or see her photographs; cannot be around strangers
Ritualized thoughts and behaviors	Behavioral Rituals: All rituals conducted in multiples of six (minimum six, maximum seventy-two times a day)
	Washing: Hands (usual: thirty-six times a day), taking lengthy showers (twice a day)
	Checking: Checks to see the knives are in place (usual: thirty-six times a day); checks to see if husband is all right either by calling him or by going to him if he is in another room (usual: six times a day)
	Mental rituals: All mental rituals conducted in multiples of six (minimum six, maximum twelve times each up to eight to ten hours a day)
	Prays in a ritualized way ("God is mighty")
	Repeats phrases (Mercy, mercy," "how shall I fly")
	Repeats numbers ("6, 6, 6, 6, 6, 6," or "not 3, 3, 3")
Treatment eligibility	Eligible for CBT. Moderately depressed only, not psychotic, does not abuse alcohol or other substances, is not at risk for suicide or a psychotic breakdown, previously compliant with pharmacotherapy treatments, is using adjunctive medication and is being helped by it

The clinician identifies all the specific internal and external triggers that induce anxiety and asks the patient to rate (1) the degree of anxiety experienced, and (2) the amount of avoidance exhibited to each and every stimulus on a scale (e.g., 1 to 100) in order to generate a hierarchy of phobic stimuli that may be used later on during the exposure phase (described in Chapters 6, 7, and 8). This phase often requires a detailed investigational effort on the part of the therapist and the patient until all the pieces of the puzzle are linked to each other. Although this phase may induce anxiety in some patients, many express a sense of relief in being able to discuss their innermost fears with someone who not only handles them in a matter-of-fact manner but understands and expects the patient to have them.

External anxiety triggers.   Often, individuals with OCD experience tremendous anxiety when they confront specific environmental stimuli (Riggs and Foa 1993). Specific objects (e.g., toilets, knives, garbage, chemical products), people (mother, husband, etc.), situations (talking to a friend, driving over a bump on the road), and places (restaurants, public toilets) may become associated with their obsessions, thereby creating anxiety. Such individuals may avoid these stimuli or may ritualize following exposure to them.

A host of environmental stimuli triggered Allison's anxiety related to her obsessions. For example, she could not bring herself to touch knives. Merely glancing at them, especially at the blades, triggered her obsessions about Michael's face being mutilated. Not only had she given up using knives, she could not tolerate observing others, particularly Michael, using them in her presence. As a result, Michael and Allison were restricted to eating foods that did not require the use of knives or, alternatively, were forced to order out on a regular basis. Bathrooms were another source of fear for Allison. She refused to use public toilets. Although she would enter certain "clean" restrooms to freshen up, she would use gloves so she would not have to come in direct contact with the door, faucets, or other objects. When she felt compelled to wash her hands, she carefully opened the tap, removed her gloves, placing them carefully in her purse, and then used her own bottled water and bar of soap to wash her hands. Allison also feared using the bathrooms in other people's homes, even those of her close friends and family. Although she would enter their bathrooms, and even wash her hands without using gloves or bottled water, she still used tissue paper to open and close the door and taps, and refused to use their toilets, preferring instead to wait until she returned home. As a result, traveling outside or even visiting friends and family became significantly difficult.

Often, fears of specific stimuli generalize to other related stimuli, thus increasing the number of stimuli capable of inducing anxiety and/or avoidance. As a result, the individual's life becomes more and more restricted. For example, Allison's fear of becoming contaminated by soiled clothes led her to fear the laundry bin, the washing machine, and even the neighborhood laundromat and dry cleaner. Although a majority of patients understand the association between their obsessions and the avoidant behaviors, at times they may require assistance in understanding this relationship. For example, during treatment Allison professed a growing fear of being around her sister-in-law, a fear that she did not understand but that greatly troubled her. On close investigation, it became apparent that she had developed this fear after the two had gone on a shopping trip. During this trip, her sister-in-law had excused herself to use the public restroom and had later explained to Allison that she had had a bout of diarrhea. Following this incident, Allison had stopped meeting her sister-in-law quite as frequently because she feared that the contaminants from the public toilet would spread to her via her sister-in-law.

Internal anxiety triggers. Anxiety may also be triggered by stimuli experienced internally (e.g., internal images, thoughts, or impulses) (Riggs and Foa 1993). Most of these internal cues are embarrassing or disgusting to the patient and hence must be obtained by direct questioning, perhaps with examples of triggers experienced by other OCD patients so that the patient feels reassured that he or she is not alone, immoral, or disgusting. For example, a patient may feel ashamed at images of himself having sex with the Virgin Mary. Explaining that up to 90 percent of people in the "normal" population experience intrusive thoughts, images, urges, or impulses may also help to provide patients with as much information about their internal triggers as possible.

Other internal triggers that may give rise to obsessions include internal bodily cues, such as indigestion, which then lead to obsessive thoughts about getting infested with bacteria. Obsessions may also be triggered by numbers, patterns, sounds, or music in one's mind. Although these cues are less shameful, they also tend to be more subtle; thus careful questioning is still essential in examining all the possible internal triggers of anxiety.

> Allison's internal anxiety triggers, which led to an increase in obsessions, included the following: spontaneous images of Michael getting injured in a car accident, having a heart attack, getting stabbed, or getting strangled. Other triggers included the words of the song "Devil in a Blue Dress," which would play in her mind every now and then, as well as seeing the color blue in her mind (incidentally as a result of the association with the song), and physical sensations such as her heart skipping a beat, or feeling hot or tingly.

Catastrophic Fears

What does the patient fear will happen if he has obsessions or if he does not ritualize?

A majority of individuals with OCD fear that their obsessions may cause something disastrous to occur if they do not perform their rituals (Riggs and Foa 1993). For example, a father who has obsessions about strangling his child may fear that he will kill his child in reality, or at the very least increase the probability that his child may actually die, or a person with contamination fears may fear that he will get infected with bacteria if he handles garbage. Although most contamination fears surround the possibility that one will become infected and most obsessions about inflicting harm are associated with an increased fear that a loved one might die or get harmed, no two individuals will necessarily fear the same catastrophe. For example, one individual may fear that his child will die if he does not check the gas stove to ensure that it is off, while another may fear that his child will suffer great pain and permanent damage if the gas permeates the air in the house.

> Allison's obsessive thoughts of Michael's face being mutilated with knives were especially disturbing to her because she believed with all her heart that they would somehow increase the chances of something bad happening to him in reality, and that if it did it would be all her fault. She specifically feared that Michael's face would get horribly mutilated if she did not check the kitchen to see if the knives were in place, or if she did not call Michael at least six times a day, to check on his well-being and to reassure herself.

It is important to ascertain all the specific fears and to continue questioning until each and every one is understood. Novice therapists often make the mistake of ending their questioning before the "ultimate" consequence is obtained. For example, one individual may fear that his wife will come to harm because of his obsessions, whereas another, who may have a similar fear, may have an even greater one—that in the event that his wife did come to some harm, he would be struck down by a bolt of lightning as his punishment for having these obsessive thoughts.

A significant minority of patients do not have specific fears, but may have more nonspecific fears about what may happen because of the obsessions, or what may happen if they do not ritualize. For example, an individual may fear that the anxiety itself—from the obsessive thought or from not performing rituals—will be intolerable, without necessarily fearing that something catastrophic may occur to him or loved ones. Yet someone else may not feel "right" or "comfortable" unless all rituals are performed. In many cases, individuals who on assessment appear to have nonspecific fears may, over the course of treatment, turn out to have specific fears that were previously not known to them. For example, the individual who merely states that the "anxiety from not performing the ritual will be intolerable" may eventually come to realize that he is fearful of going crazy or having a nervous breakdown if the ritual is not performed.

Eliciting all the fears is crucial for treatment to be effective. In the case of the individual who fears that a bolt of lightning will strike him if his wife comes to harm because of his obsessive thoughts, merely countering his fears about his wife's death would not be sufficient to alleviate his anxiety. Only if treatment also addresses his fears of being struck down by an act of God will his anxiety truly diminish. As will be evident later, establishing whether a patient has specific fears, or whether he merely finds it difficult to tolerate the anxiety, is important in deciding which components of treatment to use (see Chapter 6).

Avoidance and Rituals

What does the patient avoid or do over and over again to lessen his anxiety?

As discussed in Chapter 1, avoidance behaviors are central to all anxiety disorders, including OCD, and theoretically develop in order to reduce the anxiety provoked by the phobic stimulus (e.g., a restaurant). However, because of the intrusive nature of obsessions ("I may have become infested with bacteria from the food I ate in the restaurant" as opposed to "I am afraid of getting a panic attack in the restaurant"), passive avoidance and escape behaviors, although used, are usually insufficient to alleviate the anxiety aroused.

For example, leaving the scene is sufficient to reduce the fear of having a panic attack in the restaurant. However, because contamination may have already occurred, leaving the scene does not prevent the bacteria from the food eaten in the restaurant from spreading throughout one's body. Hence, compulsive or ritualized behaviors are developed by individuals in order to "undo the harm," thereby reducing the anxiety created by the phobic stimulus (If I clean my hands fifty times, maybe the contamination will leave my body), and are maintained by their success in doing so (I did not get infected with a disease from the food I ate only because I washed my hand fifty times).

During the information-collecting phase, the clinician attempts to compile an exhaustive list of maneuvers used by the individual to reduce anxiety. What does the patient do when he begins to feel anxious? How does he cope with his anxiety when he has an obsessive thought? Essentially, the goal is to collect a list of (1) avoidance behaviors (e.g., does not take the garbage out, avoids using the public toilet), (2) mental rituals (counts numbers, prays, repeats certain phrases), and (3) behavioral rituals (washes hands, checks the stove, rearranges objects around the house).

Allison exhibited a variety of maneuvers to alleviate her anxiety associated with her obsessions. Avoidance maneuvers included *not* doing the following: touching knives, using public toilets, taking the garbage out, handling soiled clothes, allowing Michael to touch knives, seeing her sister-in-law, and so on. Mental rituals included praying ("God is mighty, I challenge you not"), repeating phrases such as "safe Mike," "how shall I fly," and numbers such as "6, 6, 6, 6, 6, 6," or "not 3, 3, 3." Allison also exhibited a variety of behavioral rituals. Most frequently, she washed her hands, checked to see that the knives were in place, and called Michael at work multiple times a day. She always ritualized in multiples of six. For example, she called Michael six times a day and would usually check the knives and wash her hands thirty-six times a day. On "good days" she checked the knives or washed her hands six times, but on certain "bad days" Allison could not stop until she had repeated the rituals seventy-two times (twelve times six).

Degree of Insight

How much does the patient believe that his obsessions are senseless or that his compulsions are excessive or unreasonable?

Although insight into illness at all times is no longer needed to meet *DSM-IV* criteria for diagnosis for OCD, the *DSM-IV* (APA 1994) specifies that *at some point during the course of the disorder*, the person has recognized that the obsessions are excessive or unreasonable. In contrast, the *DSM-III-R* required that patients recognize the "senselessness" of their obsessions and recognize that their compulsions were "excessive or unreasonable" but also noted cases of overvalued ideation (patients who exhibited a strong belief that obsessions or compulsions are realistic). The *DSM-IV* criteria were modified after a variety of studies suggested that OCD patients differed significantly on whether or not they had insight into their symptom but that most patients had exhibited insight at some point during their illness (see Riggs and Foa [1993] for a list of studies).

Why should the clinician assess degree of insight into illness if it is no longer needed at all times to meet diagnostic criteria? Unfortunately, the answer is not definitive. Although patients who have more insight do not always respond better than patients with a lower degree of insight, experts such as Foa (Riggs and Foa 1993) believe that patients who exhibit overvalued ideation in their obsessions and compulsions or have extremely poor insight do not respond to behavior therapy as well as those with a greater degree of insight. Hence, assessing the degree of insight enables the clinician to modify treatment as necessary or consider conjunctive treatments (e.g., low doses of antipsychotic medication may be useful).

It is important that patients with OCD who exhibit fluctuating insight not be placed in the category of overvalued ideators. Most

OCD patients, or for that matter most anxiety-disordered patients, fluctuate in the degree of insight they exhibit. A majority of such patients are able to express that their fears are unreasonable (or, in the case of OCD patients, realize that their obsessions are senseless, or that their compulsions are excessive or unreasonable) when they are not faced with the phobic stimulus. However, as soon as they face the phobic stimulus (e.g., garbage), this insight vanishes and their belief in the obsessions and compulsions becomes complete. In fact, cognitive-behavioral treatment is targeted toward improving insight when patients are confronted with the feared objects or situations.

When Allison was first interviewed at intake, she stated that her obsessions and compulsions made sense and that it showed that she was just being cautious. However, a few weeks later, during her comprehensive assessment, she was able to express that she "knew that having a thought about Michael's face becoming maimed could not really cause him harm," or that "washing hands so many times a day was completely unnecessary." In fact, Allison usually dissolved into tears and expressed immense sadness when she experienced insight into the senselessness of her symptoms. It brought on a sense that she had "wasted" and was continuing to waste the better part of her life, doing the most "bizarre and unnecessary things."

From then on, Allison continued to exhibit relatively good insight during therapy sessions and was able to regularly discuss her "unreasonable" symptoms. However, when she had obsessive images about Michael during sessions, her belief in those obsessions would return momentarily, her anxiety would increase, and she would begin covertly repeating her ritualized phrases and numbers to alleviate her anxiety and the chances of Michael actually coming to harm. At home, when she confronted stimuli that triggered her obsessions (as when she entered the kitchen, thought about Michael, saw a brown spot on her skin, saw a TV show about disease, etc.), her belief in her symptoms was complete and her anxiety would escalate. She believed that the chances of Michael coming to harm unless she ritualized, and the chances of her becoming contaminated if she handled soiled laundry or garbage, were 100 percent. However, as treatment progressed, her insight during such moments also began to change.

Impairment in Daily Functioning

To what degree do the OCD symptoms interfere with the patient's life?
Impairment in the patient's daily functioning (work, marital relationships, social life) can be assessed through informal questioning during the clinical interview and with the aid of structured scales such as the Sheehan Disability Scale (Leon et al. 1992). Understanding the degree and range of impairment is essential not just to see whether the individual meets the criteria for OCD, but also in order to formulate appropriate treatment goals and to track progress in treatment over time. For example, assessing impairment in functioning enables the clinician to target those areas of the patient's life that are most affected by the disorder. That way, the patient can begin to see change in areas of his life that have been most affected by the symptoms. In addition, assessing functioning at intake and at several points during treatment enables the clinician to evaluate if the treatment is, in fact, impacting on the patient's life as intended.

Allison had difficulty taking care of her household duties, could not go back to school, had strained social interactions, and in many cases completely avoided meeting people. She also had difficulty just going out of her house even if she did not interact with people because of her generalized fear of becoming contaminated by objects that were not "safe." However, the one area of her life that was creating the most conflict for her was her relationship with her husband. In fact, Allison finally came in for treatment only after Michael threatened to leave her unless she did. Both husband and wife agreed that their relations were strained and that her symptoms were "ruining" their marriage. As many spouses do, Michael initially assisted Allison in avoiding situations or events that triggered her obsessions, reassured her multiple times a day when she expressed her fears, and enabled her to ritualize when she wanted. He did so, not because he thought he was making her worse, but because he felt sorry for her and did not want to upset her. However, the strain of living their lives trying to alleviate her ever-increasing fears had taken a toll on him.

Mood State

How depressed is the OCD patient?

Because depressive symptoms are fairly common in patients with OCD (Karno et al. 1988) and some evidence suggests that patients with comorbid severe depression may not respond well to CBT (Foa et al. 1982, Foa et al. 1983a,b, Marks 1977, Rachman and Hodgson 1980), evaluating the patient's mood at this stage is essential in determining if the patient is an appropriate candidate for CBT. Assessing the severity of the depressive mood allows the clinician to consider if treating the depressive symptoms is necessary (via medication or CBT) before treatment for OCD can begin. For example, if the patient reports that the depressive symptoms are worse (e.g., he has difficulty getting out of bed on most days, has lost the will to do much) or the clinician observes that the depression appears to be worse or is currently affecting the patient to a greater degree (the patient is extremely distraught, weeps uncontrollably during the session, is significantly motorically retarded), these symptoms may need to be addressed before the OCD symptoms are targeted.

Onset and Course of Disorder

When did the OCD symptoms begin and how have they developed or changed over time?

Unlike patients with panic disorder who vividly remember the onset and details about their first attack, OCD patients are unable to give a detailed account of how their disorder began. This is because unlike panic disorder, which has an acute onset, OCD tends to begin gradually over time. In addition, patients usually present for treatment many years after their symptoms began, often as the result of a gradual progression of symptoms, and also because of the shame and secrecy associated with the symptoms.

Despite this, the therapist should try to collect as much information as possible. Learning how the symptoms began and how they have waxed or waned for a particular individual tells the clinician what to expect during treatment. For example, understanding which stressors tend to bring on or exacerbate OCD symptoms enables the clinician to be alert to changes in symptoms during treatment (e.g., when Allison's checking behaviors lessened in the past, an increase in mental rituals necessarily followed) and to design an effective treatment plan. Learning that Allison's germ obsessions tended to become worse when she came into contact with people who had children and with older people, whom she perceived as being dirty, enabled the therapist to design an exposure hierarchy involving people with these characteristics.

Prior Treatments

What previous treatments has the patient had? Were they adequate trials of the treatment?

Knowing what treatment patients have had in the past enables the therapist to determine what treatments must or must not be repeated. For example, learning that a patient did not respond to a prior trial of cognitive behavior therapy or a certain medication allows the therapist to consider other effective but untried treatments. However, the therapist must first determine that the previous treatments were implemented adequately (e.g., did the patient receive the therapeutic dose of a certain antidepressant for the necessary length of time?) before considering other treatments in favor of the one tried before. For example, if a patient received cognitive behavior treatment in the past, but it was conducted over a short period of time or in a slipshod manner, beginning another trial of CBT is still warranted, and modifications may be necessary if treatment elements that were ineffective then can be identified. In other cases, even if the treatment was adequately implemented, the patient may not have responded to it in the past due to extraneous circumstances such as job stress, death in the family, or some other event, and the therapist may decide to repeat the treatment despite its having failed before.

Patient Motivation and Expectation

How motivated is the patient and what does he expect to get out of treatment?

Before treatment can begin, the therapist must also find out why the patient has decided to obtain CBT at the present time and what he expects from treatment. The motivation level of a patient who has opted for CBT because he has read up on it is vastly different from the patient who is only coming for CBT because his psychiatrist has told him that he will no longer receive medication unless he gets adjunctive treatment. Knowing the motivation can help the therapist judge if the patient is an appropriate candidate for therapy. In addition, knowing the source of the motivation can help guide the treatment. For example, a patient may enter CBT treatment because she wants to stop taking medication in order to become pregnant. The patient's end goal, getting pregnant, may be emphasized by the therapist throughout treatment to help keep motivation levels up. In addition, the therapist can begin working with the patient's psychiatrist to help the patient gradually get off medications as treatment progresses.

Treatment Eligibility

Is the patient a good candidate for CBT?

Based on the assessment, the therapist must decide if the patient is an appropriate candidate for cognitive behavior therapy. Using the guidelines for determining treatment eligibility in Table 2–5, the therapist can make a decision about whether the patient can proceed with treatment, whether he needs to be referred out, or if he needs to receive concomitant treatments.

PRESENTING FINDINGS

Once the pertinent information is gathered, the therapist summarizes the evaluation and presents the findings to the patient. What is the principal diagnosis? Does he have any comorbid diagnoses or symptoms that would also benefit from treatment? The therapists offers answers to these questions and helps the patient understand how his symptoms, anxiety, and the functional impairment he has suffered are all related to his illness. The therapist also offers hope to the patient by supporting his decision to begin treatment, discussing the efficacy of treatment for many, and briefly outlining the therapeutic steps that will be taken toward helping the patient improve.

NEXT WEEK

Although the importance of doing homework or assignments may not have been discussed yet, patients are still given an assignment at the end of this session. Self-report questionnaires such as the BDI, the BAI, and the Sheehan Disability Scale may be handed out now for the patient to complete over the next week. All questionnaires and forms are explained in detail and illustrative examples are provided by the therapist to ensure accuracy.

Table 2–5. Determining Eligibility: What You Should Consider Before Cognitive Behavioral Treatment Can Be Initiated

Patient Presentation	What You Should Consider
Severely depressed	Consider medication treatment and/or cognitive behavioral treatments for depression before OCD treatment can begin.
Delusional or has hallucinations	Poor candidates for CBT when symptoms are active. The therapist may either refer out for medication treatment alone or treat with CBT but refer out for medications to treat psychotic symptoms.
Abusing alcohol or other substances	Treat that first by referring to a substance abuse counselor or treatment center.
History of poor compliance with psychotherapy	Medications may be the alternative.
Risk for suicide	Hospitalization should be considered and also medication to treat depression.
Psychotic breakdown	Hospitalization should be considered.
Using medications	Many OCD patients are treated with both medication and CBT. Although a recent trial indicates that behavior therapy alone may be as helpful as behavior therapy plus medication (Foa 1994), conventional wisdom still values two interventions over one. You may decide to consider a psychiatric evaluation if the patient has never tried medication before or offer CBT for a reasonable period and then consider adding medication if CBT is not effective. If the patient is on medications with no benefit, consider adding CBT to see if two treatments together are better, or discuss the possibility of trying other medications with the psychiatrist.

Session 2: Psychoeducation

Session Goals	Check When Done

| | |

1. Review (5–10 minutes) ☐
   - Obtain feedback on Session 1
   - Review homework (BAI, BDI, SDS, monitoring forms)
   - Briefly review events that occurred over past week

2. The Session (Psychoeducation) ☐
   - *DSM-IV* definition
   - Epidemiology and course of disorder
     ( ) Prevalence
     ( ) Age of onset
     ( ) Sex ratio
     ( ) Course of illness
     ( ) Familial incidence
     ( ) Impairment in functioning
   - Bibliography and organizations
   - Evidence-based treatments
   - Cognitive-behavioral treatment rationale
   - Components of cognitive-behavioral treatment
     ( ) Psychoeducation
     ( ) Cognitive restructuring
     ( ) Exposure
     ( ) Response prevention
   - Clarify treatment expectations and goals

3. Next Week (5–10 minutes) ☐
   - Explain role of homework in treatment
   - Identify a support to help in treatment
   - Discuss homework to be completed next week
     —Monitor obsessive thinking and compulsive thinking or behavior
     —Read psychoeducation handout (see Table 3–1
     —Listen to tape of session
   - Anticipate potential stressors that may occur during the week

SESSION OVERVIEW

After a quick review of the previous session, the therapist initiates the psychoeducation phase, which is the most didactic session of all. During this session, the therapist gives the patient facts and figures on OCD and offers the cognitive behavior treatment rationale so that the patient can have an informed understanding of his problem and the treatment he is about to receive. This constitutes the bulk of Session 2. During this session, it is also important to clarify the patient's treatment expectations so that he knows what kind of improvement to expect when treatment ends. Before the session ends, a "helper" is identified to assist in the treatment, and the patient is given monitoring forms to begin recording his obsessions and compulsions.

REVIEW

A central component of CBT is a quick review of the previous session to ensure that patients have grasped the material as intended and have completed the assigned homework. It gives the patient a sense of continuity and reinforces the fact that the assigned homework is integral to the treatment. It gives the therapist a chance to ensure that the patient has grasped the material as intended and is ready to move onto the next session.

Session 2 begins with the therapist summarizing the results of the psychological assessment, including the principal and comorbid diagnoses, severity of illness, symptoms, and so on. Then, feedback and questions are elicited from the patient for purposes of clarification. For example, the therapist told Allison the following:

As we discussed during the last session, you suffer from obsessive-compulsive disorder and major depressive disorder. OCD is an anxiety disorder. In other words, you suffer from obsessions that increase your anxiety, and compulsions that reduce your anxiety about the obsessions. For example, your fears that you may become contaminated by germs or that Michael may come to harm are obsessions because they are unwanted thoughts, they come again and again, and they make you very anxious. Your tendency to wash your hands, count numbers, and check to see if Michael is okay are compulsions, because you do them over and over again and because they make you less anxious when you do them. You feel less anxious because you believe that you're less likely to become contaminated or that Michael is less likely to die if you do these things.

You also suffer from what we call major depression. In other words, the fact that you have been feeling sad a lot of the time for the past few months, seem to have lost interest or any joy in life, have been eating and sleeping less, and are having difficulty concentrating means that you are suffering from major depression. It is likely that your depression has developed as a result of the impairment and distress caused by your OCD and will clear up as your OCD gets better. Also, the treatments you are getting will help both conditions. Is that clear, Allison? Would you like me to explain some more?

THE SESSION: PSYCHOEDUCATION

Following a quick review of the previous session, the therapist and the patient formulate the agenda for the current session. This structures the session and ensures that both therapist and patient are able to bring up what they would like to accomplish during the session. Setting the agenda also facilitates the efficient use of session time, thus increasing the chances of a rapid response to treatment.

During Session 2, the therapist first describes the reasons for beginning treatment through educating the patient about obsessive-compulsive disorder, its symptoms, types, demographics, and treatment. Learning all they can about obsessive-compulsive disorder helps patients understand the illness, clarify myths and misinterpretations that they might have, and, finally, begin the distancing process. In place of perceiving the illness as an inherent mental flaw or weakness, patients can begin to understand, perhaps for the first time, that it is a disorder shared by millions of others, one that can be diagnosed and effectively treated.

The following facts and figures on obsessive-compulsive disorder and its treatments are given to patients, but must be conveyed to each patient in your own words. The therapist should judge the patient's educational and emotional level, and provide the information to the patient at his own level. The objective is to educate the patient and provide information in a direct, yet gentle and supportive manner. Even if all the information is not communicated to the patient as presented below, you will still have this information at your fingertips if questions come up later. Patients with anxiety disorders will feel reassured that you are knowledgeable about their disorder. Knowing that you have the answers to their questions will go a long way in assuring them that you are capable of treating their problem (see Table 3–1 for a summary of facts outlined during the psychoeducation session). It is recommended that this session and others be taped for patients to use for future reference.

DSM-IV DEFINITION

Once Allison was given the results of her assessment, a detailed discussion of the definition of obsessive-compulsive disorder was also presented to her to ensure her complete understanding.

Obsessive-compulsive disorder is an anxiety disorder. People with OCD have obsessions, which are unpleasant and intrusive

Table 3–1. Psychoeducation Summary Table (Patient Handout)

DSM-IV definition	*(See Table 1–1)*
Epidemiology and course of disorder	• Highly prevalent • Equally common among the sexes • Appears to be less common in minority groups • Begins in early adulthood • Gradual onset • Chronic condition, waxes and wanes in severity • Some evidence to support a genetic basis for OCD • Some evidence that there is a biological component • Individuals suffer for years before presenting for treatment • Causes significant impairment in functioning
Bibliography and organizations	• Burns, D. D. (1989). *The Feeling Good Handbook: Using the New Mood Therapy in Everyday Life.* New York: Morrow. • Foa, E. B., and Wilson, R. (1991). *Stop Obsessing! How to Overcome Your Obsessions and Compulsions.* New York: Bantam Books. • Anxiety Disorders Association of America (301) 231-9350. • Obsessive Compulsive Foundation, 9 Depot Street, Milford, CT 06460, (203) 878-5669. • World Wide Web for OCD information: Site name: OCD—Obsessive-Compulsive Disorder http://www.cmhc.com/guide/ocd.htm • Ocd net: OCD-L@VM.marist.edu
Etiology and maintenance of symptoms	Temperament Biological Psychological
Evidence-based treatments for OCD	• Serotonergic medications —Clomipramine (tricyclic antidepressant) —Fluoxetine (SSRI) —Fluvoxamine (SSRI) —Sertraline (SSRI) —Paroxetine (SSRI)

Table 3–1. (*continued*)

DSM-IV definition	(See Table 1–1)
	• Behavior therapy —Exposure —Response prevention • Cognitive therapy
Cognitive-behavioral treatment rationale	• Short-term, symptom-focused treatment approach • Identifies and modifies maladaptive thoughts and behaviors • Reduces emotional distress and improves functioning • Alleviates the anxiety associated with obsessions, thereby reducing the frequency and persistence of these thoughts, images, impulses, or urges • Breaks the association between compulsions and the subsequent feelings of relief or reduced anxiety
Components of treatment	• Psychoeducation • Cognitive restructuring • Exposure • Response prevention
Clarify treatment limitations	• OCD is a chronic condition; symptoms wax and wane in severity, usually as a function of stress. • Patients will not be "cured" or entirely symptom free at the end of the treatment. • Anxiety will reduce substantially and symptoms will become more manageable. • Goal of treatment is for patients to: —Experience significantly less anxiety when obsessions are triggered; —Be better able to resist compulsive rituals; —Have fewer obsessions and rituals.

thoughts that keep coming to you over and over again despite the fact that they may not make sense to you and despite the fact that you don't want to have them. They may come to you in the form of ideas, thoughts, impulses, or images, and they tend to create immense anxiety when they come. For example, your images about getting infested with ticks or about your husband getting killed are what we call obsessions. You have told me how unpleasant they are and how hard it is to put them out of your mind. Almost like the ticks latching onto your skin, these obsessive thoughts seems to grab hold of your mind. Does that sound like how you think about them?

Questioning the patient to see if he agrees or if he is on the same page with you is a crucial part of cognitive-behavioral therapy. Also, asking the patient to summarize information in his own words will ensure that he understands.

Now, the second part of OCD is the compulsions. Those are the many rituals you do over and over again, that make you less anxious for the moment. For example, when you call Michael several times a day, you feel somewhat better and reassured that he's alive, but soon the relief wears off and you do it again and again. When you wash your hands you probably feel the same sense of relief for a little while, relief that the ticks or the germs are washed off. When you repeat "6" or "God is mighty" over and over again, those are also rituals that make you feel better for a little while.

So, just to summarize a little, when you have these repetitive thoughts and images that are hard to control and that make you anxious, we call them obsessions. When you actually do, think, or say something over and over again that seems to make you somewhat less anxious for a little while, we call those rituals or compulsions. Am I explaining that clearly enough?

A list of the different obsessions and compulsions is presented to the patient (Goodman et al. 1989c) at this juncture. Going over the list carefully with the patient lets the therapist check for other symptoms the patient may not have thought to share during previous sessions. It may also help patients realize that some symptoms they did not consider to be part of their OCD are indeed that.

EPIDEMIOLOGY AND COURSE OF DISORDER

Facts to cover during this session include:

- Highly prevalent
- Equally common among the sexes
- Appears to be less common in minority groups
- Begins in early adulthood
- Gradual onset
- Chronic condition, waxes and wanes in severity
- Some evidence to support a genetic basis for OCD
- Some evidence that there is a biological component
- Individuals suffer for years before presenting for treatment
- Causes significant impairment in functioning

Prevalence

Obsessive-compulsive disorder is now thought to be far more prevalent than was initially believed (Karno et al. 1988, Robins et al. 1984). The lifetime prevalence of OCD, as calculated by the largest epidemiological study on OCD to date, is believed to be 2.5 percent (Karno et al. 1988), suggesting that more than six million people in the United States suffer from OCD at some point in their lives. The one-month prevalence rate of obsessive-compulsive disorder is estimated to be 1.3, which means that over three million people in the United States suffer from OCD at any given time (Karno et al. 1988). According to these estimates, OCD is the fourth most common psychiatric disorder, following phobias, substance abuse, and major depressive disorder (Rasmussen and Eisen 1990).

OCD prevalence rates appear to be fairly consistent across different countries, including the United States, Canada, Korea, Puerto Rico, New Zealand, and Germany. The lifetime prevalence rates for OCD range from 1.9 to 2.5 within these sites while annual prevalence rates generally range from 1.1 to 1.8 (Weissman et al. 1994). The only exception appears to be Taiwan (lifetime 0.7, annual 0.4), which has demonstrated lower rates for all psychiatric disorders including OCD.

Some new studies suggest that the true prevalence of OCD may be less if trained clinicians make the diagnosis rather than trained lay interviewers (3.1 percent versus 0.6 percent) (Stein et al. 1997). However, more studies are needed to see if this finding can be replicated across different communities, using larger samples. Even so, at a lifetime rate of 0.6 percent, OCD is still not as rare (0.05 percent) as initially believed (Rudin 1953).

Up to 90 percent of people in the "normal" population (those without OCD) have obsessive thoughts (Rachman and DeSilva 1978).

Occurrence in Men and Women

OCD appears to be equally common in males and females. However, some studies show that a little over half the people with OCD are female (Rasmussen and Tsuang 1986, Weissman et al. 1994).

Occurrence in Minorities

Some studies show that OCD appears to be less common among minority groups (Karno et al. 1988). More studies are still needed to examine the impact of ethnicity on the expression and treatment outcome of OCD.

Time of Occurrence

Although OCD typically first strikes in early adulthood (mean age 19.3 to 25.6 years), in 30 percent of cases it can begin in childhood

(American Psychiatric Association 1994). It also tends to occur earlier in men than in women. Boys can develop OCD anywhere from 6 to 15 years of age but typically develop it during early adolescence (peak onset 13 to 15 years). Females tend to develop OCD symptoms anywhere from the age of 20 to 29 years but typically develop symptoms between the ages of 20 and 24 years. It is not clear why females develop OCD at a later age than males.

Gradual Onset

The onset of OCD usually tends to be gradual. However, some patients report an acute onset (Rasmussen and Eisen 1990). Some studies indicate that the onset of OCD may be linked to stressful life events, but more conclusive research is needed on precipitants.

Chronic Condition, with Varying Severity

Like the other emotional disorders, obsessive-compulsive disorder tends to be a chronic condition, with symptoms alternately increasing and decreasing in severity over time, usually as a result of stress (American Psychiatric Association 1994, Rachman and Hodgson 1980, Rasmussen and Tsuang 1986, Riggs and Foa 1993). However, a minority of patients (approximately 5 percent) tend to have episodic courses, where symptoms remit between episodes, and approximately 15 percent of patients appear to progressively deteriorate over time (American Psychiatric Association 1994). (The information about progressive deterioration may be shared with your patient at your discretion. Because patients with anxiety disorders tend to overestimate the probability of something negative happening to them, it is generally not advisable to share potentially frightening information, especially if it occurs only to a minority of individuals with OCD. One important fact to convey to patients, especially in the case of potentially alarming information, is that these data frequently refer to individual patients not receiving treatment.)

Possible Genetic Basis

There is evidence to suggest that genes may play a role in the etiology of OCD. For example, studies show that when one twin has a diagnosis of OCD, the other is far more likely to also have a diagnosis of OCD if the twins are identical than if they are fraternal, presumably because identical twins have more genes in common (Billett et al. 1998). However, since identical twins also have more similar environments than fraternal twins, a definitive conclusion may be drawn only when studies compare rates of OCD among identical twins who are raised together with those who are reared apart.

Studies also show that first-degree relatives of individuals with OCD have elevated rates (3 to 12 percent) of OCD over what would otherwise be expected in the general population, thereby providing further support for a genetic basis for OCD (Billett et al. 1998).

Biological Components

Biological theories propose a link between OCD and a variety of neurochemical and neuroanatomical deficits, including increased levels of the neurotransmitter serotonin, deficits in the frontal lobe, deficits in the basal ganglia, and increased metabolic activity in the prefrontal cortex (Baxter et al. 1990, Charney et al. 1988). Although there is evidence to suggest that obsessive-compulsive disorder has a biological component, more research is still needed before definitive conclusions may be drawn about the relative influence of biological and psychological factors in the development of OCD. What is important to convey is that whether or not OCD has a biological component, patients still have a good response to CBT.

Individuals May Suffer for Years before Presenting for Treatment

A majority of patients with OCD tend to suffer for years before presenting for treatment (Steketee 1993). This may be attributed to the shameful nature of their symptoms, which can keep persons with

OCD in the closet for years, as well as to a lack of publicity about the disorder and available treatments.

Functioning May Be Severely Impaired

Studies show that obsessive-compulsive disorder appears to cause significant impairment in functioning. It can lead to the development of other illnesses, such as depression; it can lead to job loss; and it can destroy relationships. Some studies show that individuals with OCD are less likely to have social contacts or to get married than other groups (Ingram 1961, Khanna et al. 1986, Kringlen 1965, Lo 1967), while others show that approximately 50 percent of married OCD patients have significant problems with their spouses (Emmelkamp et al. 1990, Riggs et al. 1992).

BIBLIOGRAPHY AND ORGANIZATIONS

Self-help books are enormously helpful to patients and play an adjunctive role in cognitive-behavioral treatment. During this session, the therapist outlines reading materials, may give specific reading assignments (e.g., a chapter a week), and also makes patients aware of the different organizations that exist for patients with obsessive-compulsive disorder. These organizations may provide information on OCD, support groups, qualified professionals, and related matters. Some, like the Anxiety Disorders Association of America, also offer patients the opportunity to attend conferences and seminars to keep up to date with the research literature. See Table 3–1 for a list of resources for patients.

ETIOLOGY AND MAINTENANCE OF SYMPTOMS.

People with OCD often ask, Why me? Why am I afflicted with this illness? Although the answer to that is not entirely clear, most experts believe that both biological and psychological factors play an important role in its development. As mentioned earlier, individuals with OCD tend to have more first-degree relatives with OCD than those without OCD, suggesting that there is a genetic component to the illness. In addition, temperament and biological and psychological factors also play a role in the development of OCD. In terms of more immediate triggers, it appears that symptoms first begin for many individuals when they are faced with some life stress. However, symptoms continue even after the stressor has remitted. In fact, most people continue to have symptoms until they are treated.

EVIDENCE-BASED TREATMENTS

To date, there are essentially three evidence-based treatments: (1) serotonergic medications, (2) behavior therapy, and (3) cognitive therapy.

Discussing all the available treatments gives your patient the opportunity to consider alternate or conjunctive treatments that are in line with his desires. A quick run-through of all available treatments, specifying which ones have been demonstrated to be effective, is ethically warranted so that the patient can make an informed decision about treatment. In addition, obtaining this information allows the patient to see that the treatment he is about to receive has been scientifically studied, has been conducted on other patients with OCD, and has led to substantial improvements for a majority of patients.

Traditionally considered to be refractory to treatment, OCD now has many effective treatments. However, psychodynamic psychotherapy and many psychotropic medications have not proven effective in treating OCD (Black 1974, Knight 1949, Malan 1979, Perse 1988), and hence should not be considered first-line treatments. Instead, treatments with scientific evidence supporting their efficacy for a majority of patients should be implemented.

Serotonergic Medications

Research studies indicate that up to 60 percent of patients exhibit some response to treatment with selective serotonin reuptake inhibitors (SSRIs) and clomipramine. Treatment effects may also be augmented or improved by adding other agents (behavior therapy, antipsychotics, intravenous clomipramine) (Greist 1994). However, the average therapeutic effect appears to be moderate (Greist 1990, McCarthy and Foa 1990) and symptoms tend to recur within a few weeks in up to 90 percent of patients when drugs are discontinued (Pato et al. 1988, Thoren et al. 1980). See Table 3–2 for a list of medications used in treating obsessive-compulsive disorder.

Tricyclic Antidepressants

Although a majority of tricyclic antidepressants have been ineffective in treating obsessive-compulsive disorder, Anafranil (clomipramine) is not only effective but is currently the most widely studied medication for OCD. Experts suggest that clomipramine works where other tricyclics have failed because, in contrast to the others, it primarily increases serotonin levels in the body. (Most tricyclics work by increasing noradrenergic levels.) Although tricyclics generally tend to have more side effects than SSRIs, side effects are better tolerated by OCD patients than by patients suffering from panic or depression (Greist 1994).

Clomipramine (Anafranil) is the only tricyclic antidepressant medication shown to be effective in controlled research trials, and is the medication most extensively studied in the treatment of OCD (DeVeaugh-Geiss et al. 1989, 1990, Greist et al. 1990, Insel et al. 1983, Jenike et al. 1989a, Katz et al. 1990, Marks et al. 1980, Mavissakalian et al. 1990, Stein et al. 1992, Thoren et al. 1980, Zohar and Insel 1987). It was the first medication approved by the Food and Drug Administration for the treatment of OCD.

Table 3–2. Session 2: Summary Table for Medications Used in the Treatment of Obsessive-Compulsive Disorder (Adults)[1]

Generic name	Brand name (pharmaceutical company)	Pharmacology	Recommended dosage range	Minimum duration required to access therapeutic effect	Demonstrated to be effective in controlled research trials	Approved by the FDA for treatment of OCD
Clomipramine hydrochloride	Anafranil (Novartis)	Tricyclic antidepressant	max 250 mgs	2–3 weeks	✓	✓
Fluoxetine hydrochloride	Prozac (Eli-Lilly)	Selective serotonin reuptake inhibitor (SSRI)	20–60 mgs	4–6 weeks	✓	✓
Fluvoxamine maleate	Luvox (Solvay)	Selective serotonin reuptake inhibitor (SSRI)	100–300 mgs	4–6 weeks	✓	✓
Sertraline hydrochloride	Zoloft (Pfizer Inc.)	Selective serotonin reuptake inhibitor (SSRI)	50–200 mgs	2–3 weeks	✓	✓
Paroxetine hydrochloride	Paxil (Smith Kline Beecham)	Selective serotonin reuptake inhibitor (SSRI)	20–60 mgs	6 weeks	✓	✓

1. Information on the medications was obtained through the product information departments of the respective pharmaceutical companies.

Selective Serotonin Reuptake Inhibitors (SSRIs)

Fluvoxamine (Luvox) has been demonstrated to be superior to placebo in the treatment of obsessive-compulsive disorder (Goodman et al. 1990, Goodman et al. 1989a, Jenike et al. 1990a, Mallya et al. 1992, Perse et al. 1987, Price et al. 1987). It is approved by the Food and Drug Administration for the treatment of OCD.

Fluoxetine (Prozac) (SSRI) has been demonstrated to be superior to placebo in the treatment of obsessive-compulsive disorder (Fontaine and Chouinard 1985, Jenike et al. 1989b, Montgomery et al. 1993, Tollefson et al. 1994). It is approved by the Food and Drug Administration for the treatment of OCD.

Sertraline (Zoloft) (SSRI) has been demonstrated to be superior to placebo in the treatment of obsessive-compulsive disorder in controlled trials (Chouinard et al. 1990, Greist et al. 1995, Jenike et al. 1990b). It is now approved by the FDA for OCD indication.

Paroxetine (Paxil) (SSRI) has been evaluated in a multicenter trial to determine if it is an effective treatment for OCD (Zohar and Judge 1996) and now has FDA approval for OCD indication.

As the psychotherapist, you may or may not be directly involved with the patient's medication treatment. However, some understanding of the available medications is prudent even if you are responsible only for providing psychotherapy. As part of the psychoeducation phase in CBT, you will be informing your patient about the range of medication treatments available to him and answering questions that the patient may have in response to this information. In addition, when your patient has been previously treated with medications and has not responded, you may be in the position of determining if a referral to a psychopharmacologist is still indicated. For example, if your patient was treated with a medication not indicated for OCD, was not treated with an adequate dose of an effective medication, or was not given the medication over the recommended duration, you may still decide to refer the patient for medication despite the patient's reports that he "did not respond to medications." In addition, skilled psychopharmacologists may also consider trying the patient on more than one medication.

Finally, even if the patient has received an adequate trial of medication treatment without response, another trial may still be warranted because conjunctive behavior therapy and medication treatment may work for your patient when medication alone did not.

Cognitive Behavior Therapy

Behavior Therapy

A vast body of uncontrolled and controlled research trials conducted over many sites throughout the world attests to the effectiveness of behavior therapy (i.e., exposure and response prevention) as a treatment for obsessive-compulsive disorder (Boersma et al. 1976, Boulougouris and Bassiakos 1973, Catts and McConaghy 1975, Cobb et al. 1980, Emmelkamp et al. 1985, Emmelkamp and Kraanen 1977, Emmelkamp et al. 1980, Emmelkamp et al. 1989, Emmelkamp et al. 1988, Fals-Stewart et al. 1993, Foa and Goldstein 1978, Foa et al. 1983b, Foa et al. 1992, Foa et al. 1984, Hodgson et al. 1972, Hoogduin and Hoogduin 1984, Julien et al. 1980, Marks et al. 1975, Marks et al. 1988, Meyer 1966, Meyer and Levy 1973, Meyer et al. 1974, Rabavilas et al. 1976, Rachman et al. 1971, Rachman et al. 1973, Roper et al. 1975, Steketee et al. 1982).

These and other trials, conducted to examine the efficacy of exposure and response prevention, generally show that between 50 and 75 percent of patients with obsessions and compulsion exhibit a substantial decrease in their symptoms, and that a majority appear to maintain gains in treatment even years after they discontinue treatment. (For a comprehensive and detailed review of studies demonstrating the efficacy of behavior therapy, please see Abramowitz [1997], Foa et al. [1998], Foa et al. [1985], and Steketee [1993]). A recent meta-analysis by Abramowitz (1997) examining only controlled trials confirms the finding that combined exposure and response prevention leads to a substantial improvement in patients with obsessive-compulsive disorder, and also finds that the effectiveness of behavioral treatments increases as more hours are spent in therapist-guided exposure.

Exposure appears somewhat less effective in the treatment of pure obsessionals (patients who present with obsessive ruminations but no compulsions) (Emmelkamp and Kwee 1977, Kasvikis and Marks 1988, Salkovskis and Kirk 1997, Steketee 1993, Stern 1978). However, experts believe that many pure obsessionals may present with covert rituals that are not classified as such and that the untreated rituals may thus serve to hinder the treatment of obsessions (Steketee 1993).

An examination of the relative efficacy of behavioral techniques for the treatment of obsessive thoughts indicates that obsessive thoughts respond primarily to exposure (Foa et al. 1984, Foa et al. 1980a), and that combined in vivo and imaginal exposure appears to be superior at maintaining long-term gains, particularly for those patients who cognitively avoid their catastrophic fears (Foa et al. 1980b). Efficacy studies also indicate that ritualized behaviors and thoughts respond primarily to response prevention (Foa et al. 1984, Foa et al. 1980a, Mills et al. 1973, Turner et al. 1980).

Cognitive Therapy. A number of case reports have suggested that cognitive therapy is an effective treatment for obsessive-compulsive disorder (Headland and McDonald 1987, Roth and Church 1994, Salkovskis 1983, Salkovskis and Westbrook 1989), especially when used adjunctively with behavioral techniques such as exposure and response prevention (Freeston 1994, Kearney and Silverman 1990, Salkovskis and Warwick 1985, 1986). Recent evidence from controlled studies not only confirms that cognitive strategies are effective in treating OCD, but finds that they may be as effective as behavioral strategies when used alone (Emmelkamp and Beens 1991, Emmelkamp et al. 1988, van Oppen et al. 1995). A recent meta-analysis combining only controlled trials confirms the finding that cognitive strategies are at least as effective as behavioral treatments (Abramowitz 1997).

Cognitive therapy has also been used to treat patients who are resistant to behavior therapy alone (Salkovskis and Warwick 1985, 1986), especially pure obsessionals or patients without overt rituals who tend not to respond well to exposure and response prevention alone (Salkovskis and Kirk 1997). However, more controlled research trials are needed to better determine the effectiveness of cognitive therapy as a treatment for OCD.

Cognitive Behavioral Treatment Rationale

Because many patients have no familiarity with cognitive behavior therapy and, in fact, may have prior experience with traditional dynamic therapies, orienting them to CBT is crucial, as it enables the patient to understand what is expected of him and to decide whether or not he is willing to make the commitment.

Before the treatment components are outlined, patients are given a brief summary of the cognitive-behavioral therapy and the model underlying the treatment. At this juncture, a general explanation is offered, with a more detailed rationale of the cognitive and behavior model of obsessive-compulsive disorder presented when the respective treatment components are introduced.

Again, the following explanation is written in a style that is simple and clear for patients. However, you may choose to further simplify the language (or not), based upon your sense of the patient's background. Do not assume that patients know more than they do, as it is better to err on the side of being redundant than not presenting the information.

Cognitive Behavior Therapy:
- Short-term, symptom-focused treatment approach
- Identifies and modifies maladaptive thoughts and behaviors

- Reduces emotional distress and improves functioning
- Alleviates the anxiety associated with obsessions, thereby reducing the frequency and persistence of these thoughts, images, impulses, or urges
- Breaks the association between compulsions and the subsequent feelings of relief or reduced anxiety

Cognitive behavior therapy (CBT) is a short-term, symptom-focused treatment approach that attempts to reduce emotional distress and improve functioning in patients with psychological disorders. CBT achieves this by examining and modifying thoughts and behaviors that such individuals tend to exhibit, which are believed to perpetuate the symptoms and problems. As these characteristic thoughts and behaviors are modified, patients feel significantly better, their symptoms improve, and they are able to function more effectively. CBT has been demonstrated to be effective for a variety of psychological disorders, including obsessive-compulsive disorder, as we discussed earlier.

With regard to OCD, CBT targets symptoms such as obsessive thoughts and compulsive rituals. We spoke earlier about how your obsessions make you feel anxious and how you try very hard to reduce your anxiety by performing your rituals. However, performing your rituals makes you feel better only for a short period of time, and before long, your obsessions come back, you feel anxious again, and you go back to performing your rituals. As a result, you begin to ritualize more and more until the rituals become so time consuming that you have no time left for anything else. It becomes like a drug, and you need to do more and more to get the same effect. And ironically, because you try so hard to stop thinking about your obsessions, you think about them more and more, and so you need to ritualize more and more.

In CBT, we try to understand why your obsessions make you so anxious in the first place, and once we understand we try to reduce your anxiety associated with the obsessions. As your anxiety drops, you'll see that your obsessions will become less frequent and less persistent. As part of this treatment, we also work on reducing the amount you ritualize. Cognitive behavior therapy does this by breaking the association between your rituals and your subsequent feelings of relief. Through therapy, as you begin to realize that your anxiety will go down even if you do not ritualize, thus showing your rituals serve no purpose, you will no longer need to perform the rituals.

COMPONENTS OF
COGNITIVE-BEHAVIORAL TREATMENT

The different techniques to be used in treatment are briefly described here so that patients have a general understanding of how cognitive behavior therapy works. In particular, the clinician should emphasize that patients will experience temporary increases in anxiety during the course of therapy and that this evocation of anxiety is necessary for the anxiety to ultimately be diminished. Although this discussion will inevitably trigger anxiety and some patients may choose not to continue treatment, it is essential to prepare them at this stage, when the discussion is still abstract, in order to help ensure future compliance with treatment. It is better to address concerns at this point, rather than waiting until later on when the patient may lose trust in the therapist after being unpleasantly surprised by increases in anxiety.

Presenting the Components

CBT for OCD comprises four broad, essential techniques: psychoeducation, cognitive restructuring, exposure, and response prevention. I am going to describe psychoeducation in some detail because that is what we have been doing today. I will then briefly outline the other techniques we will be using in our therapy together and then we will discuss them at greater length when we actually begin to use them over the next few sessions. It is important to keep in mind that we will always go at a pace that is relatively comfortable for you, so you are always in control, and so there is no need for you to fear the process.

Psychoeducation

Today I have been telling you all about OCD because I believe that as you understand the illness, realize that it is a problem shared by millions of other people, and know that it is a problem that can be diagnosed and treated, your anxiety about having OCD will begin to drop. My goal in teaching you these facts is so that you realize that OCD is not a mental flaw or weakness, and that having it doesn't mean that you're crazy. Although you may still not be entirely convinced of this today, my goal is that over the course of our work together, you will slowly come to see it for what it is, an illness that can be diagnosed and treated.

Cognitive Restructuring

During our next session, we will begin to systematically modify some of your assumptions and beliefs about OCD, and about people and the world in order to reduce anxiety associated with your obsessions and compulsions. For example, much of your anxiety stems from what you believe it means to have these obsessions, and that you believe you are bad or are an evil person for having them. We will begin by examining these and other thoughts that go through your mind every day, and then as we understand how these thoughts make you anxious, we will work on giving you skills to change this inner dialogue or self talk so that you ultimately feel less anxious.

Exposure techniques

Once you have the skills to reduce your anxiety, we will begin to help you to directly confront or face what makes you anxious. For example, we know through research that when people are exposed to situations that they fear, their anxiety gradually declines over time. They habituate or become accustomed to these situations as they realize that their fears do not come true. For example, people who are afraid of flying would be helped to confront their fears by slowly approaching a plane, sitting in one, flying shorter distances, then longer ones, and so on, until they are no longer afraid. In the same way, you will be helped to confront your fear of using public toilets, of Michael being stabbed or harmed, and so on, in small, gradual steps until your fears about them go down. Although the very idea of confronting these fears may seem out of the question at the moment, remember that you will have already developed some skills to reduce your anxiety by then. In addition, remember that we will be confronting your fears in a slow, gradual fashion, and you and I will both decide which step to take next. Although our goal is to expose you to all your fears, particularly your worst fears, if you feel that you are too afraid to confront a particular situation, we will stop and take even smaller steps until you feel ready to go ahead. Everything will be broken down in small portions so that you don't feel overwhelmed.

Response Prevention

We are also going to be working to reduce your compulsions so that you are able to take your life back and not spend hours performing these rituals. It will also become easier for you to become accustomed to your obsessions if we stop you from doing your rituals. But since it is a habit you have developed over the years, we will have to work together actively to break it. We may even need to call on Michael or someone else to help you not perform your rituals outside the session. My goal is to help you see that your anxiety will go down even if you do not perform your rituals. I also want to help you realize that your fears about Michael getting stabbed, or you being contaminated with ticks, are not only very unlikely to occur, but that if even on the unlikely chance they were to occur, performing your rituals wouldn't prevent them from happening anyway. I know that the thought of not performing your rituals is making you anxious right now, but I want you to know that you and I will be working together to decide how to proceed, and that you will just be taking small steps at a time.

CLARIFY TREATMENT EXPECTATIONS
AND GOALS

It is also important to clarify the limitations of CBT so that patients begin treatment with realistic expectations and do not expect a "cure" by the end of treatment. OCD is a chronic condition and one should expect symptoms to wax and wane in severity, usually as a function of stress. Hence, patients will not be symptom free at the end of the treatment, and indeed, in many cases, may never be completely free of all symptoms. Even in cases where complete symptom remission is ultimately possible, it may take many months or years for that to occur. However, patients should expect that their anxiety will be reduced substantially and that their symptoms will become more manageable. Patients may also be told that the goal of treatment is for them to experience significantly less anxiety when their obsessions are triggered, to be better able to resist their rituals, and, as a result, to have fewer obsessions and rituals. Once they learn these skills, they can continue to implement them until the symptoms disappear or become negligible.

NEXT WEEK

Explaining the Importance of Homework

The patient is informed that homework, from monitoring thoughts and rituals, to performing cognitive restructuring during episodes of anxiety, to conducting exposure and response prevention at home, will become an integral part of treatment. Patients are helped to realize that homework is assigned in cognitive-behavioral treatment so that therapeutic results may be generalized outside the session, and that although assignments will be examined to ensure that accurate learning is taking place, no effort will be made to grade the assignments.

Selecting a Co-therapist

For outpatient treatment to be successful, it is critical that a supportive friend or family member be identified to function as a co-therapist outside therapy sessions. The co-therapist can help in providing support and tracking symptoms, and, most important of all, help patients conduct homework on the outside. Enlisting a co-therapist is particularly useful when assisting patients to block ritualized behaviors.

At the end of this session, the therapist and patient work together in deciding who may be an effective co-therapist. Ideally, the person should be someone who lives with the patient. It is equally important that this person be empathic and noncritical. Often, the spouse—who may spend the most time with the patient—may not always be an appropriate candidate if he is unable to control his feelings of frustration and anger toward the patient's symptoms.

Once the co-therapist is identified, the individual is brought in during a therapy session, where the therapist explains the treatment rationale, how exactly he should offer constructive, noncritical support, and steps he should take if the patient fails to do the appropriate homework. The identified co-therapist person should be in regular contact with the therapist.

Assigning Next Week's Homework

Forms that monitor the type and frequency of obsessions and rituals are handed out at the end of this session (see Table 3–3). The Obsession-Compulsion Monitoring form is one such example, and it is given to patients to fill out over the next week. The therapist describes the purpose of monitoring symptoms and explains how to fill out the form. Although it is primarily intended to get an accurate estimate of the frequency with which patients ritualize and in response to what obsessional triggers, some patients' rituals may actually decrease in frequency and/or duration merely through the process of self-monitoring.

The psychoeducation summary table (Table 3–1) and a tape of the session are also given to the patient so that facts learned in this session may be strengthened and used for future reference.

Table 3–3. Obsession-Compulsion Monitoring Form

Name_____ Date_____

Time of day	Describe obsession (intrusive images, thoughts, urges, ideas, impulses that create anxiety and/or the urge to ritualize) or the trigger that elicits the urge to ritualize	Record level of anxiety (0–100)	Describe compulsive ritual (mental or behavioral acts that create a sense of relief or reduction in anxiety)	Record time spent on ritual	Record level of relief (0–100)
6–6:30 A.M.					
6:30–7 A.M.					
7–7:30 A.M.					
7:30–8 A.M.					
8–8:30 A.M.					
8:30–9 A.M.					
9–9:30 A.M.					
9:30–10 A.M.					
10–10:30 A.M.					
10:30–11 A.M.					
11–11:30 A.M.					
11:30–12 P.M.					
12–12:30 P.M.					
12:30–1 P.M.					
1–1:30 P.M.					

1:30–2 P.M.

2–2:30 P.M.

2:30–3 P.M.

3–3:30 P.M.

3:30–4 P.M.

4–4:30 P.M.

4:30–5 P.M.

5–5:30 P.M.

5:30–6 P.M.

6–6:30 P.M.

6:30–7 P.M.

7–7:30 P.M.

7:30–8 P.M.

8–8:30 P.M.

8:30–9 P.M.

9–9:30 P.M.

9:30–10 P.M.

10–10:30 P.M.

10:30–11 P.M.

11–11:30 P.M.

11:30–12 P.M.

12–6 A.M.

Session 3:
Cognitive Restructuring
(Phase I)

IDENTIFYING AUTOMATIC THOUGHTS

Session Goals	*Check When Done*

1. Review (5–10 minutes)   ☐
   - Obtain feedback on Session 2
   - Review homework (thought record and ritual monitoring form)
   - Briefly review events that occurred over past week

2. The Session (Cognitive Restructuring Phase I)   ☐
   - Provide rationale for cognitive restructuring
   - Defining automatic thoughts
   - Monitoring automatic thoughts
   - Tackling complications

3. Next week (5–10 minutes)   ☐
   - Discuss homework to be completed
     —Obsession-Compulsion Monitoring form (OCM) (see Table 3–3)
     —Automatic Thought Log (ATL) (see Table 4–1)
   - Anticipate potential stressors that may occur during the week

SESSION OVERVIEW

This session marks the beginning of cognitive restructuring, which is described over a two-session period for purposes of illustration. However, cognitive restructuring, once introduced, continues on an ongoing basis throughout therapy. In Phase I, the rationale for cognitive restructuring is provided and patient's obsessions and automatic thoughts are identified.

Following a review of the prior session, assigned homework, and events over the past week, the therapist describes the specific elements and rationale for cognitive restructuring. What is it? How is it conducted? How does it help reduce obsessions and compulsions? What is an "automatic thought"? What effect does it have on anxiety? Answers to these questions form the bulk of the first half of the session. Following this, a "thought log" is filled out so that patients can observe how obsessions and automatic thoughts should be recorded. The session ends with a discussion of next week's homework, and potential events and troublesome situations that may come up for the patient.

Forms used during this session include the Automatic Thought Log and the Cognitive Distortions Sheet (Burns 1989, pp. 8–11).

REVIEW

The session begins with a quick review of Session 2, including any feedback or reactions the patient may have had to the previous session. Did the patient receive the information as it was intended? Was it helpful? Does he still have any myths or misinterpretations, or did he develop any new ones?

The therapist also collects the homework. The therapist takes a few minutes to see if the Obsession-Compulsion Monitoring form was filled out accurately, and whether the patient experienced any difficulties identifying obsessions, noting the frequency and length of each compulsion, and so on.

THE SESSION:
COGNITIVE RESTRUCTURING PHASE I

RATIONALE FOR COGNITIVE RESTRUCTURING

Why Is a Rationale Necessary?

Before cognitive restructuring can begin, and because a theoretical understanding is believed to improve treatment compliance and efficacy, the rationale for cognitive restructuring is offered to patients. In simple language, the therapist defines the concepts (e.g., What is cognitive restructuring?), describes the rationale (How does it work?), and cites evidence to demonstrate its efficacy (studies have shown that it works).

The Rationale

Why Is Cognitive Restructuring Used in the Treatment of OCD?

Cognitive theorists suggest that faulty cognitive processing is a central component in OCD because unwanted thoughts, images, ideas, and impulses are cardinal features of the illness. Cognitive models hypothesize that a *faulty appraisal style* may underlie the dysfunction in obsessive-compulsive disorder (A. Beck 1976, Beech and Liddell 1974, Carr 1974, Foa and Kozak 1985, Guidano and Liotti 1983, McFall and Wollershein 1979, Pitman 1987, Reed 1985, Salkovskis 1985, Warren and Zgourides 1991, Wegner 1989). As discussed above, having obsessions is not believed to be dysfunctional in and of itself. In fact, research shows that up to 90 percent of the "normal" population report having cognitive intrusions (Rachman and De Silva 1978). According to Salkovskis (1985, 1989), individuals who develop obsessive-compulsive disorder differ from the normal population in that they have dysfunctional, anxiety-provoking automatic thoughts in the presence of intrusive obsessions. These automatic thoughts, in turn, are based on certain core assumptions and beliefs held by individuals about themselves and others. In other words, the dysfunction lies not in the obsessions themselves but in the way these obsessions are processed or appraised by individuals with a particular *belief system*. Due to this faulty appraisal, these individuals experience greater anxiety in response to the obsessions, find it more difficult to dismiss them or ignore them, and end up ritualizing in order to alleviate the anxiety associated with them.

Cognitive restructuring is employed to identify and challenge these faulty appraisals (as well as the assumptions and beliefs on which they are based) and replace them with more realistic perceptions, so that the anxiety provoked by the obsessions can decline without requiring the use of pathological coping methods such as compulsive rituals. If successfully done, this will lead to a decrease in the frequency and intensity of obsessions and compulsions.

What Kinds of Distorted Beliefs Occur in OCD?

Several irrational beliefs have been linked to obsessive-compulsive disorder (see Steketee 1993). For example, obsessions allegedly cause discomfort or anxiety because the individual believes that having obsessions means that some harm may come to himself (e.g., I may infest myself with germs) or others around him (my mother will die if I have obsessions about her dying). Individuals with obsessive-compulsive disorder presumably *overestimate the risk associated with everyday concerns* about health, safety, death, sex, morality, and concern about others, and, as a result, experience excessive and unrealistic anxiety in the presence of obsessional stimuli (Carr 1974, Foa and Kozak 1985, Salkovskis 1985, Steiner 1972). OCD patients may also have unrealistic demands for safety, and assume that a situation is dangerous unless proven safe even though common logic and previous experience may dictate otherwise (Kozak et al. 1987). In addition, individuals with obsessive-compulsive disorder also tend to *underestimate their ability to cope with this risk or harm*, which leads to heightened feelings of helplessness, uncertainty, and discomfort that the individual believes can only be reduced by ineffective coping methods such as performing compulsive rituals (McFall and Wollershein 1979).

Some research supports the notion that individuals with obsessive-compulsive disorder tend to be filled with *doubt and uncertainty* (Beech and Lidell 1974, Guidano and Liotti 1983, Reed 1985). Because they are never quite sure if their conclusions are accurate, individuals with obsessive-compulsive disorder perform ritualistic behaviors such as checking in order to relieve themselves of the discomfort of potentially being wrong. As a result, decision making becomes arduous if not impossible, and such individuals need an inordinate amount of information before they can make a decision. Frequently, they catastrophize about the result of making a wrong decision.

The belief system of individuals with obsessive-compulsive disorder is also characterized by a sense of *perfectionism, rigidity, and moralism* (McFall and Wollershein 1979, Steketee et al. 1991). Such individuals believe that they must be perfect in all endeavors, tend to have rigid ideas of right and wrong, have a more "tender conscience" than others (Reed 1985), and believe that failure to live up to these ideals could lead to punishment. Such beliefs create tremendous anxiety and lead to an overconcern with precision and control.

However, according to Salkovskis (1985, 1989), the key dysfunction in obsessive-compulsive disorder and one that encompasses all others involves distorted beliefs about *responsibility and self-blame*. Obsessions lead to compulsive thoughts and behaviors rather than just heightened anxiety because individuals believe that, unless they do something to prevent it (i.e., perform rituals), they are responsible for the harm that may occur (it will be my fault if my mother dies unless I repeatedly check the gas stove to make sure that it's off). They do not merely overestimate risk or harm, as do individuals with other anxiety disorders; they additionally hold themselves accountable or responsible for the potential harm. This sense of responsibility leads to tremendous shame or guilt, which the individual finds intolerable. Along these lines, other theorists have suggested that individuals with OCD tend to *fuse thought and action*, meaning that they tend to equate thinking (if I have an obsession about killing my son) with doing (I will succeed in killing him in reality), thus heightening their sense of responsibility, guilt, and shame (Rachman 1993).

As a result, the individual seeks a variety of methods to diminish his exaggerated sense of responsibility. By suppressing or neutralizing the obsessions (e.g., escaping or avoiding situations that trigger obsessions, seeking reassurance from others, performing rituals), this perceived responsibility declines temporarily, and thus leads to a reduction in feelings of shame and guilt. Ironically, it is the very attempt to suppress or neutralize obsessions that creates more discomfort in the long run and leads to an increase in obsessions, thereby creating a vicious cycle of alternating obsessions and compulsions.

How Does Cognitive Restructuring Work?

Cognitive restructuring works to modify the faulty appraisal style (e.g., distorted beliefs about responsibility) manifested by individuals with OCD, and in doing so reduces anxiety and the frequency of the obsessions themselves. By identifying the automatic thoughts that trigger anxiety, by challenging the erroneous beliefs and assumptions on which they are based, and by substituting more realistic (and invariably less anxiety provoking) ways of appraising the world, the individual experiences less anxiety when obsessions occur, and as a result has fewer and fewer obsessions. Why? Because anxiety is believed to fuel obsessions; as it declines, obsessions decline accordingly. For example, as the automatic thoughts that stem from distorted beliefs about responsibility are challenged and modified, the individual experiences less anxiety when they occur, and therefore, in the long run, has fewer obsessions.

Clinical Vignette

THERAPIST: Although I briefly outlined the different components of treatment during the last session, I'm now going to more fully describe what we'll be doing during the next few sessions. We will soon begin examining and modifying some of your thoughts using a technique called "cognitive restructuring." Let me begin by telling you what it is and why it's useful for us to do it.

ALLISON: Okay.

THERAPIST: Our goal is to reduce your obsessions and the amount of time you spend ritualizing, so that you feel better and are able to function more effectively. In order to do that, we have to look at why your obsessions recur and what makes you say or do something repeatedly. Most people have obsessions now and then, and on occasion most people will repeat certain actions even though they know there is no need to do so. For example, let's say someone is sitting in church and has a sexual thought about the person next to him even though he may not even be sexually attracted to that person and even though he may want to concentrate on the sermon. What this person just had was an obsession, an intrusive thought or image. It's just like you do, for example, when you have an obsession about Michael getting strangled. Let's consider another example. A person who is scheduled to fly checks her purse to make sure she has her airline tickets. She checks them when she wakes up, right before she leaves, and a few times on her way to the airport, even though she knows that the tickets are exactly where she left them. She does it because it reassures her. She believes she is "better safe than sorry." That's similar to a ritual you have when you check to see if the gas stove is off or when you call Michael repeatedly to make sure he is all right even though you know you just did it a moment ago.

ALLISON (incredulously): I see what you're saying but you are going to have a hard time persuading me that most people have thoughts like I do. It isn't that I don't trust you. I do. But that's a hard sell. If most people have obsessions and compulsions, then why am I in a shrink's office and the rest of humanity is out there having a good time?

THERAPIST (smiles): We don't know if everyone out there is having a good time but you're right, there are very good reasons why you need treatment and those without obsessive-compulsive disorder do not. Consider this. Up to 99 percent of people report that they have obsessions every now and then. This has been demonstrated in several research studies. However, most people don't have *recurring* obsessions and compulsions to the point where they can't function well. So first we need to understand why you and others who suffer from this disorder have obsessions over and over again, and why you ritualize the way you do when most people don't.

ALLISON: The difference is that they have it sometimes and I have it a lot of the time.

THERAPIST: Yes, that's one of the differences and we need to understand why. But if you're still having trouble believing that most people have occasional obsessions and compulsions, what you could do is check with people in your life who don't suffer from obsessive-compulsive disorder. Why don't you ask Michael, for example, if he has ever had an intrusive thought or image like that or whether he has ever done something more than once even if he knows that he just did it? I can tell you that it happens to me at times.

ALLISON: Believe me I will. I will even ask my I-never-do-anything-wrong friend, Rachel.

THERAPIST (laughs): Good. Ask as many people as you can and let me know what they say in the next session. Now let's go ahead in understanding this some more. Very simply, the theory on which cognitive therapy is based says that the reason you cannot stop your obsessions is that you try too hard to stop them in the first place. And the reason you try to stop them in the first place is because these obsessions make you anxious for some reason.

ALLISON: You would feel anxious too if you had such weird thoughts.

THERAPIST: Actually, Allison, what I'm saying is that a lot of people have weird thoughts or obsessions but that they don't necessarily make everyone anxious. They certainly make you feel very anxious and so you try very hard to stop them from entering your mind. And here's the catch-22. The more you try to stop them from coming, the more they come. In fact, it's because you try to stop them from coming that they come repeatedly. It's like the old joke: stop thinking of a white elephant. Now all you can do is think of a white elephant, right.

ALLISON (acknowledges): Uh-huh.

THERAPIST: Another good example is dieting. People will usually report that the more they try not to think about food, the more obsessed they become with it. That is similar to what occurs in obsessive-compulsive disorder. It's because you try so hard to get rid of the obsessions that they come back at you like a boomerang. The reason you try to stop them is because they bother you, because they make you feel so anxious. It's your way of taking the anxiety away. And that brings us to the rituals. Because you can't stop the obsessions, you come up with other ways of reducing your anxiety. You distract yourself, you avoid doing things that will trigger your obsessions, you seek reassurance from others, and most of all you ritualize over and over again to reduce your anxiety. And the irony here is that the more you distract, avoid, and ritualize, the more obsessions you ultimately have. And the vicious cycle continues because the more obsessions you have, the more you distract, the more you avoid, and the more you ritualize.

ALLISON: Hmm, that's interesting. I'm not sure I understand everything you just said, especially the last part about why avoiding or ritualizing makes my obsessions increase, but what you're saying makes some sense to me. I know that my obsessions do bother me tremendously, they make me sick to my stomach. But that's natural, isn't it? For example, I don't want my husband to die, so thinking about it is bound to make me anxious, right?

THERAPIST: I will explain why distracting, avoiding, or ritualizing increases your obsessions before we end today, but let me first address what you just said. Is it natural or inevitable for obsessions to make someone anxious? Actually, I'm saying that it is not natural or inevitable. And that's the reason why we will be doing cognitive restructuring. What I'm saying is that the obsessions themselves don't make you anxious. What makes you anxious is what it *means* to you that you are having obsessions—what you think about the fact that you are having obsessions, or what you take the obsessions to mean. For example, I know you believe that it's wrong to have such obsessional thoughts and, as a result, you cannot discuss or ignore them.

ALLISON: But it is wrong.

THERAPIST: I know you think that. And it's because you believe it that you feel so anxious when you have obsessions. You also believe that your obsessions will come true, that you should be able to control them, and mostly that you will be at fault if something bad happens to you or someone else when you fail to ritualize. For example, you believe that Michael will actually die if you have obsessions about him dying. So of course, if you believe that, having these obsessions is very dangerous, and you try your best to get rid of them. So what I'm saying, and what cognitive therapy says, is that your obsessions make you anxious because you believe they are dangerous.

ALLISON: But it's true, it's not that I just happen to believe these things.

THERAPIST: I know you think that they're true. And given that you think these things, it is completely understandable that you get so anxious and cannot stop yourself from ritualizing over and over again. If I believed, like you do, that having thoughts about my husband dying might actually lead to his death, or at the very least that it means that I want him to die, I would feel very upset and anxious too, and would do all I could to stop the obsessions. And if I thought that doing something over and over again would stop him from dying, I would most certainly keep on doing it. No matter what anyone else thought. Even if they thought I was crazy.

ALLISON: (begins crying).

(Pause)

THERAPIST: Allison, what made you cry just now?

ALLISON: Just hearing you say that you understand. No one has ever said that to me before. Everyone thinks I'm cuckoo, a kook for doing all this crazy stuff. Even if they don't say it, I know from the way they look at me.

THERAPIST: I know, it must be hard to believe that people around you think you're crazy and to have people not understand what you're going through. Allison, you may not believe me now, but you are quite sane. I am not saying that your thoughts are true or that we don't need to change them, because I do not believe that they are true—and yes, they do need to be changed in order for you to get better. What I am saying is that having these thoughts does not mean you're crazy, and in fact, given that you have them, it makes perfect sense that you do what you do over and over again.

ALLISON: Okay (pause). You know, I feel a little better hearing that.

THERAPIST: I'm glad. Allison, I want to make sure we're on the same page, so can you tell me in your own words what you remember from our discussion today?

ALLISON: I can try. You said that almost everyone has obsessions now and then but because they don't try to stop them, they wind up not having that many.

THERAPIST: Exactly. Because the more you try to stop thinking about something, the harder it is not to think about it.

ALLISON: And the more you try and stop it, the more obsessions you have.

THERAPIST: Yes. And the reason people with obsessive-compulsive disorder want to control the obsessions is because . . . (pause)

ALLISON: Because they think it is wrong to have them.

THERAPIST: Right. People with obsessive-compulsive disorder have many beliefs about their obsessions, such as that it's wrong or dangerous to have them. They also tend to believe that harm will come to themselves or the people they love, that they may be responsible for this harm, that they should be able to control their thoughts, and that making mistakes is not acceptable. Having these beliefs makes them so anxious that they do whatever they can to reduce the anxiety by avoiding, ritualizing, distracting, and so on. Think about it, it is quite a burden to feel this way.

ALLISON (closes her eyes): So let me see if I have it. Because we have these beliefs, these obsessions make us nervous; because they make us nervous, we try and stop them; and because we try and stop them, they increase.

THERAPIST: Exactly.

ALLISON: But wait, you said earlier that ritualizing can also increase obsessions?

THERAPIST: Yes, ironically, it can. Let me see if I can explain. Let's say that you call Mike repeatedly because you think that that will keep him alive. He stays alive and so you believe that you kept him alive. You are flooded with relief and feel that you're off the hook, that you are no longer responsible for his death. And so you keep on calling him each time you have a vision of him dying. But the relief from ritualizing only lasts for a short time, and before you know it, you have another image of him dying, so you call him some more, and some more. But because the effects are temporary, bang comes another image, and so the vicious cycle continues, and increases the obsessions and compulsions.

When you ritualize and the things that you fear don't happen, you conclude that the rituals prevented them from occurring. And so, you don't learn that there is no connection between ritualizing and bad or good things happening. By ritualizing, you never truly learn that there is no connection between your telephone calls and Michael dying, or for that matter, between your obsessions of him dying and his actual death. You don't learn that thoughts cannot kill or save anyone. You also don't learn that the anxiety about the obsessions would have decreased naturally anyway. When you stop ritualizing, you learn that what you feared would happen does not, in fact, happen. For example, you believe that Michael is alive because you keep calling him. If you did not call him, and he did not die that day, you would hopefully start considering that maybe your obsessions cannot kill him whether you call him or not.

ALLISON: Hmm. He could have gotten lucky one day, though.

THERAPIST: He could, but if it kept happening and he remained alive, then we would either have to believe that he is the luckiest man in the world or consider the more realistic alternative.

ALLISON: Maybe, but you would have to get me to stop ritualizing to find out and I'm not sure if I'm ready to do that just yet. In fact, I'm regretting starting therapy at this moment, I'm feeling a little panicky, like you're going to force me to stop ritualizing—and I know I can't.

THERAPIST: I know this is hard, Allison, and I'm sorry you feel panicky. Would it help to know that you won't be forced to do anything and that most patients react this way in the beginning? Your anxiety is completely understandable. This conversation has probably even generated some obsessions, and you're probably ritualizing right now or feel pressured to leave my office so you can ritualize. Am I right?

ALLISON (smiles tearfully): Aren't I pathetic? I'm repeating "safe Mike" because I know I can't call him now. And yes, I am waiting for the session to end so I can call him. I was even wondering if I saw a pay phone on my way here.

THERAPIST: Hmm, that must be so distressing. I can understand why you feel pressured to ritualize. Let me just assure you on one point, though. You are not going to be forced to do anything in here. Before we begin each component, you and I will agree to proceed. We will also agree on how to handle the inevitable misgivings you will have during treatment. You will have misgivings and will never be entirely "ready" or at ease about not ritualizing—if you were, you wouldn't need treatment. So both of us will have to agree on how I can remind you to do certain things, ask you to do things, and even cajole you to do things you are nervous about doing. That is my job. But if at any point you want to put the brakes on because you simply are not ready for the next stage, all you have to do is to let me know and we'll stop. Is that a deal?

ALLISON: Yes.

DEFINING AUTOMATIC THOUGHTS

Once the rationale and the principles are presented, the actual tasks of cognitive restructuring can begin. During the remainder of this session, patients learn about automatic thoughts and how to identify and record them. A "thought log" is filled out during the session in order to model the desired behavior and to teach patients how and when to fill out the record.

What Are Automatic Thoughts?

Although patients have been given a general sense of what types of thoughts are being examined, they should now be provided with a detailed description of automatic thoughts to help them understand what they are specifically required to record on a continuous basis.

As initially defined by Beck (1969), an automatic thought (or image) is a quick, discrete evaluation a person makes of his life situation. Such thoughts may represent an explanation of the past (e.g., Michael was sick last week because I didn't ritualize enough), the present (she thinks I'm crazy), or may be a prediction about the future (Michael will die unless I call him twenty-one times). Automatic thoughts are not specific to individuals with obsessive-compulsive disorder or even to individuals with psychological illnesses but are experienced universally. However, the types of automatic thoughts that individuals with OCD have are often very similar.

Automatic thoughts generate emotional states such as anxiety, depression, and even pleasant emotional states such as happiness (e.g., my husband loves me). However, dysfunctional automatic thoughts such as those occurring in OCD create persistent negative emotional states and hence are the ones targeted in treatment. Automatic thoughts also influence behaviors (Allison makes twenty-one phone calls to Michael), and can lead to a variety of physiological reactions (tensing muscles, increased heart rate).

Automatic thoughts are so called because they occur rapidly, automatically, without deliberate reasoning, and are uncritically accepted by individuals as being true, in contrast to what they think about a situation. Automatic thoughts are typically outside of awareness, and are initially difficult to identify because individuals are not used to thinking about their thoughts (although the feelings they generate may be easily identified). However, automatic thoughts are not unconscious and, with training, are readily accessible for most patients.

As outlined in Beck's seminal work on depression (1976), automatic thoughts (e.g., Michael will be killed unless I call him now) form the most superficial level of cognition and are based on dysfunctional assumptions (my behavior is related to what happens to others), which in turn are based on core beliefs held by individuals about themselves and others (I am an evil, harmful person). Core beliefs represent the most fundamental level of cognition and are hypothesized to develop in childhood, as a result of repetitive and often dysfunctional interactions with significant others. However, cognitive therapy does not usually explore childhood origins and experiences in order to correct these distorted beliefs. Instead, current, situation-specific automatic thoughts held by the patient become the conduit through which assumptions and core beliefs are ultimately changed. In other words, as the daily automatic thoughts are gradually challenged and replaced with more realistic appraisals of the world, over time the underlying assumptions and core beliefs also get modified. Later on in therapy, assumptions and beliefs are often addressed directly in order to maintain gains and prevent relapse (J. Beck 1995).

Automatic Thoughts in Obsessive-Compulsive Disorder

Individuals with an underlying belief system characterized by themes of *responsibility* and the like (see above for description of other core beliefs in OCD) have automatic thoughts when intrusive obsessions occur, and as a result are filled with high levels of anxiety and distress. The automatic thoughts are appraisals or evaluations of the obsessions (e.g., my obsessional image of Michael dying will cause his death) and reflect the individual's underlying belief system (I am an evil person). Automatic thoughts or appraisals that occur upon the performance of rituals generate feelings of relief because they alter the appraisals that follow obsessional urges (by checking to see that Michael is alive, I have, in effect, kept him alive by my actions).

Clinical Vignette

THERAPIST: Let's try and spend some time understanding what automatic thoughts are and how they affect how you feel and what you do. As I was saying earlier, automatic thoughts are the inner dialogue people have with themselves. It's a silent, inner dialogue that goes on in our heads all the time and is our way of making sense of the events in our lives. They can just pop into our minds and have a profound effect on how we feel. For example, you had mentioned a few weeks ago that you had suddenly begun feeling anxious around your sister-in-law.

ALLISON: Yes, I still am.

THERAPIST: Do you remember what we figured out? About when the anxiety first began and how?

ALLISON: Yes, I was afraid that she caught something in the mall restroom and that she would pass it along to me.

THERAPIST: Exactly. You had an automatic thought when she came out of the restroom, something like, "Lauren probably caught something in there and I will get it if I touch her or if I am close to her." That was your quick take on the situation, which made you very nervous and made you avoid her, and which is still making you avoid her.

ALLISON: I see.

THERAPIST: An automatic thought can be an explanation of something that happened in the past or is occurring in the present, or it can be a prediction of what will happen in the future. These thoughts occur so automatically, so rapidly, that you barely realize that you're having a thought.

ALLISON: You said that everyone has them, not just people with OCD.

THERAPIST: Yes, that's true. But there are certain thoughts that occur to people with obsessive-compulsive disorder that you and I need to focus on. What I had said earlier was that soon after an obsession strikes you, your mind gets filled with various types of automatic thoughts that make you so anxious that you try your best to stop yourself from having the obsessions. You either distract yourself, perform your rituals, or actually avoid certain things in order to reduce your anxiety.

ALLISON: Sorry, which thoughts? You mean when I picture Michael dying?

THERAPIST: No, those are your obsessions, and as we discussed before, up to 99 percent of people have obsessive thoughts. Remember we talked about what those obsessions mean to you or the thoughts that come soon after. For example, your thoughts that "because I am thinking about Michael dying, it must mean that I want him dead," or "if I think about him dying it may cause him to die" make you feel anxious, and understandably so.

ALLISON: Right, right, right. It's hard for me to separate them like that. Very confusing.

THERAPIST: It is confusing in the beginning but I promise that it will get easier as we go long. What I'm saying is that these automatic thoughts often turn out to be irrational and not necessarily based on fact. In fact, last week you remarked to me that on occasion you "know" that many of your thoughts are "way out." You acknowledged last Wednesday, for example, that thinking of Michael dying cannot lead to his death.

ALLISON: I know I said that. But I'm having a hard time understanding why. I know that deep down I do believe that he will die unless I do something to prevent it. It's just that if I didn't believe that, why would I call him a hundred times even though I know he'll get angry with me? And why would I get so scared when I try not to call?

THERAPIST: You're quite right, Allison. If you didn't believe those thoughts, you would not do what you're doing and you would not feel so afraid. But there is a part of you that pops up every now and then that does think differently, right? A part of you that thinks these thoughts may not be true?

ALLISON (grudgingly): I suppose.

THERAPIST: Hmm, so what you are saying is that there is a possibility, however small, that your thoughts such as "Michael will die if I imagine him dying" or that "Michael will die unless I call him eighteen times on the telephone" may not necessarily be true.

ALLISON: A very small possibility.

THERAPIST: Small it is. All right, so getting back to what I was saying earlier, it isn't the obsessions that create the anxiety, it is your beliefs and assumptions about what they mean that create the anxiety, like "I shouldn't be having such thoughts," or "I had better say 'safe Mike' twenty-four times, otherwise it will come true," and so on and so forth. Having these thoughts does not mean you're crazy, and as I said earlier, given that you have them and believe them, it makes perfect sense that you do what you do over and over again.

ALLISON: I'm relieved to hear you say that but I still feel somewhat skeptical. Can my thoughts really change? How?

THERAPIST: Yes, thoughts can change and that is one of our goals in therapy. What you and I are going to do is to examine a lot of your thoughts to see if they're true or not. We are going to set out like scientists, meaning that we will only accept these thoughts if we get hard facts—evidence—to back them up. For example, you will ultimately have to convince me that your thought "If I have obsessions of Michael dying, he will most certainly die" is true. You will have to convince me with some real facts, and not just because you believe them to be true.

ALLISON: I'm not sure I would know how to do that.

THERAPIST: That's perfectly all right, I would not expect you to know how to do that just yet. We'll figure it out together along the way. For now, I want you to imagine that you will be the defense lawyer who has the burden to prove that these thoughts are accurate or adaptive. By the same token, I will be like the prosecuting attorney who has to convince the court that they're not true or helpful to you. I can't believe you just because you say so and you can't believe me just because I say so. Based on the evidence, if we ultimately decide that they are not true or helpful to you, then my job will be to help you slowly restructure the way you think, to make your thoughts more realistic and more adaptive. We will slowly chip away at your anxiety-provoking thoughts so that your obsessions and compulsions can naturally decrease in the long run.

ALLISON (smiles): And what if we find that they *are* true?

THERAPIST: Good question. If we find that your thoughts are true but we agree that they are still dysfunctional to you, we may still use cognitive restructuring or we may utilize more of the behavioral exercises I referred to during our first session. I will describe them in some detail in a few sessions. These behavioral techniques are also designed to reduce your obsessions and compulsions.

MONITORING AUTOMATIC THOUGHTS

Once automatic thoughts are defined, the patient is instructed to begin filling out the "thought record" (Table 4–1) whenever he experiences a sudden rise in anxiety associated with his obsessions. In other words, patients are asked to begin documenting their thoughts when obsessions strike, when they experience an increase in anxiety, or when they experience an urge to perform rituals. They are also asked to note the specific situation when the anxiety was triggered and to document the level of anxiety they experienced (on a scale of 1 to 100) during these moments.

Table 4–1. Automatic Thought Log

Fill out when you have a negative feeling or if a negative feeling becomes worse

1. Feeling
   How do you feel now? Check √ and rate how much on a scale of 0 (usual) to 100 (worst I can imagine).
   Anxious —( )
   Sad   —( )
   Guilty —( )
   Angry   —( )
   Other   —( )   Specify which one _____

2. Situation
   What were you doing when you felt this way?

3. Automatic thought
   What went through your mind that could have made you feel this way? List all thoughts here and rate each thought on how much you believe it—0 (not at all) to 100 (completely).

4. Behavior
   What did you do? How did you cope with the situation?

The goal of monitoring is to increase patients' awareness of the anxiety-provoking appraisals they make on a routine basis. Making patients cognizant of the fact that they are thinking in specific ways creates the awareness and distance necessary to ultimately modify cognitions. Monitoring automatic thoughts also enables the therapist to identify common thoughts and distortions that tend to occur during moments of increased anxiety.

The first automatic thought log is always filled out during the session by the therapist. Not only does this provide patients with a concrete example of the task, but it also enables the therapist to resolve any problems (e.g., anxiety generated by the task) that may come up when the task is performed outside the office. The thought log should be filled out using an anxiety-provoking situation that occurred closest in time to the current session so that the associated automatic thoughts can be remembered with comparable ease. Ideally, anxiety generated during the session should be utilized to fill out the record, because the therapist will be able to elicit "hot cognitions" with skillful probing and questioning (J. Beck 1995).

Using basic cognitive techniques such as Socratic questioning, guided discovery, and the downward arrow technique (see J. Beck 1995 for a full description of the techniques), the therapist helps Allison identify and record her automatic thoughts during a specific situation when she experienced increased anxiety over the last week

Clinical Vignette

THERAPIST: Take a look at this thought log, Allison [see Table 4–1]. We are going to fill this out together here so that you have some idea of when and how to begin recording your automatic thoughts. Can you remember the last time you felt very anxious or had a very strong urge to ritualize?

ALLISON: I'm always anxious. I always ritualize.

THERAPIST: You're right, you are anxious a lot of the time, but are there moments when you are less anxious or more anxious?

ALLISON: I guess so.

THERAPIST: So can you think back to the last time you experienced a sudden increase in anxiety? A change from your usual or baseline level of anxiety?

ALLISON: Over the last week? Hmm, so many times, let me think (pause). Well, maybe when my in-laws came over on Saturday. I felt really bad—they brought us dinner.

THERAPIST: How anxious did you feel on a scale of 1 to 100, with 100 being the worst anxiety you have ever experienced?

ALLISON (smiles): 150.

THERAPIST (smiles in response): That bad, huh? How about we call it 100 though just because it's easier to think of a scale from 1 to 100 rather than 1 to 150.

ALLISON: Okay.

THERAPIST: So in the box where it says "Feeling," I am putting down "anxious" and "100." Now what was going on when you got so anxious?

ALLISON: Well, they came for dinner.

THERAPIST: Can you be more specific? When was the exact moment you realized you felt anxious. Did it begin when they stepped through the door?

ALLISON: Well, no, I mean I was getting anxious that they were coming over but that started the moment I woke up.

THERAPIST: So you woke up and that's when . . .

ALLISON: Well, yes, uh no. What I was just talking about was not my anxiety in the morning. I was talking about after they came over.

THERAPIST: All right. So we know it started after they came over. Can you remember exactly when?

ALLISON: Well, they brought us dinner because they know I am too wacked out to make dinner for their precious son.

THERAPIST: Hold on. That's a thought you just had, an automatic thought, that was your take on the situation that probably made you feel anxious or bad in some way.

ALLISON (acknowledges): Yes.

THERAPIST: But for our purposes now, it is not a description of what actually happened. The description in this case would be "mother-in-law entered with dinner for us."

ALLISON: But it's true. She does think I'm a psycho.

THERAPIST: You may be right but we'll have to figure that out later. Right now I need to separate out what was going on, and what you were thinking or saying to yourself about what was going on. Right now we are just writing down what was going on when your anxiety shot to 100. We'll get to what you were thinking in a minute.

ALLISON: Oh, okay. But that wasn't when my anxiety shot up to 100, that was later. Sorry.

THERAPIST: You don't have to apologize, Allison, there's nothing to be sorry about. Part of what we're doing here is that I am helping you sort out your feelings, your thoughts, your actions, the whole situation, and it isn't easy. It's all jumbled up in your head because you're not used to unscrambling these things, none of us are. This is part of the process of learning how to record these thoughts on your own. I would like you to be comfortable questioning or challenging me in any way.

ALLISON: Thanks. Well, let me think (closes her eyes). I feel like a detective. What was going on at the exact moment was—that's it . . . his mom insisted that I help out in the kitchen. They had brought over dinner and salad stuff and she asked me to make the salad. When I said that I didn't feel comfortable doing that, she got really mad at me, she went like "humph" and started to make the salad herself. That was it, as soon as she started making the salad, boom! I felt so nervous, I thought my heart would stop. I ran out of the kitchen and locked myself in my bedroom.

THERAPIST: Very good. That is exactly how specific I want you to be. Let me write that down now [see Table 4–2].

Situation

What were you doing when you felt this way?

My in-laws came over. They brought us dinner. His mom insisted that I help out in the kitchen. She asked me to make the salad and when I said that I didn't feel comfortable doing that, she got really mad at me and started to make it herself. As soon as she started making the salad, I felt very nervous, I thought my heart would stop. I ran out of the kitchen and locked myself in my bedroom.

THERAPIST: Is that okay?

ALLISON: Uh huh. Yes.

THERAPIST: Now, let's get to your automatic thoughts. What was going on in your mind when the anxiety struck? What were you saying to yourself?

ALLISON: I just thought that I had to get out of there. I knew that I had to get out of there, I thought my heart would stop.

THERAPIST: You knew that you had to get out? Why?

ALLISON: I don't know.

THERAPIST: Let's see. What would have happened if you had been unable to get out of the kitchen?

ALLISON: I would have died, for sure.

THERAPIST: Was that your fear? That you would have died? How?

ALLISON: Well, not died exactly. I guess I was afraid that I wouldn't get to complete doing, uh, saying my, uh, my, well, ritual. I was saying "safe Mike, safe Mike" and was afraid I would not be able to say it forty-eight times unless I got out of there.

THERAPIST: I see. Why did you suddenly feel that you had to say "safe Mike" forty-eight times?

ALLISON: You know, because . . .

THERAPIST: I think I have some idea, but tell me, Allison, I'd like to hear what specifically went through your mind.

ALLISON (agitatedly): IwasafraidthatMichaelwould . . . I can't say it.

THERAPIST: "Die"?

ALLISON: Yes (looks preoccupied).

THERAPIST: Are you saying "safe Mike" now? Are you afraid that Michael will die now unless you say "safe Mike"?

ALLISON: Sort of, yes.

(Pause)

THERAPIST: Are you done? Shall we go on?

ALLISON: Okay.

THERAPIST: I know this is upsetting, Allison, but do you understand how important it is for us to get at your thoughts?

ALLISON (with tears in her eyes): I know, I know. We can go ahead, I'm ready. I'm all right.

THERAPIST: Let me know if you want me to stop at any time. You suddenly became concerned that Michael would die after your mother-in-law began making the salad. What about that could have triggered that fear?

ALLISON: The knife. I have always been nervous about knives, I guess, and now especially. I just got afraid looking at her using a knife.

THERAPIST: Looking at the knife made you afraid that Michael would die? Can you help me understand what about the knife did that?

ALLISON: No, I can't, I'm sorry (starts sobbing).

THERAPIST (gently): Allison, should we stop for a minute?

ALLISON: No, it's okay, I don't mean to cry, I do want to continue. You know, as soon as I saw her using the knife, I started having these really gory visions of Michael getting stabbed, I pictured the knife cutting his stomach. I was trying so hard to stop thinking it, but I kept seeing the blood, the gore, and then I began to worry, oh my God, he'll die, Michael is in danger.

THERAPIST: And then?

ALLISON: Just that I had to do something, otherwise he would die and it would be my fault. I had to save him. That's when I began saying "safe Mike."

THERAPIST: I see. Let me begin writing that down.

ALLISON: I think I actually said it aloud once. I'm sure she heard me but I didn't care. I had to make sure that nothing and no one would stop me from saying it. That's why I had to run and lock the door because I knew that even one second free in my head and he would be dead.

THERAPIST: (continues writing).

ALLISON: All I could think was that Michael would die and that it would all be my fault. I kept saying to myself, "You better be careful, Allison, you can't even get through a family dinner without seeing Michael brutally stabbed."

THERAPIST: Careful of what?

ALLISON: Going to hell. I'm headed there. What else would you expect if a wife constantly imagines her husband's head on a guillotine, being flung down from buildings, stabbed viciously? I must subconsciously want him dead.

THERAPIST: I see. May I read out what you just said to me?

ALLISON: My thoughts? Okay.

THERAPIST: Let me know if I've omitted anything [see Table 4–2].

Automatic Thought

What went through your mind that could have made you feel this way? List all thoughts here and rate each thought on a scale of 0 (not at all) to 100 (completely).

As soon as she picked up the knife all I could see was Michael being stabbed all over. All I could think was that Michael would die and that it would all be my fault. I ran from the room and tried to get the thoughts out of my head. I began saying "safe Mike, safe Mike," I think I actually said it aloud once. I'm sure she heard me but I didn't care. I had to make sure that nothing and no one would stop me from saying it. That's why I had to run and lock the door because I knew that even one second free in my head and he would surely die. I better be careful, I can't even get through a family dinner without seeing Michael brutally stabbed. I will go to hell, I'm headed there. What else would you expect if a wife constantly imagines her husband's head on a guillotine, being flung down from buildings, stabbed viciously? I must subconsciously want him dead.

ALLISON: (begins ritualizing).

THERAPIST: We're almost done, Allison, you're doing very well. How much did you believe your thought that Mike would die unless you said "safe Mike"?

Table 4–2. Allison's Automatic Thought Log

Fill out when you have a negative feeling or if a negative feeling becomes worse

1. Feeling
   How do you feel now? Check √ and rate how much on a scale of 0 (usual) to 100 (worst I can imagine).

Anxious	√ (100)
Sad	√ (95)
Guilty	√ (100)
Angry	— ( )
Other	— ( ) Specify which one _____

2. Situation
   What were you doing when you felt this way?

   My in-laws came over. They brought us dinner. His mom insisted that I help out in the kitchen. She asked me to make the salad and when I said that I didn't feel comfortable doing that, she got really mad at me and started to make it herself. As soon as she started making the salad, I felt very nervous. I thought my heart would stop. I ran out of the kitchen and locked myself in my bedroom.

3. Automatic thought
   What went through your mind that could have made you feel this way? List all thoughts here and rate each thought on how much you believe it—0 (not at all) to 100 (completely).

   As soon as she picked up the knife all I could see was Michael being stabbed all over. All I could think was that Michael would die (100) and that it would all be my fault (100). I ran from the room and tried to get the thoughts out of my head. I began saying "safe Mike, safe Mike," I think I actually said it aloud once. I am sure she heard me but I didn't care. I had to make sure that nothing and no one would stop me from saying it. That's why I had to run and lock the door because I knew that even one second free in my head and he would surely die (100). I better be careful, I can't even get through a family dinner without seeing Michael brutally stabbed. I will go to hell, I am headed there (95). What else would you expect if a wife constantly imagines her husband's head on a guillotine, being flung down from buildings, stabbed viciously? I must subconsciously want him dead (90–95).

4. Behavior
   What did you do? How did you cope with the situation?

   I ran into the bedroom and locked the door and lay on my bed crying.

   I ritualized, I said "safe Mike" forty-eight times.

ALLISON: 100.

THERAPIST: How convinced were you that it would be your fault, that you would be responsible?

ALLISON: Most assuredly, 100.

THERAPIST: What about the thought, "I will go to hell"?

ALLISON: Hmm, maybe 95?

THERAPIST: And finally, what about your thought, "I must subconsciously want him dead"?

ALLISON: Is this really necessary? I mean, I'm not absolutely sure, 90 to 95, you know.

THERAPIST: I know it must be hard to put numbers to your thoughts when you're not even used to thinking about the fact that you're thinking. Actually, it is very necessary that we rate how much you believe your thoughts but your best estimate is good enough, 90 to 95 is fine.

It will also get easier to work with these numbers as we go along. One of the reasons we do it is so that you and I can decide if the thought is bothersome enough to work on changing. Since you are having automatic thoughts all the time, this allows me decide which ones we should focus on in therapy. If a particular thought doesn't distress you too much or if you don't believe it too much then we can move on to other thoughts that you believe much more. Also, once we begin working on changing your thoughts, I would like to see whether you believe it less and less as therapy progresses.

ALLISON: I see. I'm just feeling tired. Are we done?

THERAPIST: I know you're tired and anxious but you've done very well. I'm really pleased with our progress today. It's hard to talk about what makes you so anxious when you would like to not even think about it. We just have a little more to go. I just want to note down what you did, your behavior, right after you felt anxious. I am going to put down what you just said, that you said "safe Mike" over and over again, ran out of the kitchen, and locked yourself in your bedroom. Did you do anything else?

ALLISON: No, I don't think so.

THERAPIST: Good. During the next week, can you fill in the automatic thought log on your own the next time you have a sudden burst of anxiety?

ALLISON: I can try.

THERAPIST: That's all I need. Then we can go over it together during our next session. But remember what I said earlier, Allison—filling out this log may create some initial anxiety because usually you try to avoid the thoughts and you are not used to focusing on the things that make you anxious. You are used to ritualizing as soon as the thoughts come to you, not to writing them out in detail. I would still like you to try filling it out because it's necessary for treatment to work. As therapy progresses, the anxiety will decrease. Perhaps reminding yourself that this will help in the long run may help you tolerate the anxiety while you write it down.

TACKLING COMPLICATIONS

Identifying automatic thoughts is a difficult task for OCD patients (and for patients with anxiety and depressive disorders in general) because of the immense emotion these thoughts generate. Patients with OCD have learned to cope by ritualizing as soon as the obsessions and automatic thoughts occur so that the anxiety quickly diminishes. In fact, they are not aware of the automatic thoughts, but merely of the obsessions themselves and the intense anxiety that floods them. Having them attend to the automatic thoughts goes against their natural impulse to neutralize them with some other thought or action, and hence can be extremely anxiety producing. In the patient's mind, postponing the ritual to identify and document his thought may not only flood him with anxiety, but may also bring about the very outcome he fears.

Therapists need to understand that patients are not resisting treatment if they initially do not fill out the thought log or state that they do not know what they are thinking. The therapist must gradually help patients understand and cope with the anxiety associated with the task. In fact, predicting that the task may be difficult before it is assigned goes a long way in ensuring compliance. If patients continue to be anxious, the task should be broken down into small, manageable steps until the patient is able to complete the homework in between sessions (e.g., first the therapist, then the patient fills out the thought log during the session itself). Finally, automatic thoughts that may be preventing them from accomplishing the task itself (this won't work for me, so why bother doing it) should be identified and challenged during sessions so that the anxiety associated with the task declines.

NEXT WEEK

Patients are asked to record their thoughts on the Automatic Thought Log (ATL) when they have episodes of anxiety related to obsessional triggers, or if they have the urge to ritualize over the next week. Potential stressors that may come up over the course of the next week are identified as examples of when to fill out the thought log. Patients are also asked to continue recording the Obsession-Compulsion Monitoring form (OCM).

Session 4:
Cognitive Restructuring
(Phase II)

REVISING AUTOMATIC THOUGHTS

Session Goals	*Check When Done*

1. Review (5–10 minutes) ☐
   - Obtain feedback on Session 3
   - Review homework
     —Automatic Thought Log (ATL)
     —Obsession-Compulsion Monitoring
       form (OCM)
   - Briefly review events that occurred over past
     week

2. The Session (Cognitive Restructuring Phase II) ☐
   - Linking automatic thoughts, feelings, and
     behaviors
   - Understanding automatic thoughts within a
     larger framework
     —Beliefs
     —Assumptions
     —Automatic thoughts
   - Examining the validity of automatic thoughts
   - Identifying cognitive distortions in the automatic
     thoughts
   - Revising automatic thoughts
   - Assessing effectiveness of cognitive restructuring
   - Tackling complications

3. Next Week (5 minutes) ☐
   - Discuss homework to be completed
     —Obsession-Compulsion Monitoring form (OCM)
       (see Table 3–3)
     —Revised Thought Log (RTL) (see Table 5–1)
   - Anticipate potential stressors that may occur during
     the week

SESSION OVERVIEW

Once the patient has learned to identify automatic thoughts, feelings, and behaviors, he is ready for the second phase of cognitive restructuring, where dysfunctional automatic thoughts are replaced with more rational ways of thinking. Again, Phases I and II are described as occurring over a two-session period for purposes of illustration. Depending on how long it takes the patient to accurately identify his automatic thoughts, Phase I may continue for multiple sessions before Phase II is introduced. In addition, the task of restructuring and modifying dysfunctional and erroneous thoughts, which begins in Phase II, continues on an ongoing basis throughout therapy.

Following a review of the previous session, the assigned homework, and events over the past week, identified automatic thoughts are evaluated through Socratic questioning, guided discovery, and collaborative empiricism. Inherent cognitive distortions are identified, and the patient learns to replace distorted thoughts with more rational and adaptive ways of thinking. The session ends with a discussion of next week's homework and the potential events and troublesome situations that may come up for the patient.

Forms used during this session include the Revised Thought Log (RTL) (Table 5–1) and the Common Misconceptions Observed in Obsession-Compulsion Disorder form (Table 5–3).

REVIEW

The therapist begins with a quick review of the patient's mood over the past week. Did the patient experience any significant increases or decreases in depression or anxiety over the course of the week? How does he feel today? Did he experience any other negative emotions? Additionally, the therapist elicits any feedback or reactions the patient may have had to Session 3. Did the previous session in-

Table 5–1. Revised Thought Log

Fill out when you have a negative feeling or if a negative feeling becomes worse

---

1. Feeling.
   How do you feel now? Check √ and rate how much on a scale of 0 (usual) to 100 (worst I can imagine).
   Anxious___ (   )   Sad___ (   )   Guilty___ (   )   Angry___ (   )
   Other___ (   )   Specify_____

---

2. Situation
   What were you doing when you felt this way?

---

3. Automatic thought
   What went through your mind that could have made you feel this way? List all thoughts here and rate each thought on a scale of 0 (not at all) to 100 (completely) on how much you believe this thought.

---

4. Behavior
   What did you do? How did you cope with the situation?

---

5. Cognitive distortions
   What mistakes am I making in my thinking? Enumerate.

---

6. Revised thoughts
   Are there more realistic or useful ways to look at the same situation? List alternate thoughts here and rate each on how much you believe it, from 0 (not at all) to 100 (completely).

---

7. Outcome
   How do you feel now? Did you behave any differently?

---

crease his anxiety? Did he understand the rationale for cognitive restructuring? Does he require further clarification on the differences between automatic thoughts, feelings, and behaviors? After the patient offers his understanding of the concepts learned in the previous session, the therapist strengthens this learning by offering a summary of the previous session.

Finally, the therapist attempts to ascertain if the patient experienced increased anxiety while filling out the thought log at home. If so, did it prevent him from filling out the form? If not, did he have any difficulties filling it out? And finally, was he able to correctly identify his automatic thoughts and label his feelings and behaviors?

THE SESSION:
COGNITIVE RESTRUCTURING PHASE II

Once identified, automatic thoughts are examined carefully in session (1) to determine if they are distorted or unhelpful, (2) to understand which emotions they generate, and (3) to understand the dysfunctional assumptions and beliefs on which they may be based. Because the targeted automatic thoughts are dysfunctional and tend to generate negative emotional states such as anxiety, restructuring them is crucial for change in obsessive-compulsive disorder. As stated in Chapter 4, restructuring dysfunctional cognitions is purported to reduce the anxiety associated with obsessions, and thereby reduce the frequency of the obsessions themselves.

LINKING AUTOMATIC THOUGHTS,
FEELINGS, AND BEHAVIORS

As therapist and patient review the thought log, and/or as the patient spontaneously reports them during the course of a session, the therapist helps the patient clarify the differences and links between

automatic thoughts, feelings, and behaviors. In the beginning, helping patients understand the differences between the three predomi-
nates. For example, patients often use "I feel" when discussing a
thought, or respond with a thought when asked to state how they are
feeling. Clarifying which is which helps patients to understand and
begin thinking in terms of the cognitive model. Emphasis is also placed
on distinguishing between different emotional states so that patients
are able to better link different thoughts with different feelings.

Patients are also helped to understand how the three states are
linked to each other and to situational triggers (e.g., when this happened, I thought this, then I felt this, and then I did this) in order to
(1) further consolidate their grasp of the cognitive model, and (2)
begin the process of demystifying what appear to be a series of spontaneous, out-of-the-blue events. For example, using the previous
session as an example, the therapist helped Allison see how her idiosyncratic obsessive-compulsive sequence unfolded as her mother-
in-law began making the salad. The therapist explained that her
anxiety and urge to ritualize did not appear out of the blue, but instead were triggered by a specific event. Allison was helped to see
that as soon as she saw the knife (situational trigger), she had repetitive images of Michael being stabbed (obsession), followed up
by appraisals that Michael would die, that she would be responsible
for his death, and so on (automatic thoughts), which then led to
heightened anxiety (feeling), palpitations (physiological components
of feeling state), and finally to her running out of the room (escape
behaviors) and counting (ritualized behaviors).

Her subsequent reduction in anxiety (feeling) was also traced to
appraisals that her rituals would reduce the chances of Michael dying
and reduce her sense of responsibility about the harm (automatic
thoughts), which led her to subsequently perform her rituals (behavior).

Since much of the success in therapy comes from reiterating concepts until they are strongly wedged into the patient's belief system,
linking the thought to the corresponding feelings and behaviors each
time a thought is discussed strengthens the patient's conviction that

there is a reason that he feels so anxious and performs rituals, and escapes or avoids certain situations. The therapist uses Socratic questioning each time to elicit thoughts and does not presuppose that the patients "already know" it just because it has been discussed before.

UNDERSTANDING AUTOMATIC THOUGHTS WITHIN A LARGER FRAMEWORK: ASSUMPTIONS AND BELIEFS

As stated earlier, *automatic thoughts* form the most superficial level of cognition and are based on dysfunctional assumptions. *Dysfunctional (conditional) assumptions* in turn are based on *core beliefs* held by individuals about themselves and others (J. Beck 1995). Although much of therapy targets the current situation-specific automatic thoughts reported by patients, the therapist still places them within the larger framework of the assumptions and beliefs upon which they are based. Based on the common themes observed in sessions, the therapist gradually formulates the patient's unique cognitive conceptualization (automatic thoughts → assumptions → beliefs) and thereby focuses on automatic thoughts based on central beliefs and assumptions. For example, if the patient's automatic thoughts appear to be largely based on beliefs about responsibility, such thoughts must be modified in order for therapy to be successful. In contrast, thoughts based on less central beliefs need not be the focus of such sustained work (see Table 5–2 for ways to link common beliefs, assumptions, and automatic thoughts observed in obsessive-compulsive disorder).

Automatic Thoughts

What thoughts went through your mind?
    As the patient continues to record the specific images or words that flash through his mind during periods of increased anxiety, the

Table 5–2. Common Beliefs, Assumptions, and Automatic Thoughts in Obsessive-Compulsive Disorder

Core Beliefs	Assumptions	Automatic Thoughts
1. **Overestimating risk or harm.** I am (and my loved ones are) vulnerable to harm (falling ill, dying, being out of control, or of being immoral).	(1) If I take even the slightest risk, I will be harmed. (2) If I take even the slightest risk others will be harmed.	(1) I will catch salmonella poisoning unless I wash my hands over and over again. (2) If I touch my sister-in-law, I will be contaminated. (3) I will have a nervous breakdown if the anxiety continues.
2. **Responsibility.** I am responsible for causing harm to myself and others (infecting myself or others, causing my death, causing the death of others).	(1) If I think about something, it is the same as doing something. (2) If I don't prevent or do not try to prevent harm to myself or others, it will be like I caused the harm in the first place. (3) I continue to be as responsible for bad things happening even if the chances of them occurring are minimal. (4) If I do not neutralize when an intrusion occurs, it will be like I wanted what was involved in that intrusion to actually happen. (5) One should and can exercise control over one's thoughts.	(1) I will harm my children unless I check the gas stove, count numbers, or repeat phrases. (2) I may have killed someone on the road so I better go back and check to make sure. (3) I should not imagine my husband dying, I should be able to control it.
3. **Underestimating own ability to do things.** I am incapable (of coping, remembering things, making decisions).	(1) If I am not able to control everything, it means that I am out of control. (2) I cannot trust myself to do even simple things let alone things of any consequence.	(1) I don't remember if I checked to see if the stove is off, so let me check again. (2) I cannot cope with the anxiety. ·
4. **Perfectionism.** I am flawed (I make mistakes, errors, fall short, I don't have everything in order).	(1) If I am not competent in all the things I do, it means that I am flawed, not worthwhile. (2) Making mistakes is unacceptable.	(1) If every object in my room is not exactly the way it should be, I will have a nervous breakdown. (2) If I miss checking one of the knobs, I had better start the whole thing again.

Table 5–2. (*continued*)

Core Beliefs	Assumptions	Automatic Thoughts
5. **Rigidity, morality, superstition.** I am immoral, evil, wicked (I sin, I think blasphemous things).	(1) Having bad thoughts is unacceptable, blasphemous. (2) Having good thoughts is my only hope for redemption. (3) Ritualizing can prevent harm from happening.	(1) I will go to hell because I imagined my mother dying. (2) I sinned because I imagined myself having sex with the priest.

therapist begins to see if certain types of thoughts come up more frequently than others. As certain themes become evident, the therapist begins to make hypotheses about which assumptions and beliefs may have given rise to these automatic thoughts.

Although a full range of automatic thoughts observed in obsessive-compulsive disorder cannot be enumerated, as they differ from patient to patient as well as within a given patient from day to day, some examples are provided in Table 5–2 above.

Assumptions

What does this thought mean to you?

Although automatic thoughts directly affect the patient's moods and actions, the thoughts themselves are based on unarticulated assumptions, rules, or attitudes the patient has developed over the years—what psychologist Judith Beck refers to as "intermediate beliefs" (J. Beck 1995). Although these intermediate beliefs dictate the patient's daily inner dialogue, they are not as easily identified (or modified) as automatic thoughts. However, they may be inferred from themes found across automatic thoughts themselves.

Drawing on frequently occurring automatic thoughts, the therapist has already begun making tentative hypotheses about the patient's assumptions, rules, or attitudes, and now attempts to confirm or reject these formulations. For example, one way to elicit intermediate beliefs is to work with the patient to understand the tangible meaning of a specific thought (e.g., it means that I should be careful at all times).

Salkovskis (1985) has enumerated five dysfunctional assumptions that characterize individuals with obsessive-compulsive disorder: (1) if I think about something, it is the same as doing something; (2) if I don't prevent or do not try to prevent harm to myself or others, it will be like I caused the harm in the first place; (3) I continue to be as responsible for bad things happening even if the chances of them occurring are minimal; (4) if I do not neutralize when an intrusion occurs, it will be like I wanted the harm involved in that intrusion to actually happen; and (5) I can and should be able to exercise control over my thoughts (p. 579). These and other assumptions that characterize obsessive-compulsive disorder were presented in Table 5–2.

Beliefs

What does this thought mean about you?

Core beliefs, considered to be the deepest level of cognition, are hypothesized to develop in childhood as a result of repetitive and often dysfunctional interactions with significant others (J. Beck 1995). They are rigid, all-encompassing beliefs about oneself and others and are not easy to identify or modify. Core beliefs give rise to, and hence may be gleaned from, assumptions people make about life, and from the specific automatic thoughts they have about day-to-day events. One way to ascertain core beliefs is to ask the patient what particular thoughts mean about the way he is (e.g., it means that I am evil).

As outlined in the previous chapter, an overarching sense of *responsibility and self-blame* is considered to be the core belief in individuals with obsessive-compulsive disorder. Although they *overestimate the risk* associated with everyday concerns about health, safety, death, sex, morality, and concern about others, and *underestimate their ability to cope* with this risk or harm; above all, they hold themselves responsible for harm to themselves and others.

Individuals with obsessive-compulsive disorder also tend to distrust their memory for thoughts and actions, tend to fuse thought and action, and are consumed by *doubt and uncertainty*. As a result, they tend to have difficulty making decisions and try very hard to exert control over their own thoughts. They are also thought to be unduly *perfectionistic, rigid, and moral*. In fact, some observers note that individuals with obsessive-compulsive disorder tend to have a more "tender conscience" (Reed 1985) than others, which may, in part, explain why negative thoughts are hard for them to dismiss.

Clinical Vignette

Note: Although the conversation below (linking Allison's automatic thoughts from the last session to the assumptions and beliefs on which they are based) may not occur until later in therapy when themes or patterns in her thinking become apparent, it is explored here for purposes of illustration. It would otherwise be premature to conclude from one situation that the resulting automatic thought is based on a certain assumption or belief, or that it reflects a core assumption and belief. At this stage, the therapist would only begin to form hypotheses. The therapist may decide to share them with the patient only later on in therapy, once further evidence for the belief has been collected.

THERAPIST: Allison, you said that you would go to hell because you had obsessions about Michael getting stabbed.

ALLISON: Yes, that's right.

THERAPIST: I've noticed that thoughts like this come up frequently, that you will be punished, you deserve to be punished, go to hell.

ALLISON: They do? They do, don't they?

THERAPIST: What about having the obsessions is so bad that you think you will go to hell? I'm not sure I understand why.

ALLISON: Being preoccupied with your husband dying? I think that classifies as a sin, I would say it's blasphemous.

THERAPIST: So having the obsession means to you that you are committing a sin, because it's almost like you're killing Michael yourself?

ALLISON: Yes, not almost, it feels like I am killing him.

THERAPIST: And when you say that you are preoccupied about him dying, it almost sounds like you're saying that you're plotting to kill him. Is that what it means to you?

ALLISON: I don't know but it sure seems that way.

THERAPIST: I think I'm beginning to understand what makes you so panicked and afraid. It's not just that having obsessions is bad, it's like a sin to you. I think if I had an obsession about my husband dying and took that to mean that I was plotting to kill him, and that I would succeed in killing him, I would be extremely frightened.

ALLISON: Yes, I guess it does. It seems so real that I can't help thinking that.

THERAPIST: What do you think it means about you that you're "preoccupied" with killing him, that you will "succeed" in killing him.

ALLISON (with tears in her eyes, looking away): I don't know.

(Pause)

THERAPIST: I can't imagine that it makes you feel very good about yourself.

ALLISON (starts sobbing uncontrollably): I must be so evil. I am such a horrible, wicked person, such a wretch, I don't know why he's with me. He's such a good man. I sin against him and he still stays with me. He doesn't deserve someone like me.

THERAPIST: Allison, I can't imagine how tormented and rotten you must feel to think that you're evil, wicked, and that you deserve to go to hell.

EXAMINING THE VALIDITY OF
AUTOMATIC THOUGHTS

Once patients learn to differentiate and link situational triggers to thoughts, feelings, and behaviors, the therapist begins to examine whether the automatic thoughts generated by the patient are indeed valid, as the patient believes they are. Is it true that Allison's mother-in-law thinks she is a psycho? Will Michael die if she imagines that he will, and is she responsible for his death? Will counting numbers prevent him from dying? Will she go to hell? All the appraisals the patient makes, all the premises under which the patient operates, become the subject of scientific discussion, open to inquiry and refutation.

Although answers to some of the questions may seem self-evident to the therapist, the patient's thoughts are never directly challenged and patients are not expected to believe that their thoughts may be distorted just because the therapist believes that they are; indeed, some thoughts may not be distorted (J. Beck 1995). By the same token, the therapist does not believe that the automatic thoughts are accurate just because the patient "feels" or "knows" that they are.

Instead, the patient and therapist collaborate to discover whether the specified automatic thoughts are erroneous, dysfunctional, or maladaptive, using empirical, factual evidence (collaborative empiricism). Each thought is framed as a scientific hypothesis, and both therapist and patient provide facts or evidence to support or reject the hypothesis, and consider other ways of thinking and alternative explanations.

The process of evaluating automatic thoughts is a subtle one, where the art of cognitive therapy is very much in play. The emphasis is on guiding patients (by asking leading questions) to discover the true facts for themselves, rather than on challenging the patients or handing them the "true" facts on a platter (guided discovery).

To set up this stage, the therapist again describes how and why the thoughts will be evaluated. The rationale and method for evaluating the thoughts is once again furnished to strengthen the patient's understanding of the concepts and to make sure that the ongoing dialogue involved does not appear to the patient as a senseless harangue inflicted upon him by a know-it-all therapist. It is important that the patient understands and agrees to the therapeutic strategies that will be used to evaluate his thoughts. Hence, the guidelines for evaluating thoughts are outlined at the start, before any further discussion ensues.

Guidelines for Examining the Validity of Automatic Thoughts

Following are some questions that are used to examine the validity of automatic thoughts (J. Beck 1995). However, it is important to note that the list is not exhaustive and is merely intended as a guide for therapists. Depending on the type of thought presented, entirely different questions may have to be posed to evaluate it. Further, all questions need not be used in every situation, and on occasion none of the questions given below will be appropriate to evaluate a particular thought.

What is the evidence?

Using Socratic questioning, the therapist seeks to uncover the evidence that supports or refutes the automatic thought under investigation. The patient is first asked to provide factual evidence to support the thought (e.g., What proof do I have that thinking about something can make it happen?) rather than relying on his "feeling" that it is true. Next, the patient is asked to provide evidence that refutes this thought (Have I killed her yet by thinking anything?).

If sufficient evidence does not exist, the patient and therapist examine creative ways in which more data can be gathered to confirm or refute the thought later on. Behavioral experiments can be used as ways to gather more information (e.g., asking my friends if they have ever had an obsessive thought to determine that I am not the only one who experiences them) and to help patients arrive at more realistic conclusions (it is true, when I force myself to obsess it is much harder to do so, and I am less anxious—but when I try to stop thinking about it, I can't seem to push them away).

Because all anxiety patients tend to focus on and overestimate risk or harm, disconfirming this risk or harm by sifting through the evidence is a highly useful strategy in the cognitive behavioral treatment of anxiety-disordered patients. However, in patients with obsessive-compulsive disorder, this line of questioning may not be appropriate for some automatic thoughts, particularly for catastrophic fears that are believed to occur in the distant future (e.g., I will go to hell). In these situations, considering alternative explanations may be more useful (see below). Once the patient is able to consider other alternatives, reviewing the evidence for and against each alternative may then become a viable strategy.

What is the worst that could happen? How likely is this? Can I tolerate this?

Questioning patients about their catastrophic fears is a more specific strategy for assessing the evidence. The patient is asked to voice the worst possible outcome (e.g., Michael will not love me anymore if I tell him that I cannot go to his mother's house for dinner), and then attempt to see how likely it is (What are the chances that Michael will stop loving me just because I cannot go to his mother's house for dinner?). If so, the worst outcome gets modified by this line of questioning (the more realistic outcome is that he will be angry if I tell him that I cannot visit his mother, but he won't stop loving me). Once this is done, the patient is asked to see if he can tolerate this modified worst outcome (Can I tolerate it if Michael gets angry with me? Is that so bad?).

Often, the worst outcome is not as bad as it appears on the surface (e.g., I am afraid that people in the restroom will think I am strange). In these situations, the therapist can help realistically evaluate the worst outcome (Is that so bad? How will your life be different if people you will probably never see again think that you are strange?). Learning to tolerate the anxiety associated with the worst outcome enables patients to view the feared situation as more controllable and helps them to consider coping strategies other than escaping, avoiding, or performing rituals.

When the worst outcome cannot be disconfirmed because it is feared to occur in the distant future (e.g., I will go to hell) or if it is overly valued at a particular stage (I am 100 percent sure that I will become contaminated if I use a public restroom), or even if the smallest likelihood that it may come true is too traumatic to consider (Michael will die), then the most useful strategy is to consider alternative hypotheses or explanations (see below).

Is there an alternative (less threatening) explanation?

With anxiety comes a narrowed attentional focus that prevents patients from considering alternate or less threatening scenarios or explanations of events. To help broaden their focus, patients are asked to consciously generate alternative, less threatening explanations other than the anxiety-inducing appraisals they instinctively (automatically) formulate. Since a patient may have difficulty generating alternative outcomes, once the patient has exhausted his list, the therapist tentatively offers other possible outcomes to further broaden the patient's focus. The emphasis on the word *possible* is deliberate because the goal is to get patients to consider a full range of other outcomes, rather than judging a single one as "correct" right away. At this stage, the patient's belief in his automatic thought is complete, and getting him to consider other possibilities, rather than probabilities or certainties, is far easier to accomplish. In addition, the therapist may not yet know what, if any, is the "correct" explanation, without further collection of data.

As mentioned above, this line of questioning is particularly useful for patients with obsessive-compulsive disorder who may not be able to disconfirm their thoughts by providing evidence that refutes them, or by engaging in a dialogue about the worst outcome. Providing patients with less threatening alternatives allows them to at least consider the possibility that they may not be in danger, but that they *think* that they are, that they may not be actually doing harm but that they may *fear* that they will do harm, and so on. Once patients are able to consider other alternatives (e.g., I guess it is possible . . .), then reviewing the evidence for and against each alternative becomes more viable (see above). Behavioral experiments may also be used in this context, by testing each anxiety-provoking automatic thought against the less threatening alternatives (leaving a radio on to assess the catastrophic thought that the house may burn down versus the alternate one that it will be a waste of electricity).

Is this way of thinking helpful or detrimental to me?

This line of questioning is particularly useful when attempts to invalidate a distorted thought prove to be fruitless, or when a thought is indeed valid yet quite maladaptive to the patient's functioning. In such cases, the therapist guides the patient to assess the impact of the thought on the patient's life in order to determine if it is helpful or detrimental. For example, thinking that one is doomed to be alone is unhelpful even if someone has a history of unsuccessful relationships. In other words, thinking about being alone forever is not valid, just accurate at present. Such pessimistic thoughts may lead such a person to avoid relationships, or sabotage existing relationships, thereby increasing the likelihood of his being alone. Enumerating the pros and cons of such thoughts and their consequences can also be useful. For example, thinking that I am doomed to be alone leads me to avoid men, which may protect me from being rejected or disappointed (pro) but will ensure that I am alone (con).

Often, when thoughts are valid yet maladaptive, an evaluation may reveal that, rather than a distortion, the problem is behavioral in nature, in which case problem solving, social skills training, and so on may be used adjunctively along with cognitive restructuring. For example, someone who has never had friends and predicts that he never will is probably right, he may not. However, the thought is still maladaptive since it does not help him to make friends. A more appropriate thought may be, "Why don't I have any friends?" If it becomes evident that the person has a deficit in social skills, then social skills training may be employed even as the cognitions are restructured.

What would I tell or think of another person if he were in a similar predicament?

Asking patients to try to see how they would judge the situation if it were happening to someone else, or asking them to advise someone who presents them with a similar thought, serves a dual purpose. First and foremost, it has the benefit of automatically creating a distance between the person and his automatic thought, thereby enabling him to examine the thought more objectively. As stated earlier, creating a distance (by self-monitoring of thoughts, or thinking about the fact that one is thinking) makes the thought less automatic, less subjective, and is a necessary step in restructuring cognitions. Second, having patients evaluate someone else's problems rather than their own not only broadens their focus by helping them realize that others could potentially have similar problems, but also helps promote confidence in their own ability when they see that they may be qualified to determine how others should handle problems.

Clinical Vignette

Note: The therapist usually begins evaluating the most recent or the most upsetting Automatic Thought Log filled out by the patient over the last week and restructures it using the Revised Thought Log (Table 5–1). However, for purposes of continuity, we will illustrate how to evaluate and restructure the thoughts recorded in the previous session.

THERAPIST: Allison, let's go back to the time when Michael's mother picked up the knife to make the salad. You said to me that you "knew that Michael would die." What made you so sure?

ALLISON: Well, I saw him getting stabbed.

THERAPIST: You mean you had an obsession that he was getting stabbed when your mother-in-law picked up the knife.

ALLISON: Yes.

THERAPIST: What made you think that that would lead to his death?

ALLISON: I don't know, I just knew it. I could feel it in my bones. Haven't you ever had a feeling like you "know" something is going to happen?

THERAPIST: I can't say for sure. But let's think about this. Apart from your "feeling" that he was going to die, was there any reason for you to think that he would die? Is he ill? Does he have a serious medical problem?

ALLISON: No, no, he's completely healthy. It's just that I kept seeing it, it seemed so real.

THERAPIST: I know it seemed real, but was it real? Or were you just afraid that imagining Michael dead could kill him?

ALLISON: Yes, I guess I was.

THERAPIST: What do you think about that now? Does it seem possible to you that imagining someone dead could kill that person?

ALLISON: Anything is possible. Why take the chance?

THERAPIST: That's an interesting thought. How about we test that out right now?

ALLISON (alarmed): What do you mean?

THERAPIST: Let's see. Can you close your eyes and imagine that you are dead?

ALLISON (laughs): What? What kind of therapy is this? You seriously want me to do that?

THERAPIST: Yes, why not? Remember, we had talked about scientifically examining your thoughts to see if they're accurate or not? Well, this is a small experiment we can use to test out your assumption that having an image about Michael could kill him. The logic would follow that if an image can kill Michael, then the same should apply to you, too. Can you close your eyes and for the next minute or so imagine that you're being stabbed?

ALLISON: Okay, but I feel very silly (closes her eyes).

(Pause)

ALLISON (opens her eyes): Of course, I'm not going to die.

THERAPIST: You seem sure of that. How come?

ALLISON: I don't know. When you look at it like that, it does seem ridiculous that I would think that.

THERAPIST: When it isn't Michael that you're thinking about, it seems incredible to you that you would actually believe that imagining that someone is dead can actually cause that person's death.

ALLISON: Yes, otherwise a lot more people would be dead in this world, I guess!

THERAPIST: Absolutely. Pretty much everyone would be dead and the others in prison. So can we conclude from this that thinking that something will happen cannot make it happen?

ALLISON: I know that it's true at some level but it's hard to believe all the time.

THERAPIST: I know. How much do you believe your automatic thought now? That your obsession could kill him?

ALLISON: Oh, zero right now. I don't know how much I'll believe this when I'm faced with a knife again, but right now I don't believe it.

THERAPIST: We will be working on getting you to believe it less and less even when you're faced with such situations. For now, it's enough that you don't believe it in here. Let's continue examining what else you said to yourself that night. You said something about the fact that if he died it would be your fault?

ALLISON: Yes, I did, I still feel that. If he dropped dead, what else could I think?

THERAPIST: Let's see. If he did die, could there be any other reason for it?

ALLISON: What else could there be? He's young, healthy, doesn't have any medical problems, and even you would have to agree that that would be too much of a coincidence that I imagined him dying and he actually died.

THERAPIST: It would seem so, except I know that you have obsessions about him dying much of the day, so it wouldn't be that coincidental. If you're always thinking something, eventually you will be right.

ALLISON: I guess, but it still would seem coincidental to me.

THERAPIST: All right, let us look at this another way. Suppose you were a judge and you had two defendants before you. One had an obsession that his wife died and she did die, and the other shot his wife and she died. Which one would you send to prison?

ALLISON: Obviously the guy who shot his wife.

THERAPIST: Why?

ALLISON: I know what you're getting at. He can't be held responsible for her dying if all he did was imagine her dying. She must have died because something happened to her, not because he imagined it.

THERAPIST: Right. I have another question for you. If a friend called you and said, Guess what? So-and-so that we know from college died last night. What would your first question be?

ALLISON: How did he die?

THERAPIST: Yes, and as you asked her, what would you be thinking about the likely causes?

ALLISON: Heart attack? Car accident?

THERAPIST: Would you be thinking "Maybe his wife imagined him popping off and that's why he died?"

ALLISON: (begins giggling): Of course not.

THERAPIST: And if your friend said just that, what would you say?

ALLISON: I'd say, don't be ridiculous, it wasn't her fault. You can't kill someone by thinking about it. He must have died for some other reason.

THERAPIST: Good. So how come you have different standards for yourself? How come you wouldn't hold these people responsible but you would think it was your fault if Michael died right after you had visualized him dying?

ALLISON: I don't know. I guess I am pretty hard on myself.

THERAPIST: Yes, it seems that way to me too. You seem to worry that it will be your fault, but when you look at it objectively, it seems ludicrous that you could be responsible.

ALLISON: Yes, I guess it does.

THERAPIST: How much do you believe that it would be your fault if he died now? If all you did was imagine that he was dying?

ALLISON: I'd like to say zero, but if I'm honest there's still a part of me that doesn't agree completely. Maybe 20?

THERAPIST: I'm glad to hear that you don't believe it as much. Getting back to the situation, you also said that you "had" to say "safe Mike" over and over again to save him. Do you still believe that now?

ALLISON: I must. I've been saying it as we've been doing this exercise.

THERAPIST: I'm glad that you were able to tell me that. What is the worst thing that could happen if you had not said "safe Mike" that night or if you didn't say "safe Mike" just now?

ALLISON: He could have died. He could die now.

THERAPIST: Now that you don't believe that thinking about him dying could kill him, what do you think is the worst thing that could have happened that night, or now, if you had not ritualized?

ALLISON: Nothing, I guess, but why take the chance, just in case?

THERAPIST: How do you think saying "safe Mike" could help protect him even if he was going to die?

ALLISON: Well, I know it doesn't seem logical right now. I mean if thinking about something can't make it happen, it should apply here too.

THERAPIST: Are you saying that just as thinking about him dying cannot lead to his death, saying "safe Mike" cannot save him?

ALLISON: Yes, I guess so.

THERAPIST: Why?

ALLISON: Because thinking cannot cause something to happen, good or bad.

THERAPIST: Good.

ALLISON: But what's the harm in saying it? You know, just in case, why take the chance?

THERAPIST: You're right, we should examine that. Do you think there is any harm in saying it or doing your other rituals?

ALLISON: Not really. Except that . . . no, there is no harm. I would rather not take the chance.

THERAPIST: Except that what? Can you tell me what you were just about to say?

ALLISON: Well, I guess it just takes up so much of my time.

THERAPIST: Yes, it does, doesn't it? And why is it that bad?

ALLISON: Sometimes it seems that's all I do. If I'm not checking on him to make sure he's alive, I'm saying inane things all day. And the rest of the time, I'm washing my hands. I feel so weary sometimes.

THERAPIST: I know. Although it makes you feel less anxious for a short period, these things have become a burden in and of themselves.

ALLISON (quietly): You have no idea. I *hate* the fact that I have to do them. I feel so tortured by them. I sometimes see my whole life stretch ahead of me, completely wasted. When I reach judgment day, and someone asks me what I accomplished in my life, there's not much I'll have to say if I continue on like this. Counting, checking, washing, counting, checking, washing (begins crying).

(Pause)

THERAPIST: Oh, Allison, I'm sorry that you feel so miserable. You're right, I can only imagine how you feel, but only you know how it feels inside. Tell me if I'm wrong, but it sounds like you're saying that they've become more and more of a burden than beneficial to you.

ALLISON: Yes, ironic, isn't it? How I wish I didn't have to do them. Sometimes I think they bother me more than the obsessions.

THERAPIST: Remembering that they are more harmful than helpful is an important first step in stopping them.

ALLISON: But you know, it's so difficult to stop. Maybe I just have to suffer in order to protect my husband.

THERAPIST: Do you think that it's better for you to torment yourself to the extent that you have no life to speak of even though there is a zero percent chance that Michael will die if you imagine him dying, and a zero percent chance that he could be saved by these rituals even if he were going to die by a real cause?

ALLISON (smiles weakly): I guess if you put it that way, no.

THERAPIST: Can you put it any other way right now, Allison?

ALLISON: I'm sure I could come up with something if I thought about it some more. But not right now. You're very persuasive.

THERAPIST: The evidence is very persuasive, I think. I'm merely presenting it to you, but thank you for the compliment. Now let's get to the rest of your thoughts. You said that you were wretched, wicked, that you would go to hell. You also said, "What kind of a wife imagines her husband's head on a guillotine, being flung down from buildings, stabbed viciously? I must subconsciously want him dead." Let's examine them. First, let's look at your thought that you're wicked and deserve to go to hell.

ALLISON (laughs): Dr. M., even you cannot persuade me to believe that I won't go to hell for sure.

THERAPIST: You're right. Why is it that I can't?

ALLISON: Because no one can, only God can.

THERAPIST (smiles): Hmm, then why is it that you can predict that you will go to hell for sure?

ALLISON (smiles back): Touché. I guess I can't say for sure either. But I can certainly increase my chances by doing bad things.

THERAPIST: Well, let's talk about that. You say that you're wretched, wicked because you have obsessions of Michael dying.

ALLISON: I do believe that, yes.

THERAPIST: Can you remember what I told you about what obsessions are, about why you have them?

ALLISON: I do—you said that most people have obsessions but they don't have many because they don't try to stop them.

THERAPIST: Very good. And you, and others with obsessive-compulsive disorder, have recurring obsessions because . . .

ALLISON: I, *we* try to stop them.

THERAPIST: Yes. Can you tell me why you want to stop them?

ALLISON: Because I think they're bad.

THERAPIST: Exactly. You try to stop them because having them means a lot of different things to you. You believe that they are bad, that you're wicked for having them, you think they will come true, and so on. Now that you know this, can you consider the possibility that you are not wretched or wicked or that you are not going to hell, but that you just have more obsessions than most people because you think it's bad or wicked to have them and are trying so hard to stop them?

ALLISON: I guess it is possible. But why do I have such horrible thoughts? Why don't I have good, happy obsessions that I can't shake off?

THERAPIST: You probably have good, happy thoughts but you don't become preoccupied with them because you don't think it's bad to have good thoughts, and you're not afraid that they'll come true. And so you don't try to shake them off.

ALLISON: I see, yes.

THERAPIST: And because you believe that it's bad or wicked to have thoughts such as those about Michael, and because you're afraid they'll come true, you try your best to stop them. And so you can't forget them.

ALLISON: Right, right, I get it.

THERAPIST: So, is it possible that you're not wicked or evil, just that you are afraid you're wicked or evil because you have obsessions?

ALLISON: I guess so.

THERAPIST: And is it possible that you are not hell bound, just that you are afraid you are headed that way because you have obsessions?

ALLISON: Yes.

THERAPIST: All right, now what about your fear that you may subconsciously want him dead?

ALLISON: I do fear that. I told you, another therapist actually said as much to me.

THERAPIST: You had mentioned that to me before. It is hard for me to think that that's what he meant but I'm sorry you had to go through that. From what I can gather, you love Michael very much and do not want him to die, in fact, you are morbidly afraid that he will die.

ALLISON: I know, but who knows about the unconscious?

THERAPIST: You're right, who knows? But let's look at it this way. Is it possible that you are not a bad wife and that you do not want him dead, but that you are so afraid that he will die that you worry about it all the time?

ALLISON: Hmm, I guess it is possible. Thinking that certainly makes me feel better even if it isn't true.

THERAPIST: Good. Of course, there could be other possibilities too. Is it possible that you had an image of Michael dying once when you were very angry with him, and then got so upset that you had such an image that you tried to shake it off and couldn't. And because you tried so hard to shake it off, it kept coming back at you even though you weren't angry with him anymore?

ALLISON: I guess that's possible too.

THERAPIST: So there are other ways to look at it rather than the fact that you may subconsciously want him dead.

ALLISON: I suppose.

IDENTIFYING DISTORTIONS

During the monitoring and evaluation process, it usually becomes evident that patients are exhibiting a consistent trend in their thinking or are exhibiting a "systematic negative bias" in the way they process information (Beck 1976). The therapist notes these errors, cognitive distortions, or misconceptions as soon as the discussion of automatic thoughts commences. Consistent biases or themes are identified and described to the patient, with the ultimate goal of having patients identify the misconceptions themselves.

The therapist can furnish the patient with the entire list of cognitive distortions first elaborated by Aaron Beck (1976) (see J. Beck [1995] and Burns [1989] for the complete list of cognitive distortions), or provide him only with a list of common errors made by individuals with obsessive-compulsive disorder (see Table 5–3), or provide him only with the errors he makes consistently. The decision is based on the therapist's judgment about what the patient will be able to handle. If the patient will be too overwhelmed by the entire list, then describing only the errors he is making will be far more useful to him. However, if it is judged that the patient's organizational or intellectual sensibilities will be stimulated by having a list and identifying his distortions, then giving him the entire list may be a good idea.

Clinical Vignette

THERAPIST: Allison, do you remember that we had talked about the fact that people with obsessive-compulsive disorder make

Table 5–3. Common Misconceptions Observed in Obsessive-Compulsive Disorder

1. **Catastrophizing**
   I will have a nervous breakdown if the anxiety continues any longer.
   My family will die in a fire unless I unplug all the electrical appliances in the house.
   If Michael didn't call to say he will be late, it means that he is dead.

2. **Overestimating risk of harm or danger**
   I will become ill if I use the public restroom.
   I better wash my hands over and over again; otherwise I am liable to fall sick.
   Planes crash so Michael shouldn't fly.

3. **Underestimating ability to cope**
   I am no good at handling my anxiety.
   I am not sure if I remembered to check, so let me check again.
   I don't trust myself to decide one way or the other. What if I am wrong?

4. **Personalization/self-blame**
   If Michael dies, it will be my fault.
   I had better call and check to see if he is alive, or else I will be responsible for his death.
   If I don't check the gas stove to see that it is off, it is as good as saying that I want him dead.

5. **Negative labeling**
   I am a sinner because I imagine my husband dying.
   I am wicked, evil, wretched, a degenerate.
   I am weak.

6. **All-or-nothing thinking**
   If I make even one mistake, it means I am no good.
   Even the slightest anxiety is intolerable.
   Everything must be in perfect order; even the slightest disorder is not okay.

7. **Magical reasoning**
   Michael will die if I touch the knife.
   If I say "safe Mike" I will prevent his death.
   If I have an obsession over and over again, it is a sign that it will come true.

8. **Should and must statements**
   I should be able to control my obsessions.
   I should never make a mistake.
   I should not feel anxious.

certain consistent mistakes in their thinking or think in certain ways that are not helpful to them?

ALLISON: Uh huh. I remember.

THERAPIST: Here is a list of the common mistakes in thinking made by people with obsessive-compulsive disorder. I would like you to take a look at it at your leisure and ask me any questions you have once you look over it.

ALLISON: Is this for me to take home?

THERAPIST: Yes, it's for you to keep. Right now we're going to use the list to identify some of the thinking mistakes you made the night Michael's parents came over for dinner.

ALLISON: Is that different from what we just did?

THERAPIST: Yes and no. We just got through examining the different automatic thoughts you had that night and we discovered that some of your thoughts were not necessarily based on fact and that there were other ways to look at the same situation. Now we are going to name the different mistakes or errors of logic that you made in your thinking that night. Giving them a name makes it easier to remember and allows us to keep track of which ones you usually tend to make.

ALLISON: So what we did before is to see whether I made any mistakes and now we're naming the mistakes I did make that night.

THERAPIST: Yes, exactly. Very good. So let's go back to your first thought where you predicted that Michael would die because you had an obsession about dying. If you take a look at the list here, can you tell me what mistake(s) you may have made?

ALLISON: Hmm. Was I *catastrophizing* by saying that Michael was going to die?

THERAPIST: Very good, you were *catastrophizing* by thinking of the worst thing that could happen to him. Because Michael was not in the slightest danger of dying at that moment, that's catastrophizing. Anything else?

ALLISON: I'm not sure.

THERAPIST: How about *magical reasoning?* Look at number seven on the list. You were predicting a cause and effect connection that is magical rather than actual.

ALLISON: Yes, that's what we were discussing before, isn't it? Thinking that something will happen because I have an obsession about it?

THERAPIST: Yes, that type of thinking is very common in obsessive-compulsive disorder. If I think a bad thought, then it will happen. If I think a good thought, it will prevent the bad thing from happening. This error also applies to a thought you had later on the same night, when you believed that you had better say "safe Mike" to prevent him from dying.

ALLISON: I see.

THERAPIST: I am going to write these errors down here. Over the next week when you fill out the Revised Thought Log, I would like you to begin identifying these errors on your own. You can refer to the list when you begin evaluating your thoughts, and jot down whichever error you think you're making at that moment. Ultimately, you will get so good at identifying the mistake you're making you won't need to refer to the list.

ALLISON: But what do I do if I don't think I'm making a mistake?

THERAPIST: Excellent question, Allison. If you don't think you're making an error at the moment but you recall that you considered it an error in the past, note it down anyway.

ALLISON: I'm not sure I follow. How can I think it was an error in the past but not at the moment?

THERAPIST: Remember you said just a few moments ago that you hope you will remember that Michael cannot die if you have an obsession about him dying when you're faced with a knife? That's what I mean.

Let me give you an example. If you have a magical thought about Michael dying again, but at the moment that the anxiety strikes the thought doesn't seem so magical anymore, jot down the distortion anyway. Why? Because if you think back, you will remember that you decided the thought was magical and not real when you examined the objective evidence not so long ago. With practice, it will be apparent to you that the thought is magical rather than realistic even during an anxiety-provoking situation. However, at this point, you may have to force yourself to note down this information.

ALLISON: I see. But that's assuming I will be collected enough to remember what I thought in the past. When I get so nervous, I can barely think of anything else but how I can get out of there and just do my rituals.

THERAPIST: In that case, put nothing down but try to evaluate the thought a little later on, or bring it up during our next session and we can put our heads together. If you do that enough, over time it will get easier to identify the mistakes closer and closer to the moment when the automatic thought actually strikes. And that's our goal. The sooner you can correct the thought, the less anxiety it will produce.

MODIFYING AND REVISING
THE AUTOMATIC THOUGHT

Once the distortions have been identified, the task turns to formally modifying the maladaptive thought. Emphasis is placed on logical reasoning and on instituting a more realistic, adaptive thought in the place of the automatic thought. For example, after a series of questions Allison was able to acknowledge that there was no connection between her obsessive thoughts of Michael being stabbed and his actual death. After she was helped to identify the mistakes in her thinking, she was helped to construct an argument against her initial automatic thought, which had told her that there was such a connection between the two.

Just as the Automatic Thought Log (ATL) was first filled out in therapy, a formal argument against a central automatic thought is now written out by the therapist to both clarify the task and model the appropriate behavior. However, the argument itself is formulated by both the therapist and patient. Through a series of Socratic questions, the therapist elicits the logical, rational thought from the patient and records it on the Revised Thought Log (RTL) (see Table 5–1), which is similar to the ATL but has added space to document the cognitive distortions, the revised thoughts, and the outcome (e.g., Do I feel better after doing this exercise?).

Over the next few sessions, the patient is instructed to fill out the RTL on his own. Once the patient demonstrates the ability to frame a well-thought-out, logical way to rebut and replace each of the central automatic thoughts, the revised thoughts can be put on index cards or audiotapes to be used as prompts when the automatic thoughts are triggered. Indeed, since the bulk of the work in cognitive therapy occurs outside the session, it is imperative that patients have the tools to begin restructuring cognitions when obsessions strike.

It is important to note that the process of changing cognitions is a gradual and difficult one. Change does not occur overnight. Patients do not and cannot be expected to completely believe the revised thought even if they have crafted it themselves. Although the degree of belief in the automatic thought can fluctuate from time to time, at the beginning of therapy most patients tend to completely believe that their primary appraisals are accurate. After the automatic thoughts are thoroughly evaluated, patients may begin to acknowledge that the initial thoughts may be invalid or maladaptive. For example, their belief may decline from 100 to 75 percent during the therapy session. However, as soon as an obsession strikes, this belief will, in all likelihood, shoot up to 100 percent again. Patients are encouraged to challenge their automatic thought *despite* the fact that they now completely believe that it is true. If they find it hard to challenge the thought unless they believe that it is inaccurate, they are encouraged to remind themselves that they were able to think differently during the session, and to try to recall the conversation with the therapist.

Indeed, it is the process of challenging and modifying the automatic thought *each time* it is triggered that leads to changed cognitions. Automatic thoughts, and the assumptions and beliefs on which they are based, are slowly chipped away whenever a revised thought is used to replace an already existing automatic thought. Over time, the patient exhibits a decreased belief in his automatic thought and an increased belief in his revised thought. With enough time and practice, the revised thought begins to occur closer and closer in relation to the time when the obsession and the automatic thought are triggered, thereby decreasing or eliminating the anxiety associated with the obsessions. In other words, the revised thought eventually becomes the "automatic" dialogue that patients have with themselves instead of the initial, dysfunctional automatic thought.

Guidelines for Restructuring Thoughts

Just as automatic thoughts vary from person to person, and from situation to situation, revised thoughts must also be specific to the individual and the context. However, we offer general guidelines to help therapists structure rational, logical arguments against the patient's automatic inner dialogue. Below is a list of functional assumptions and sample adaptive thoughts that can be generated. While these adaptive thoughts and assumptions challenge the core dysfunctional beliefs held by individuals with OCD, they must be specifically tailored to the belief system of the particular patient.

1. Experiencing obsessional thoughts will not cause harm to occur to myself or others because thinking is not the same as doing.

Sample revised thoughts:

a. *Thinking that I will be contaminated with bacteria will not lead me to become infected because* . . .

b. Thinking that Michael will be stabbed will not lead to his death because . . .

2. Neutralizing my obsessions will not prevent harm from occurring

Sample revised thoughts:

a. Washing my hands over and over again when I have obsessions of getting infected will not prevent the infection from occurring because . . .

b. Calling Michael twenty-one times will not prevent him from dying because . . .

c. Saying "safe Mike" over and over again when I have visions of him getting stabbed will not lead to his death because . . .

d. If I don't say "safe Mike," it does not mean that I will have caused his death because . . .

e. My anxiety will naturally decrease even if I don't say "safe Mike" because . . .

3. If I want to control my obsessional thoughts, I need to first learn that the exercise of control is unnecessary.

Sample revised thoughts:

a. I know from experience now that the more I try to control or suppress my thoughts about Michael dying, the more I wind up having such thoughts.

b. I know now from experience that the less I try to control or suppress my thoughts about Michael dying, the less I seem to have them.

c. I cannot expect to control my obsessional thoughts at all times; no one can.

d. The more I ritualize, the more I seem to increase my obsessions and compulsions in the long run.

4. Having bad thoughts is not a sign of immorality.

Sample revised thoughts:

a. If I think that Michael will be strangled, it does not mean I am an evil, wicked person.

b. If I imagine that Michael will be stabbed, it does not mean that I want him to be stabbed.

c. If I don't ritualize, it does not mean that I am an evil, wicked person.

d. One of the reasons I get so anxious when I have visions of Michael dying is because I think that it is bad, evil, and wrong to have such thoughts.

5. Harm is not likely to occur to me or others, I just worry that it is. Sample revised thought:

a. Michael is not really in any imminent danger of dying, I just worry that he is.

6. If I am not competent in all the things I do, it does not mean that I am flawed, or not worthwhile.

Sample revised thought:

a. If I am not able to go to school now it does not mean that I am flawed or worthless—I have an illness that is making it hard for me to focus on work, that's all.

7. I am capable of coping with the anxiety from the obsessions. Sample revised thought:

a. I will not have a nervous breakdown if I don't ritualize, because . . .

Clinical Vignette

THERAPIST: Allison, now we are going to begin writing another dialogue, a more rational, helpful dialogue that you can have with yourself when your obsession about Michael being stabbed strikes again.

ALLISON: And saying this new dialogue will help prevent the obsession next time?

THERAPIST: Not right away, but it will reduce the obsessions in the long run. But that's not our immediate goal. Our goal is to change the dialogue you have with yourself after the obsession strikes so that you are not as troubled by this obsession. Over time, as you get less and less troubled by it, the obsession will be less likely to occur.

ALLISON: You mean I have to grin and bear it and then it will go away?

THERAPIST: Kind of. Picture that the anxiety is the fuel that keeps your obsession going. As we change your inner dialogue, over time you get less anxious, and as the fuel runs out, the obsession will occur less and less frequently and intensely.

ALLISON: I'll have to see it to believe it.

THERAPIST: And you will. Shall we get started?

ALLISON: (acknowledges).

THERAPIST: If it's possible that there is no connection between what you think and what happens to Michael, what can you say to remind yourself of this on those occasions when you are absolutely sure that thinking about him dying will cause his death?

ALLISON: You mean like what can I say to myself when I'm faced with a knife again?

THERAPIST: Yes, exactly.

ALLISON: I can just say to myself, Allison, he cannot die if you think it, don't be so ridiculous and stupid.

THERAPIST: I like the idea about reminding yourself that imagining something cannot make it happen. But do you think that you could say that without getting down on yourself? How do you think you will feel if you call yourself ridiculous or stupid.

ALLISON: Kind of bad, I guess.

THERAPIST: Yes, that's how I would feel too if I said that to myself. In fact, I've noticed that you tend to give yourself negative labels quite frequently.

ALLISON: I know, I do.

THERAPIST: In fact, I would like you to note down when you do that, identify the mistake, and then try to replace that dialogue too. What kind of mistake would you be making if you call yourself stupid or ridiculous.

ALLISON (scanning the list): *Negative labeling?*

THERAPIST: Very good. And how would you replace such a thought?

ALLISON: I'm not sure. *"Don't call yourself ridiculous."*

THERAPIST: Not bad—how about adding something like, "It is not helpful to call myself ridiculous or stupid, it only makes me feel bad and guilty and does not help me change?"

ALLISON: That sounds reasonable.

THERAPIST: Getting back to the automatic thoughts you had that night. What else could you say to yourself instead?

ALLISON: How about, "Thinking about something cannot cause it to happen. If wishing someone dead could make it happen, most people would be in jail by now."

THERAPIST: Excellent. Why don't we make that a little more specific to the automatic thought you had that night, starting with the automatic thought you're trying to replace? Something like, "When I saw the knife . . ."

ALLISON: When I saw the knife, I began having images of Michael getting stabbed and began thinking that he would actually die because I had the obsession about him getting stabbed, and then it would all be my fault. But, the truth is . . .

THERAPIST: Wait, before you try to replace the thoughts, how about adding how that thought made you feel and what you did?

ALLISON: I felt anxious and I wanted to do all I could to stop that from happening.

THERAPIST: Good.

ALLISON: But the truth is that he was not and is not actually going to die because I know that thinking about something does not make it happen.

THERAPIST: How about adding, *"That is magical reasoning, just as saying 'safe Mike' is not going to save him even if he was in danger of dying (which he is not)."*

ALLISON: Yes, that's right. Saying it over and over again just temporarily makes me feel less anxious because there is a part of me that thinks it will actually work. That is also magical reasoning because it doesn't.

THERAPIST: Not only that, what other harm can ritualizing do in the long run.?

ALLISON: I'm not sure.

THERAPIST: We had talked about how ritualizing can actually increase obsessions and anxiety in the long run.

ALLISON: Hmm. I could say, "Saying 'safe Mike' will ultimately increase my obsessions and anxiety in the long run, which is not what I want."

THERAPIST: Good, you're doing very well. Now let's get to the other thoughts, where you call yourself wicked and evil for having such thoughts. We just talked about that a few moments ago.

ALLISON: Hmm, it's possible that I think about Michael dying because I love him more than anything else in the world and don't want him to die, and not because I subconsciously want him to die, I'm a good person, I am not evil or wicked. Thinking that is just going to make me feel depressed, guilty, and bad about myself.

THERAPIST: Very good. Now I know that you think it's wrong to have such obsessions when you say these things to yourself. How about adding something about how it's normal to have obsessions and how you cannot control them like this?

ALLISON: Okay. Let's see. I cannot possibly expect to control all my obsessions; no one can. I know that it's normal to have obsessions. Most people have them every now and then, so it's not my fault that I have them and it's not a sign that I'm wicked. Mine just come more frequently because I worry that they will come true and so I try hard to stop them from coming. If I tried to hang on to the obsessions instead of trying to get rid of them, I would have them less and less. I already tried that in session with Dr. McGinn and it worked.

THERAPIST: Good, I think we're about done. I'm going to write this down on the Revised Thought Log (see Table 5–4 for Allison's completed Revised Thought Log) so that you can not only use it the next time this obsession strikes but so you can use it as an example the next time you fill out the log on your own.

Table 5–4. Allison's Revised Thought Log

Fill out when you have a negative feeling or if a negative feeling becomes worse

1. Feeling.
   How do you feel now? Check √ and rate how much on a scale of 0 (usual) to 100 (worst I can imagine)
   Anxious √ (100)   Sad √ (95)   Guilty √ (100)   Angry ___ ( )
   Other ___ ( )   Specify _____

2. Situation
   What were you doing when you felt this way? *My in-laws came over. They brought us dinner. His mom insisted that I help out in the kitchen. She asked me to make the salad and when I said that I didn't feel comfortable doing that, she got really mad at me and started to make it herself. As soon as she started making the salad, I felt very nervous, I thought my heart would stop. I ran out of the kitchen and locked myself in my bedroom.*

3. Automatic thought
   What went through your mind that could have made you feel this way? List all thoughts here and rate each thought on a scale of 0 (not at all) to 100 (completely) on how much you believe this thought. *As soon as she picked up the knife all I could see was Mike being stabbed all over. All I could think was that Michael would die (100) and that it would all be my fault (100). I ran from the room and tried to get the thoughts out of my head. I began saying "safe Mike, safe Mike," I think I actually said it aloud once. I am sure she heard me but I didn't care. I had to make sure that nothing and no one would stop me from saying it. That's why I had to run and lock the door because I knew that even one second free in my head and he would surely die (100). I am so wretched (95), I can't even get through a family dinner without seeing Michael brutally stabbed. I am so wicked (95), I will go to hell (95). What kind of a wife imagines her husband's head on a guillotine, being flung down from buildings, stabbed viciously? I must subconsciously want him dead (90–95).*

4. Behavior
   What did you do? How did you cope with the situation. *I ran into the bedroom and locked the door and lay on my bed crying. I ritualized, I said "safe Mike" forty-eight times.*

5. Cognitive distortions
   What mistakes am I making in my thinking? Enumerate. *Catastrophizing, overestimating risks of danger, personalization/self-blame, underestimating ability to cope, labeling/mislabeling, magical reasoning.*

Table 5–4. (continued)

6. Revised thoughts
   Are there more realistic or useful ways to look at the same situation?
   Enumerate alternate thoughts here and rate each on how much you believe
   it—0 (not at all) to 100 (completely).

   When I saw the knife, I began having images of Mike getting stabbed and began thinking that I would actually cause his death just by having obsessions about him dying. This naturally made me afraid and I wanted to do all I could to stop that from happening. But the truth is that he was not and is not actually going to die because I know that thinking about something does not make it happen. That is magical thinking. By the same token, saying "safe Mike" is not going to save him even if he was in danger of dying (which he is not). Saying it over and over again just temporarily makes me feel less anxious because there is a part of me that thinks that it will actually work. That is also magical thinking because it does not. Not only that, ritualizing actually increases my obsessions and anxiety in the long run which is not what I want.

   It is possible that I think about Mike dying because I love him more than anything else in the world and do not want him to die and not because I subconsciously want him to die. I am a good person, I am not evil or wicked, thinking that is just going to make me feel depressed, guilty, and bad about myself. I cannot possibly expect to control all my obsessions, no one can. I know that it is normal to have obsessions, most people have them every now and then, so it is not my fault that I have them and it is not a sign that I am wicked. Mine just come more frequently because I worry that they will come true and so I try hard to stop them from coming. If I tried to hang on to the obsessions instead of trying to get rid of them, I would have them less and less. I already tried that in session with Dr. McGinn and it worked.

7. Outcome
   How do you feel now? Did you behave any differently? *I am not sure if I believe all this, but I feel a little better, a little less anxious (60), and somewhat less guilty (70). I was not in the situation when I filled this out so I don't know if I would have done anything differently. I would like to think so. I do feel a tiny bit optimistic.*

ASSESSING THE EFFECTIVENESS OF
THE REVISED THOUGHT

Once the rational, adaptive thought has been formulated in the session, patients are asked if their belief in their automatic thoughts has declined, and if so, by how much. They are also asked to rate if they believe the revised thought, and how much. If a change is observed, even if it is minimal, patients are asked to rate how they feel now following the exercise, and if they would do anything differently as a result. Did the anxiety associated with the obsessions decrease? Would they be less likely to escape or ritualize?

Belief in the revised thought (and a corresponding decrease in the automatic thought) is linked to the decrease in affect and any changes in behavior (predicted or performed), so that patients are able to see that although the situational triggers (what occurred, the obsessional image) have not changed, modifying the automatic thought following these triggers has led to the decrease in affect and a change in behavior.

THERAPIST: We are coming to the end of our session. How do you feel now?

ALLISON: You know, I feel a little bit more hopeful that things will change. Just talking to you today makes me feel that all is not doom and gloom. I actually laughed today, I can't believe I did. I feel like all I've been doing lately is crying.

THERAPIST: It makes me very glad to hear that. How do you feel when you think of your obsession now?

ALLISON: Less nervous, I guess. I almost feel as if I'm looking at it from a distance, like it's happening to someone else.

THERAPIST: That's interesting. Do you think you would do anything differently if the obsession struck right now?

ALLISON: I don't know, it's hard to say. I know I would at least try not to ritualize, but I'm not sure if I would succeed.

THERAPIST: That's a good beginning. It will get easier as we go along.

TACKLING COMPLICATIONS

Although restructuring cognitions helps diminish the anxiety associated with the obsessions, the process of restructuring itself may inadvertently become ritualized for some patients. For example, someone who used to repeat "safe Mike" may now begin ritualistically saying "Thinking is not the same as doing" to reduce the anxiety, or may begin overutilizing the thought logs. In this case, it is no longer the logical rationale that is reducing the anxiety but the ritualistic way of repeating the phrase or the ritualistic way of filling out the logs that is causing the anxiety to lessen. Beginning therapists must consider the possibility that this side effect may occur and should be attentive to any sign that the patient is ritualistically repeating rational thoughts instead of logically reasoning out why automatic thoughts may be erroneous or maladaptive. One way of reducing this risk is by preempting it. Discussing the issue with patients beforehand and reviewing ways to handle it will enable both therapist and patient to be on guard if such restructuring rituals occur. In addition, if they do occur, attempts should be made to make the restructuring process less ritualized for that particular automatic thought. For example, altering the wording or phrasing of the substituted thought is one way to make it less ritualized.

A related concern is that substituting revised thoughts should not promote avoidance of the automatic thought. When the anxiety associated with an obsession is triggered or the urge to ritualize occurs, patients must first be encouraged to identify the specific, maladaptive automatic thought and only then substitute a specific revised thought to replace it. If the automatic thought specific to that particular situation is not elicited by the patient, who merely voices general or nonspecific rational thoughts during moments of anxiety (e.g., you will be okay, he will be fine), then the revised thought will only serve to avoid the affect associated with the automatic thought. In other words, the patient will be suppressing the thought and not countering it. The therapist must be watchful of this tendency all throughout therapy, even if the patient feels that he "already knows" what his automatic thoughts are after awhile.

NEXT WEEK (AND FUTURE WEEKS): APPLYING COGNITIVE RESTRUCTURING OUTSIDE THERAPY

As indicated earlier, cognitive restructuring takes place within but also, most importantly, outside sessions. Patients are instructed to record and revise automatic thoughts using the Rational Thought Log (RTL) as and when their anxiety or discomfort is triggered. As patients become skilled at revising their automatic thoughts at the moment their anxiety is triggered, their discomfort associated with obsessions will decrease over time.

Once patients have generated several Revised Thought Logs, common themes are explored and generated more formally for patients to utilize as the need occurs. For example, flash cards may be developed during the session, where negative automatic thoughts are written out on one side of an index card and revised thoughts on the other. Then, when situational triggers eliciting a particular automatic thought arise, patients are encouraged to first verbalize and then revise the automatic thought in question using the appropriate card for that situation. Reading out the automatic thought allows patients to face and fully process the extent of their fears rather than avoid it as they are otherwise inclined to do. Revising the thought immediately afterwards modifies the dysfunctional assumptions and beliefs and leads to a reduction in obsessional anxiety.

As stated in Chapter 2, although patients are often able to understand that their thoughts may be irrational when they are not faced with the triggering stimulus, their insight vanishes as soon as they confront the stimulus. Hence, revising the automatic thought while confronting the triggering stimulus is therapeutically essential, in that it leads to improved insight during moments when there is none.

Session 5: Exposure and Response Prevention (Phase I)

RATIONALE AND PREPARATION

Session Goals	*Check When Done*

1. Review (5–10 minutes) ☐
- Obtain feedback on Session 4
- Review homework
  - Revised thought Log (RTL)
  - Obsession-Compulsion Monitoring Form (OCM)
- Briefly review events that occurred over past week

2. The Session (Exposure and Response Prevention Phase I) ☐
- Rationale for exposure and response prevention
- Preparing for exposure
  - Imaginal versus in vivo exposure: deciding which to use
  - Preparing for in vivo exposure hierarchy
  - Preparing for imaginal exposure hierarchy
- Planning for response prevention
  - Listing rituals
  - Deciding on the strategy: abstinence versus graded response prevention
  - Outlining the strategy
- Tackling complications

3. Next Week (5 minutes) ☐
- Discuss homework to be completed
  - Obsession-Compulsion Monitoring form (OCM) (see Table 3–3)
  - Revised Thought Log (RTL) (see Table 5–1)
- Anticipate potential stressors that may occur during the week

SESSION OVERVIEW

The behavioral phase of therapy, comprising exposure and response prevention, begins in Session 5 and is described over a four-session period. However, general principles and the rationale have already been introduced in Session 2, and the patient has already begun monitoring obsessive triggers and rituals on a daily basis. Like cognitive restructuring, exposure and response prevention then continue to be implemented throughout therapy.

Once events of the past session and week are discussed, the rationale for behavior therapy is provided during this session. Although a brief treatment rationale was presented as part of the general psychoeducation in Session 3, a more detailed behavioral rationale is now offered. The following topics are covered: What is behavior therapy? What does exposure mean? What is response prevention? How does it differ from cognitive restructuring? Why is triggering anxiety helpful?

Following this, a hierarchy of the patient's obsessional fears is created so that he can begin the process of exposure. A list of all ritualized thoughts and behaviors is also developed using the Obsession-Compulsion Monitoring form (see Table 3–3), so that response prevention can begin. The therapist and patient work collaboratively toward formulating the treatment plan for this phase. Which obsession is the least anxiety provoking? Which one is more easily implemented this week? Can the patient agree to stop performing all rituals or at least to some extent? Who can assist him at home? The session concludes after the homework for the next week is assigned. Potential sources of difficulties, especially with regard to the homework, are also addressed.

REVIEW

The therapist begins the session by requesting feedback on the previous session, and in doing so not only determines the patient's reactions but also assesses how much of the previous session the patient remembers. The therapist then fills in the blanks, thereby strengthening the patient's understanding of the previous session. Specifically, automatic thoughts and their link to feelings and behaviors are discussed, along with the relationship between automatic thoughts and the assumptions and beliefs that give rise to them. The process of examining and revising automatic thoughts, identifying cognitive distortions, and assessing the effectiveness of cognitive restructuring is also briefly reviewed.

The therapist then elicits significant events or episodes of anxiety that may have occurred over the past week, and ties them to the assigned homework. Did the patient successfully fill out Rational Thought Logs when episodes of anxiety occurred? Were the relevant thoughts appropriately restructured? Did he experience a reduction in anxiety? The therapist helps resolve problem areas and then brings the discussion around to the current session.

THE SESSION: EXPOSURE AND
RESPONSE PREVENTION PHASE I

A fundamental shift now occurs, beginning with this session and continuing until the end of treatment. Previously, sessions were focused on giving the patient ways to cope with the anxiety generated. Treatment components such as psychoeducation and cognitive restructuring teach the patient about his illness and ways to restructure misinterpretations he holds about his illness and himself. With the introduction of exposure and response prevention (Riggs and Foa 1993, Steketee 1993), the patient's anxiety is now directly triggered in therapy with the purpose of ultimately reducing it over time. In essence, the patient systematically confronts his fears in and out of sessions and learns to stop ritualizing when obsessional anxiety strikes. To ensure that patients are able to tolerate this process, coping strategies learned in prior sessions are mustered and anxiety is triggered in a structured, graded fashion.

Once events of the previous week are reviewed, the therapist introduces the behavioral part of treatment, and discusses which elements of this phase will be covered during this session. The rationale, the specific techniques to be utilized (exposure and response prevention), and the manner in which they will be implemented will be covered during the first half of the session. The patient is then told that the remainder of the session will be spent developing the exposure hierarchy and generating a list of rituals that must be addressed.

PRESENT RATIONALE FOR BEHAVIORAL STRATEGIES

Why Is a Rationale Necessary?

Offering the rationale for why behavioral strategies will be used is crucial, not just because a theoretical understanding is believed to improve treatment efficacy, but because without it the patient will probably not tolerate the anxiety provoked, and will more than likely not comply with treatment. Explaining how fear develops and how it is maintained helps the patient understand that the therapist is not being sadistic, but that the production of anxiety is necessary for it to ultimately reduce over time. To illustrate the efficacy of the process, it is often useful to find a situation in a person's life that initially caused anxiety, but that, with repeated exposure, it decreased (e.g., driving a car, speaking in public, or starting a new job).

Although many of the concepts may initially be difficult for the patient to grasp, giving the theoretical rationale is a necessary prerequisite for the patient to truly understand why behavioral strategies are used and why they are effective. To promote easy comprehension, the therapist must explain the concepts in the simplest possible terms and not use unnecessary jargon. We find that illustrating key concepts on a blackboard or using pen and paper often facilitates understanding.

The Rationale

Why are exposure and response prevention used in the treatment of OCD?

Obsessional anxiety is learned. According to behavioral theory, obsessional anxiety becomes learned via a process of classical conditioning, just as do other phobias, and hence can be unlearned (see Table 6–1). According to classical conditioning theory, if a neutral stimulus is paired with an unconditioned stimulus that naturally produces fear or anxiety, the neutral stimulus now becomes a conditioned stimulus, meaning that it becomes capable of producing anxiety when presented alone. In simpler terms, if objects, people, or situations that do not typically elicit anxiety on their own (e.g., a toaster oven) occur in the context of things that naturally elicit anxiety (house catches fire when toaster was on), these previously neutral stimuli (e.g., toaster oven) become capable of creating anxiety (using the toaster oven is now anxiety producing).

How does the individual cope with this anxiety? Individuals with obsessive-compulsive disorder develop a variety of passive avoidance and escape behaviors (e.g., not using the toaster oven) and active avoidance behaviors or compulsive rituals (checking to make sure the toaster oven is off) in order to reduce the anxiety created by the conditioned stimulus and to ward off feared consequences.

Obsessional anxiety continues if left unchecked. Behavioral theory also helps explain why these learned fears continue and do not naturally extinguish over time. In other words, why does fear continue even if the conditioned stimulus (toaster oven) does not continue to be paired with naturally fear-producing events (fire) as would be posited by classical conditioning? That is, if the fear developed because they occurred contiguously, why doesn't it extinguish if they

Table 6–1. Behavioral Explanations of How Obsessions and Rituals Are Learned and Unlearned

1. How Obsessive Fears and Rituals Are Learned
   - *Development of fear/anxiety*
     —A stimulus which does not automatically elicit anxiety or fear (a neutral stimulus) becomes associated with a stimulus (an unconditioned stimulus or UCS) that naturally elicits anxiety or fear (an unconditioned response or UCR) by being paired with it.
     —Through this pairing, the previously neutral stimulus (the conditioned stimulus or the CS) now becomes conditioned or capable of eliciting fear or anxiety on its own (the conditioned response or CR).
   - *Maintenance of fear/anxiety*
     —Avoidance and escape behaviors are developed in order to reduce the anxiety elicited by the CS and, by doing so, the individual is negatively reinforced by the cessation of anxiety that follows.
     —The individual never learns that the CS is not anxiety provoking in and of itself. The fear response does not extinguish because the individual does not learn that the CS is no longer being paired with the UCS.

2. How Obsessive Fears and Rituals Are Unlearned
   - *Goal of exposure*
     —Break or disconnect the associations between sensations of fear or anxiety and the phobic but objectively safe stimuli (extinction); and
   - *Goal of response prevention*
     —Break or disconnect the associations between the reduction of anxiety and the escape or avoidance of the phobic stimulus.

no longer occur together? Simply because the individual, in his attempts to avoid or escape the conditioned stimulus, does not stay in the situation long enough to learn that the two are no longer paired. In other words, if the individual avoids using the toaster oven or constantly checks to make sure that the toaster oven is off, he never truly learns that using the toaster oven, without repeatedly checking to see that is off, will not lead to a fire. In fact, what he does learn is that the fire is not occurring *because* he is not using it or *because* he is constantly checking to see that it is off. Thereby, a connection is created between avoiding the situation or ritualizing, and the reduced anxiety that follows. The sense of relief that follows therefore negatively reinforces his avoidance and ritualized behaviors. What this means is that because his anxiety decreases when he performs them and the disastrous consequences do not occur, he learns to perform rituals over and over again.

Obsessional anxiety can be unlearned. The individual "unlearns" the anxiety by learning that the conditioned stimulus is not truly to be feared, and by learning that the anxiety associated with this conditioned stimulus will naturally decrease as he realizes that it is not intrinsically threatening. This is accomplished by two behavioral techniques, exposure and response prevention.

Exposure. This technique involves gradually exposing the individual with obsessive-compulsive disorder to anxiety-provoking stimuli (e.g., toaster oven) for a prolonged period of time until his anxiety reaction decreases. This may be done either directly (in vivo) or in imagination, and may be done within and outside therapy sessions. As the individual gradually confronts these anxiety-provoking stimuli, and the disastrous consequences (a fire) do not occur, his anxiety about these stimuli (using the toaster oven) will naturally decrease over time. In classical conditioning terms, the previously neutral, now conditioned stimulus (toaster oven) is presented alone, without pairing it with the unconditioned stimulus (fire), so that this conditioned stimulus goes back to being neutral again. The connection between the conditioned stimulus and the unconditioned stimulus will be weakened because they are no longer paired and because the association between the conditioned stimulus and the conditioned anxiety response is therefore weakened, and a new association develops to the previously feared stimulus (no anxiety).

Response Prevention. Used in conjunction with exposure, response prevention involves blocking the avoidance behaviors that the individual has developed to cope with his anxiety. Rituals must be blocked, otherwise prolonged exposure to obsessive fears will be ineffective. As he confronts the feared situation (exposure) without using any avoidance or ritualized behaviors (response prevention), he finds that the disastrous consequence he fears does not occur and that his anxiety naturally goes down anyway. As a result, he learns that there is no need to ritualize to ward off fearsome consequences or to relieve his anxiety. From a theoretical perspective, the individual unlearns the connection he has made between his avoidance or rituals and the reduction of anxiety and it is no longer negatively reinforced by their performance.

Clinical Vignette

THERAPIST: For the past few sessions we've been focusing on ways you can feel better by modifying the way you think when you become anxious. And you mentioned to me earlier that you found it helpful.

ALLISON: Yes, I have. Of course, I feel best when I'm here because everything you say makes a lot of sense. But you were right. When I examine my thoughts and try to modify them, I feel better even if I don't believe a word of what I'm saying initially, even though my brain is saying, "Allison, you are going to get sick," or "Stop it, you will kill him." I just tell myself, "You believed it in Dr. McGinn's office so just try and say it."

THERAPIST: I'm very glad to hear that. Do you find that you're able to believe some of the other thoughts more and more now?

ALLISON: I do. I really do. When I don't, I actually picture myself talking to you. I picture you saying (imitates therapist), "Is there any other way to look at this?" When all else fails, that seems to work.

THERAPIST (laughs): Good, I'm glad I can be of some use even outside the session. (Pause). Allison, today we begin with something new. If you remember, we had briefly talked about how we would be slowly helping you face the things that make you anxious.

ALLISON (in a panicky voice): Yes, I do, somewhat. I don't feel ready though. You had said we would only do it when I was ready.

THERAPIST: I know the thought of confronting your fears makes you anxious, Allison. Today we are just going to talk about what we want to do and then we will start working on your fears during the next session, and I assure you we will only start with things you feel ready to do. First, I am going to explain again why it's important to confront your anxiety and how we will go about confronting it. We'll spend the rest of today's session looking through your list to see what you avoid, what makes you anxious, and what makes you ritualize so we can decide how to begin. We will also look through your list of rituals to see how we want to reduce them. Is that okay with you?

ALLISON: Sure, I feel better now. Now that we're just talking, I mean.

THERAPIST: Let's get started. Do you remember what we discussed earlier about why it was important to confront your fears?

ALLISON: I think so. You said that I avoid and so it gets worse.

THERAPIST: Yes it does. Let's start from the beginning. About how you may have started becoming scared of certain things. For example, knives have become scary to you because somewhere down the line they became connected with Michael getting hurt. Perhaps your fear of knives began because you had an image of Michael getting stabbed with knives. So now each time you think of a knife, or having to use it, you think of Michael getting hurt. That's why you avoid using them. Why would you want to use one if it means hurting Michael, right?

ALLISON: Right.

THERAPIST: But then, avoiding is not always enough because you are not just afraid of using knives, you don't even want to think about it. So you begin to ritualize when you imagine him dying, you check on him over and over again, for example. And then you feel less anxious when you avoid or check on him, so you do it more and more. But here's the catch. Although you feel better temporarily, you feel more anxious in the long run because what you are learning is that knives are dangerous to Michael, and that if you think about knives or if you use them, you could really kill him. And the more you think that, the more anxious you are, and the more obsessions you have in the long run.

You also start associating your rituals with feeling better, and there is a strong part of you that believes that checking up on him, not using knives, and so on, keeps him from getting killed. Am I right?

ALLISON (sheepishly): Yes.

THERAPIST: So, if you keep ritualizing and feeling better, and terrible things do not happen to Michael, you feel justified in continuing your rituals. For example, when he doesn't die, you may think, "See, that's why I have to do more rituals." And so you do more. But since the effect is only temporary, you do more and more to feel better. And before you know it, all you're doing is checking on Michael, calling him, checking knives. And your brain doesn't get the opportunity to learn that if you hadn't ritualized, Michael wouldn't have died anyway, and your anxiety would have gone down naturally. And the funny thing is that the more you ritualize, the more obsessions you have in the long run, which is exactly the opposite of what you want.

ALLISON: You mean that I'm being self-defeating then?

THERAPIST: Well, what you're doing is self-defeating, because it defeats the purpose you're trying to serve, which is to feel less anxious. So in order to help your anxiety go down more permanently, we are going to conduct two exercises—one is called exposure and the other response prevention.

ALLISON: To make me face my fears without running away.

THERAPIST: I couldn't have said it better myself. You have a good memory. We will help you gradually face all the things you're afraid of by showing you that the things you fear will happen are, in fact, not likely to happen at all. For example, we will have you confront objects like newspapers and garbage cans to help you realize that they will not give you the germs you fear. And while we're doing that, we'll also make sure that you do not avoid or distract yourself, and most important, that you do not ritualize in any way. That is called response prevention.

ALLISON: I'm not sure I can stand it.

THERAPIST: We'll be starting off slowly with things you can manage. The idea is to help you tolerate the anxiety, face it, without doing anything to take your mind off it. And before you know it, your anxiety will go down naturally, and you will realize that you are not infested with germs.

ALLISON: How do you know my anxiety will go down?

THERAPIST: Because that's how anxiety works. It goes down unless you are truly in danger of some sort. And even then it passes when the danger passes. In your situation, we are showing you that there is no danger, and that you will be fine.

PREPARING FOR EXPOSURE EXERCISES

Imaginal or In Vivo Exposure: Deciding Which to Use

Once the above rationale is presented along with a brief description of exposure and response prevention, the therapist must now decide which type of exposure is appropriate. Utilizing the information collected during Session 2 on anxiety triggers and catastrophic fears, the therapist now determines whether anxiety-provoking situations should be confronted via imagination, in vivo, or both. Indications and contraindications exist for both (see Table 6–2).

In vivo exposure is indicated for most patients with OCD and is usually the technique of choice. Several studies suggest that in vivo exposure is more beneficial than imaginal exposure when both forms of exposure are indicated for the same phobic situation (see Steketee

**Table 6–2. Imaginal Versus In Vivo Exposure:
Indications and Contraindications**

	Indications	*Contraindications*
Imaginal exposure	• Feared consequences • Internal triggers of anxiety • Insufficiency of direct exposure alone (in accessing feared consequences, reducing anxiety) • Difficulty performing in vivo exposure (due to impracticality, high anxiety and avoidance, low motivation)	• Inability to visualize • Inability to have physiological response to images
In vivo exposure	• External triggers of anxiety • Nonspecific consequences • Contamination fears • Not a good candidate for imaginal exposure (inability to visualize, inability to have physiological response to images)	• Impractical to implement • Dangerous to implement • No external anxiety triggers • Severe anxiety and avoidance • Low motivation

1993). However, as indicated below, in vivo exposure may be contraindicated or not effective for all phobic situations, in which case imaginal exposure may need to be implemented.

Other studies indicate that a combination of imaginal and in vivo exposure may be beneficial (Foa and Goldstein 1978), and that patients who receive both may be less likely to relapse than those who receive in vivo alone. However, not all patients who received in vivo exposure alone relapsed in the study, suggesting that in vivo may be sufficient for some but not for others (Foa et al. 1980a).

If both are indicated for the *same* phobic stimulus (e.g., touching garbage), imaginal exposure usually precedes in vivo exposure. Facing the anxiety-provoking situation in imagination is usually (but not always) less overwhelming, and serves to prepare or prime the patient in directly confronting the anxiety-provoking situation. If both are indicated but for *different* phobic stimuli (touching garbage versus images of Michael dying), then the decision about which to begin with can be based on factors such as which stimulus is interfering more with the patient's life or which the patient fears less.

In vivo exposure is indicated for most individuals with obsessive-compulsive disorder, but is particularly useful for those who present with nonspecific consequences, have external triggers of anxiety, and have contamination fears (Steketee 1993). In vivo exposure is also indicated if the patient is not a good candidate for imaginal exposure (see Table 6–2 for contraindications for imaginal exposure). In vivo exposure is contraindicated if it is impractical or dangerous to implement (e.g., images of mother dying), if the patient does not have external anxiety triggers, or cannot cope with the anxiety created by in vivo exposure (Steketee 1993).

Imaginal exposure is indicated from the start if the patient has many specific catastrophic fears (e.g., my mother will die if I use a knife), particularly those thought to cause future harm to others, or if the patient has internal triggers of anxiety (image of a dead child) (Steketee 1993). It may be the only form of exposure used if it is impractical to conduct in vivo exposure (fear of killing mother), or if the patient has difficulty performing in vivo exposure exercises due to heightened anxiety (Steketee 1993). In the latter case, imaginal exposure may be used first as a way of helping the patient directly confront phobic situations in later sessions. Imaginal exposure is also indicated later on in treatment if the therapist determines that direct or in vivo exposure was insufficient in accessing feared consequences or in reducing anxiety.

Confronting the anxiety-provoking stimulus in imagination is contraindicated if the patient lacks the ability to visualize or is unable to have a physiological anxiety response to images (Steketee 1993). The latter applies to patients who lack the ability to have vivid images and not to individuals who may be initially avoiding the visualization procedure because of heightened anxiety. The distinction may be made by having patients visualize content unrelated to their obsessional fears to see if they are capable of forming effective images.

It was decided that Allison would benefit from in vivo exposure and imaginal exposure for *different phobic stimuli*. Her obsessive fears of getting contaminated were triggered by many external *objects*, such as garbage cans, garbage, soiled laundry, and newspapers; *people,* such as her sister-in-law; and *situations*, such as entering a public toilet. Conducting in vivo exposure was considered to be the best and most efficient way for her to confront these fears. Priming her ability to cope with these exposure situations by having her first confront them in imagination was not considered essential at this stage. The therapist decided that imaginal exposure to these phobic stimuli would be reserved for later, if Allison was unable to directly confront these stimuli.

It was also decided at this juncture that Allison's obsessions about Michael coming to harm would primarily be confronted by imaginal exposure, as many of these did not have external triggers and involved situations that would be impractical to confront through in vivo exposure. For example, she primarily had images of Michael coming to harm in a variety of ways, having a car accident, having a heart attack, getting poisoned, getting stabbed. Not only were many of these feared disasters triggered only by internal cues, but the disasters themselves could certainly not be re-created in real life. The few external objects that triggered these obsessions (knives) were confronted using in vivo exposure.

Preparing for In Vivo Exposure

Phobic Stimuli Commonly Confronted Using In Vivo Exposure

Individuals with fears of contamination are most commonly confronted with *objects* such as garbage cans, cleaning fluids, pesticides, and so on, since these form the bulk of their fears. However, they may also be obsessively afraid of *persons* (e.g., Allison avoiding her sister-in-law) or even *situations or places* (the office, the mall, Miami, the subway).

Persons who present with obsessions about causing future harm to themselves or others may fear *objects* such as knives, cars, electrical appliances, cheese, computers, a song, and so on. They may also fear *persons* (e.g., someone may fear that his priest will die if he comes into contact with him) or *situations and places* (walking by a temple, mailing a letter, or driving a car without doing checking rituals).

Developing a Hierarchy of Obsessive Fears

The therapist and patient examine the list of anxiety triggers developed in the second session and select items for use during in vivo exposure. Together, they list all the places (e.g., restroom), people (sister-in-law), and objects (garbage can) that trigger obsessive fears, and then develop specific exposure tasks for each phobic stimulus (sitting on a public toilet). Exposure tasks should be visualized as small steps toward confronting each phobic object, situation, or place (looking at the knife, standing next to the knife, holding the knife with a cloth, holding the knife with bare hands). If there are too many steps required for each phobic stimulus, multiple hierarchies may need to be developed for different objects, persons, and places (one hierarchy for confronting the restroom, another for the knife). Otherwise, one in vivo exposure hierarchy may be sufficient for all phobic stimuli.

Each exposure task is then rated on a scale of 1 to 100 on how much it is feared and avoided by the patient (see Table 6–3). Based on this rating, phobic stimuli are then rank ordered from the least to the most feared, with the more anxiety-producing ones listed at the top of the hierarchy. Exposure begins with items creating the least amount of anxiety and ends with those creating the highest levels of anxiety. However, least-feared items should create at least a moderate amount of anxiety (30 to 40 on a scale of 100) to be considered for exposure tasks. Items creating minimal or little anxiety need not be used. Progression to the next level occurs only when anxiety to each level diminishes for two consecutive exercises. Exposure to the most feared stimuli occurs last but must occur for exposure to be successful.

Items should be ranked in such a way that the level of fear from one item to the next is relatively equidistant. Items should not be spaced too far apart with regard to level of fear (e.g., looking at knife from across the room and then holding it with bare hands), otherwise the patient may become overwhelmed. But they should also not be spaced too close (looking at knife from ten feet away, then eight feet away, etc.), making exposure somewhat inefficient.

Table 6–3. Sample In Vivo Exposure Form

Objects, people, situations	How anxious do I feel? (0–100)	How much do I avoid this? (0–100)

Clinical Vignette

THERAPIST: Now it's time for us to take a look at things that trigger your obsessions and make you afraid. We had made a list in the beginning of the different things that you find troubling (reads from Table 2–3). You had said that you tended to avoid handling garbage, garbage cans, touching newspapers, and soiled laundry. You also mentioned that you no longer met your sister-in-law after the incident at the mall restroom and that you can't even talk to her.

ALLISON: Yes, that one really bothers me. We used to be so close and now she thinks I don't want to meet her anymore and I feel bad about that.

THERAPIST: We will make sure you meet her as soon as you can. Let's see how ready you feel to do that. As I said earlier, our ultimate goal is for you to confront all these situations without ritualizing. The first step is to take this list and discuss which items you could approach first.

ALLISON: You said which items *I* could approach, so it will be based on what I think.

THERAPIST: Yes, absolutely. Take a look at this [see Table 6–2]. We have to rank each of the items on this list on a scale of 1 to 100 in terms of how anxious it makes you feel, and how much you tend to avoid it so that we can decide which items you feel ready to confront first.

ALLISON: That seems difficult. I couldn't do any right now.

THERAPIST: You're right, you may not be able to directly handle any of them right now, but perhaps you could touch some of them using a glove, or maybe even start out by looking at them. We'll begin by ranking them the way they are. If all the ranks are high up there, we will have to build in easier tasks. I want you to picture these tasks as rungs on a ladder. You will be climbing one rung at a time until you get to the top so that your anxiety is manageable along the way. If there is a rung missing and you can't reach the next one, we will add a rung in the middle. We don't want to make the ladder too hard to climb because then you might give up climbing at all.

ALLISON: That sounds simple. But what if the middle rung itself is too far?

THERAPIST: Then we'll add another one. Of course, remember that you're not going to want to do any of them because your natural tendency is to avoid all these things. So we have to be careful that we are not adding rung after rung just because you would rather not climb the ladder at all. If there are too many rungs, you will be working and working but it will take you forever to get to the top and we don't want that to happen.

ALLISON: You're right. If I had my way, I wouldn't do any.

THERAPIST: So it's my role to push you a little along the way and it's your role to tell me when you genuinely feel that any particular rung is too high for you. Deal?

ALLISON: Deal.

THERAPIST: And now, your fear of knives. That one is a little different and I think we should make a separate hierarchy for that. One reason is that knives are the only external objects on your list that have to do with your fears of Michael dying. All the rest have to do with obsessions about getting contaminated. Second, you're very afraid of them—you never use them, never even look at them, so that may require a lot of steps, and so I think we should deal with your fear of knives on a separate list.

ALLISON: Fine with me.

THERAPIST: Out of all the others, which one scares you the least?

ALLISON: I'm sorry, all of them do.

THERAPIST: Well, all right, what scares you the most?

ALLISON (scans the list): Garbage, touching garbage, that scares me the most.

THERAPIST: On a scale of 1 to 100, how much does it scare you?

ALLISON: Oh, 100 for sure.

THERAPIST: When was the last time you threw out the garbage with your bare hands?

ALLISON (laughs): Try never. Well, not for years and years.

THERAPIST: So you always avoid this. It gets a 100 then. So, right at the top will be touching garbage with your bare hands and it gets a 100 for both anxiety and avoidance.

ALLISON: Sounds like an impossible task.

THERAPIST: Well, not impossible but certainly difficult without any other rungs. Now how about telling me what is the easiest item for you, now that we know which is the hardest item. If garbage is 100, what about the rest?

ALLISON (crinkles up her nose in disgust): I guess picking up newspapers would be the easiest. I would say that's, hmm, maybe a 40. I guess I don't always avoid it. I always wash my hands after but I don't avoid it.

THERAPIST: So is the avoidance 40 then?

ALLISON: Say 45.

THERAPIST: And how anxious would it make you to pick it up if you couldn't wash your hands afterwards?

ALLISON (alarmed): Not wash my hands?

THERAPIST: Remember, we had discussed that.

ALLISON: Yes, yes, of course, I forgot. I just panicked. Maybe 40?

THERAPIST: Moving along, what comes afterwards?

ALLISON: I guess the laundry. I can't bear to touch soiled clothes. But I'm not sure I would feel ready to do that right after the newspaper.

THERAPIST: Is there anything else you would rather do first?

ALLISON: No, not really.

THERAPIST: How about we break it up then? Would it make a difference if the clothes were just put in versus if they had been there for a while?

ALLISON: Hmm, interesting thought. I guess so. I see what you mean by rungs in the ladder. I guess it would be easier if they had just been soiled.

THERAPIST: How about if they had been soiled for at least a day?

ALLISON: All right, all right, I guess I could do that. I see what you mean by pushing me.

THERAPIST: That's the role I'll be playing. So now how anxious would it make you to touch soiled laundry if it had been in the bin for a day?

ALLISON: Without washing?

THERAPIST: Yes, you can't wash after any of them.

ALLISON: Maybe 55 for anxiety, and maybe even less for avoidance—45.

THERAPIST: And how anxious would you feel if you had to handle soiled clothes from a week ago?

ALLISON: 60 for both, I think. I know that would scare me more.

Note: The therapist and patient continue in this way until the entire hierarchy has been developed. See Table 6–4 for Allison's in vivo exposure hierarchy for contaminants. A separate in vivo exposure hierarchy was developed for Allison's fear of knives (see Table 6–5.)

Preparing for Imaginal Exposure

If the therapist determines that even the smallest step toward approaching the phobic object, person, or place is too overwhelming on the in vivo exposure hierarchy, then imaginal exposure to that task should be considered before any in vivo exposure takes place. As mentioned above, facing the phobic stimulus in imagination is usually less overwhelming and serves to prepare or prime the patient for directly confronting the anxiety-provoking situation. However, in this case, a separate hierarchy just for imaginal items is unnecessary. When used as a preparation for directly confronting the phobic situation, imaginal exposure may be seen as being lower in the hierarchy than in vivo exposure, and hence a single hierarchy that includes tasks related to both is sufficient (thinking about touching a news-

Table 6–4. Allison's In Vivo Exposure Form: Fear of Contamination

Objects, people, situations	How anxious do I feel? (0–100)	How much do I avoid this? (0–100)
Touch garbage with hand (food items)	100	100
Touch garbage with hand (non-food items)	100	100
Touch garbage with clear plastic gloves (food items)	100	100
Touch garbage with latex gloves (food items)	95	100
Touch garbage with clear plastic gloves (non-food items)	90	100
Touch garbage with latex gloves (non-food items)	90	100
Use public toilet	90	95
Enter a stall in the public toilet but do not use toilet	85	90
Enter a public toilet to freshen up makeup	85	85
Have lunch with sister-in-law at a restaurant	85	85
Use sister-in-law's toilet	85	85
Have lunch with sister-in-law at her home	80	85
Have lunch with sister-in-law at your home	75	85
Use toilet at home (no washing)	75	100
Call sister-in-law on telephone	75	75
Touch garbage can with hands	75	100
Touch garbage can with clear plastic gloves	70	100
Touch garbage can with latex gloves	70	70
Handle soiled laundry from a week ago	60	60
Handle soiled laundry from a day ago	55	45
Handle the newspaper	40	45

Table 6–5. Allison's In Vivo Exposure Form: Fear of Knives

Objects, people, situations	How anxious do I feel? (0–100)	How much do I avoid this? (0–100)
Chop meat using cooking knives	100	100
Chop vegetables using cooking knives	100	100
Eat a meal with a steak knife	100	100
Eat a meal with dinner knives	95	100
Touch cooking knives with bare hands	90	100
Touch cooking knives with clear plastic gloves	90	95
Touch cooking knives with latex gloves	90	95
Touch dinner knives	85	85
Touch and use butter knife	85	85
Look at cooking knives	75	80
Look at dinner knives	70	70
Look at a butter knife	65	60
Look at a picture of a cooking knife	60	65
Look at a picture of a dinner knife	50	50
Look at a picture of a butter knife	35	40

paper and then touching something in a restroom). However, if imaginal exposure is to be used alone, for an entirely different set of phobic stimuli (fear that an obsession of Michael dying will kill him), then a separate hierarchy should be outlined. Either way, guidelines for how to construct imaginal tasks and develop imaginal scenes remain the same and are outlined next.

If it is determined that imaginal exposure is indicated but to a different phobic stimulus and will not be used in conjunction with in vivo exposure, the therapist may decide to postpone developing a hierarchy of catastrophic fears until the patient is ready to confront them in imagination.

Developing a Hierarchy of Catastrophic Fears

Utilizing the information obtained in Session 2 on anxiety triggers and catastrophic fears, the therapist and patient make a list of all the consequences the patient fears will occur if he does not ritualize. Catastrophic fears are then rank ordered in a hierarchy according to the amount of fear, anxiety, or discomfort they generate, with the more anxiety-producing ones listed at the top of the hierarchy, to be used in later exposure sessions. Patients are asked to rate their anxiety with regard to each consequence on a scale of 1 to 100 (see Table 6–6).

The level of anxiety created may vary according to but not limited to the following: (1) the type of feared consequence (e.g., imagining that Michael dies of a heart attack is less anxiety provoking and hence lower on the hierarchy than imagining that he is stabbed to death); (2) the detail of the image (brief scene about Michael dying is less anxiety provoking than a detailed one); (3) the amount of physiological reactivity generated during the scene. During later scenes, the therapist describes physiological symptoms of anxiety during the narrative and thereby increases the chances of the patient experiencing these symptoms during exposure (your stomach tightens and the blood rushes to your head as you realize that Michael is in danger). For example, a brief scene about the patient's husband dying of a medical illness is followed by a more detailed scene, then a more detailed scene replete with physiological responses of the patient, which is in turn followed by a very brief scene about the husband being stabbed, and so on.

It is important to note that multiple hierarchies may need to be developed for different obsessions. For example, Allison's imaginal hierarchy (see Table 6–7) involved different catastrophic fears in-

Table 6–6. Sample Imaginal Exposure Form

Imaginal scenes that evoke obsessional anxiety	*Expected anxiety* *(1–100)*

volving her husband. A different hierarchy was developed for her fears regarding harm coming to her mother.

Once the catastrophic fears are arranged hierarchically, the one creating the least amount of anxiety is now picked so that the first imaginal exposure session can begin. It is important to note that the least anxiety-provoking image should create at least a moderate amount of anxiety (30 to 40 on a scale of 100) for it to be used in exposure. Images creating minimal anxiety need not be utilized at all for the sake of time efficiency. However, hierarchy levels should not be spaced too far apart in terms of the level of anxiety they generate, or the patient will have difficulty moving from one scene to the next.

Table 6–7. Allison's Imaginal Exposure Hierarchy Form

Imaginal scenes that evoke obsessional anxiety	Expected anxiety (1–100)
Michael is stabbed outside his office.	100
Michael gets strangled in the garage.	100
Michael has a car accident on the way back from work and dies.	95
Michael has a heart attack and dies.	90
Michael has a heart attack at work and is hospitalized but lives.	70
Michael has a car accident on the way back from work and is injured.	55

Clinical Vignette

THERAPIST: I know from our previous conversation that the two things you fear the most are Michael's getting hurt and that somehow you will get infected with germs or ticks. Were there any other fears that we haven't discussed yet?

ALLISON: Just that I will kill him somehow.

THERAPIST: Yes, I do remember that. That's tied to your fear of him coming to harm. Let's see, we will be able to work on your fear of being infected by having you touch and handle newspapers, garbage, and so on. We are also going to reduce your fears about Michael by helping you confront a variety of knives a little later on. But you have a lot of fears about him getting hurt that will not be so easy to reduce by touching objects and so forth. So we will need to work out another way to do it.

ALLISON (puzzled): How? But wait, what do you mean less anxious about him dying? Why would I want to be less anxious about that?

THERAPIST: How about you help me out in answering that. Why would you want to be less anxious about it? Can you tell me what you remember from our previous conversations?

ALLISON: Because I'm driving him crazy (sighs). And myself, I guess.

THERAPIST: True. Anything else?

ALLISON: Yes, I'm wasting my time because he's fine.

THERAPIST: Exactly. Although it's reasonable to be concerned about your husband, especially if he is in some sort of danger, that is not what you're doing. You tend to obsess about it even if there is no chance of him coming to harm. You also get concerned that if you have an obsession about him coming to harm, it will come true and if you don't call him, you will, in essence, sign his death warrant. So, you get frightened and you call him and call him, and check knives over and over again to the point that he cannot stand your concern anymore. And you spend so much time obsessing about his death and doing your rituals that it consumes your whole life and you have no time left for anything else.

ALLISON: I keep forgetting that. I guess I was thinking that anyone would be anxious if they thought their husband was going to die.

THERAPIST: You're right. But everyone . . .

ALLISON: . . . doesn't obsess about it the way I do.

THERAPIST: Exactly.

ALLISON: But how is it done? How can I be less anxious?

THERAPIST: We help you face your fears by thinking about these things in your imagination instead of in reality. We will examine all the images or thoughts you have about Michael coming to harm, and then we'll rate them like we rated all the objects, on a scale of 1 to 100, and then we'll make another ladder.

ALLISON (mystified): And what do we do with the ladder?

THERAPIST: Scene by scene, you confront them in your imagination until you feel less anxious about them.

ALLISON (shocked): No!

THERAPIST: Yes indeed. We had briefly touched on it awhile back that there were two ways to confront what you fear.

ALLISON: I know you said that, but I guess I didn't take in what it meant. But it isn't natural for anyone to sit there and imagine that their husband is dying.

THERAPIST: You're right, it isn't natural. But this is a necessary exercise we have to use to reduce your excessive fear about Michael coming to harm. We'll be going over exactly how it's done and how it works when we begin the procedure.

ALLISON: Goodness, but will this help me?

THERAPIST: Yes, it will. Okay, let's just build a hierarchy today. I know you have many thoughts and images of Michael coming to harm. You imagine him dying of a heart attack, getting strangled, stabbed, and getting into a car accident. I know that imagining him getting stabbed is a bad one. You've mentioned that one to me before. How would you rate that?

ALLISON: 100.

THERAPIST: Where does the scene usually occur when you think about it?

ALLISON: In the office, usually.

THERAPIST: Okay, what comes next?

ALLISON: Getting s . . . I can't say it.

(Allison gets a faraway look, looks distracted)

THERAPIST: Allison, are you ritualizing?

ALLISON: Yes.

THERAPIST: What are you saying? I've noticed that every now and then you look very preoccupied and distracted and it seems that those are the times you might be doing your mental rituals.

ALLISON (smiles wanly): I do? I am? You're getting to know me very well. I was saying "6, 6, 6, 6, 6, 6."

THERAPIST: I see. Okay, let's continue. Can you point it out if it's difficult for you to say it?

ALLISON: (points to "Images of Michael getting strangled" from list in Table 2–3).

THERAPIST: How anxious would it make you to imagine that?

ALLISON: 100.

THERAPIST: So that's the same rating as "getting stabbed." Which one could you do first?

ALLISON: I guess getting strangled. (Pauses) This is such a weird conversation. I can't believe I'm sitting here and talking about this with my therapist. And you look so proper, I can't believe you're calmly sitting and writing all this stuff down. You must want to go back home to your husband and say, "Boy, did I treat a wacko today."

THERAPIST: I know all this seems weird to you, Allison. I guess it doesn't seem weird to me, perhaps because I see people with such fears all the time. These fears are commonplace in obsessive-compulsive disorder. I know you're concerned that I think you're crazy, so let me assure you that not only would I never discuss you with my husband or anyone else, but that what you're going through is not the least bit strange. You are not wacko. I know sometimes you are afraid you are.

ALLISON: I am, I guess. I know you wouldn't tell anyone, I just meant . . .

THERAPIST: I know, you thought, "I must be the strangest patient she has, so she must want to."

ALLISON (laughs):Boy, you're beginning to read my mind.

THERAPIST (laughs): Sorry to disappoint you, Allison. You're not strange at all. Now, where do you usually picture him getting strangled? In the office too?

ALLISON: No, in the garage.

THERAPIST: Let me write that down. So what comes next? After stabbing and strangling?

ALLISON: It's hard to say. I guess the car accident. I picture him getting into a car accident. Sometimes, he dies. Other times, I just picture him getting hurt.

THERAPIST: How would you rate them?

ALLISON: I guess 95 for the first one. And maybe, I don't know, about 50 or 55 when he gets hurt.

THERAPIST: So now we have the heart attack. Where does that go?

ALLISON: Again, sometimes I picture him dead and other times he lives.

THERAPIST: Can you rate them both?

ALLISON: Well, the heart attack with him dying is much scarier, of course.

THERAPIST: You rated the car accident death at 95.

ALLISON: So then this would be 90.

THERAPIST: What about the heart attack and not dying?

ALLISON: That's actually worse than the car accident and living.

THERAPIST: How come?

ALLISON: Well, because if he gets injured, he can recover completely, but to me the heart attack means he is that much closer to death the next time. It sounds so funny to talk about this. I know he's not going to die. Why is it easier for me to see it now but not when I'm at home?

THERAPIST: Well, in the beginning it was hard for you to see it here as well. It's easier for you to see it here because you've been working to change your thoughts for a while now. As you continue doing it, ultimately you will start to believe it everywhere and not just here. It's a process.

ALLISON: I feel better hearing that.

THERAPIST: Good, I'm glad. It's true.

(Pause)

THERAPIST: Now where were we? You were going to rate the heart attack and not dying.

ALLISON: If he had a heart attack and lived through it, I think my anxiety would be around 70.

THERAPIST: So the lowest rung we have is a 55, where you picture him getting injured in a car accident. That's still pretty high. We need a lower rung. Do you have any other thoughts or images about Michael?

ALLISON: No, that about covers it. I don't think so.

THERAPIST: Okay, then that will have to be the first one we attempt. The ladder is complete for now. [See Table 6–7 for Allison's imaginal exposure hierarchy.] How would you feel about starting with that?

ALLISON: I don't know. It's the best one, I suppose.

THERAPIST: Let's see how you do. We may need to start off with a very sketchy image first and then work up to making it more graphic as you're able to tolerate it. If you come up with any other images or thoughts about him that make you somewhat less nervous, let me know and we'll add them in.

Constructing Anxiety-Provoking Scenes for Hierarchy Items

Once the hierarchy is constructed, the therapist and patient prepare imaginal scenes that are judged to be capable of triggering obsessional anxiety in imagination (e.g., a scene capturing the patient's obsession about his mother dying). Imaginal scenes are usually triggered by written scripts describing the scene and are prepared in advance by the patient and therapist. Although written scripts lend themselves well to imaginal exposure, scenes may also be triggered by photographs, slides, videotapes, audiotapes, and so on, all of which can be used alone or in conjunction with written scripts. The medium used is picked according to its ability to approximate the spontaneously occurring feared obsessive situations, vividly elicit the patient's obsessional fears and concerns, and generate anxiety. However, since written scripts form the bulk of what we use in our treatment sessions, we will focus our description on their use.

At this juncture, a narrative scene is developed for the first item on the hierarchy, in Allison's case, her fear that Michael would be injured in a car accident on the way back home from work. An outline of the scene is first described or written out by the patient with no assistance from the therapist, as it is important that the scene closely approximate the patient's experience. Patients may express anxiety as they outline the scene and will probably ritualize during this exercise. They are permitted to do so since exposure has not as yet begun.

Once the skeleton of the image is completed, the therapist develops the scene as it will be used during the exposure exercise. Through questioning, the therapist obtains relevant details about the image and incorporates them into the scene. Every effort is made to make the scene realistic and to have it approximate the obsessional image as closely as possible. The following is a guide to the information needed in order to create an effective image. However, the list is not comprehensive and additional information may have to be obtained depending upon the idiosyncratic nature of the patient's obsessional image:

1. Geographical location (indoors, outdoors, home, office, mall)
2. Time of day (dawn, morning, afternoon)
3. Climate (raining, sunny, summer, snowing, etc.)
4. Number of participants
5. Description of participants (What were they wearing, what do they look like?)
6. Sequence of events
7. Sensory elements (sight, sound, smell, taste, touch)
8. Physical actions (walking, talking, running)
9. Emotional reactions (anxiety, sadness, guilt)
10. Physiological reactions (heart pounding, feeling sick to your stomach)

Although elicited questions pertain to all the participants in the image (What is Michael doing?), equal emphasis is placed on the patient's role in the image. Is the patient present in the image? What is the patient doing or feeling? The patient's perspective in the image is critical in bringing the image to life during exposure.

Using the information obtained, the therapist prepares a narrative or a series of narratives (some brief, some more detailed) that will be used during exposure exercises. As noted earlier, the hierarchy of catastrophic fears may be varied according to the detail present in the image. Hence, all elicited details may not be included right away. In general, the more detailed the image, the greater the anxiety, so that the initial exposure session may include very few details. As patients habituate to earlier images, details may then be incorporated into later exposure sessions. However, for imaginal exposure to be successful, it is important that patients ultimately be exposed to the most complete image.

Clinical Vignette

THERAPIST: Okay, Allison, why don't you tell me a little about the scene where you picture him getting injured in a car accident? Can you briefly describe the scene to me?

ALLISON (looks fearful): I'm scared.

THERAPIST: I know, but do you think you could tell me the basic story? I could ask you questions about it to fill in the details. Then all you have to do is answer questions.

ALLISON: I'll try. Can I ritualize during it?

THERAPIST: For now, yes, if you think you need to. Later on, when we begin exposure to this scene, you will not be able to ritualize.

ALLISON: Well, I see him leaving his office. He gets into his car, and then he gets struck on the highway. That's basically it.

THERAPIST: Okay, so this is in the evening then, as he's leaving work? About what time?

ALLISON: About 6:30 P.M.

THERAPIST: Is it dark? What time of year is this?

ALLISON: Well, it is dark. So I guess it's winter.

THERAPIST: And do you first see him leaving his office, or do you just see him in the car?

ALLISON: No, I see him in the parking garage, walking toward his car.

THERAPIST: What is he wearing?

ALLISON (closes her eyes, as if to remember): He's wearing a London Fog raincoat, so I think it's pretty bad weather out there.

THERAPIST: What is the weather like?

ALLISON: It's pretty misty, and damp. Drizzling rain, not heavy.

THERAPIST: What kind of a car is it?

ALLISON: It's a Honda Accord. It's silver. I wish he was driving the Jeep, I would feel safer. He just bought that car and he likes to drive it around.

THERAPIST: That is what you're thinking as he gets in?

ALLISON: Yes.

THERAPIST: What else? Is he carrying a briefcase?

ALLISON: Yes, and he looks tired.

THERAPIST: Is he thinking about anything?

ALLISON: Yes, he's thinking, "I have to get home to Allison, I hope she doesn't get on me about anything. I don't think I can handle her nuttiness today."

THERAPIST: So he's not looking forward to coming home, and you think it's because of you?

ALLISON (starts crying): Yes. Maybe that's why he doesn't pay attention on the road.

THERAPIST: I see. So now he's in the car. You said it's a new car. Does it have a new car smell?

ALLISON: Yes, I guess so.

THERAPIST: Then what? He begins driving out of the garage?

ALLISON: Then I see him getting on the Long Island Expressway. I don't picture him from the garage to the Expressway though.

THERAPIST: Okay, what do you see next. Is there traffic?

ALLISON: Yes, not a lot, but there is traffic. Lots of trucks though, tractor trailers and stuff.

THERAPIST: What is he doing in the car?

ALLISON: Listening to the news. He's drinking a bottle of water.
   And that's when it hits him.
THERAPIST: What does?
ALLISON: The huge tractor trailer. He's getting onto the highway
   when it hits him.
THERAPIST: From the left?
ALLISON: The tractor trailer is on the left and Michael is coming
   into the right lane.
THERAPIST: Then what happens?

(Therapist and patient continue with this line of questioning until
the entire scene is completed with all details included. Then, the
therapist writes it out as a coherent scene to be used during the
imaginal exposure session. See Table 8–1.)

Preparing for Response Prevention

Common Types of Rituals That Must Be Prevented

Washers Versus Checkers. Individuals with obsessive-compulsive
disorder commonly fall into one of two categories, washers and checkers. Individuals with washing rituals may repetitively wash hands or
other body parts, shower excessively or for prolonged periods of time,
and may have a variety of other rituals to decontaminate themselves
(e.g., using creams that have sanitizing agents, spraying the room with
a disinfectant).

An individual with checking rituals may check to see if the gas
stove is off, if the lights are switched off, if the front door is locked,
and so on. He may also have more bizarre rituals, such as checking
to see that he did not run over a pedestrian while driving, or checking the closets to make sure he did not accidentally lock in a child.

Allison washed her hands up to thirty-six times a day, took lengthy
showers twice a day, and checked on Michael, either by tele-

phoning him at the office or by going to the next room to see if he was fine, about six times a day on average. She also opened and shut the kitchen drawers periodically to see if the knives were in place.

Mental Versus Behavioral Rituals. As outlined earlier, rituals may be mental acts or behaviors aimed at alleviating obsessional distress. Behavioral rituals include, among others, the checking and washing rituals outlined above. Mental rituals include repeating "good" words, phrases, sounds, numbers, songs, thoughts, or images in order to neutralize the "bad" thoughts or images. While behavioral rituals are easier to document, mental rituals are not so easy, and so both assessment and treatment may have to be modified to suit the needs of these patients. For example, since mental rituals are hard to observe, the therapist may have to closely observe patients' expressions to see if they slip into a reverie and appear preoccupied, distant, or withdrawn. Patients may then be questioned to confirm if they were ritualizing and may be asked to stop if that particular ritual is not permitted. For example, Allison, who was usually active and engaged in sessions, often had a faraway look in her eyes. Upon questioning, it was revealed that Allison usually ritualized when she had this glassy expression on her face.

Mental rituals may also be more automatic than behavioral rituals, probably because they are far more easily performed (e.g., quickly thinking a good thought versus going to the bathroom to wash hands), and hence may be harder for patients to reduce. Many patients may not always be sure which thought or image is an obsession and which is a compulsive ritual, despite being informed of their functional relationship to anxiety. As noted earlier, the ritual itself may become so tedious that it may be hard for the patient to see that he is using it as a means to reduce his anxiety. To help them distinguish between the two, patients may also be asked to note which thought or image is effortless (obsession) and which requires more effort to perform (ritual).

Allison performed a variety of mental rituals. She prayed ritualisti-cally ("God is mighty") and repeated the following phrases: "mercy, mercy," "how shall I fly," "I challenge you not," and "safe Mike." She also repeated sets of numbers, "6, 6, 6, 6, 6, 6," or "not 3, 3, 3."

Explicit Versus Subtle. Some rituals are very explicit and may be noticed by any observer, while other rituals may be more subtle. Of course, behavioral rituals are usually explicit (washing hands) while mental rituals are usually more subtle (silently repeating phrases). However, the therapist should identify subtle behavioral rituals as well. For example, patients may exhibit subtle hand or body gestures such as quickly counting to six using fingers, or closing the eyes momentarily to block an image of having sex with the Virgin Mary. The list is endless and the therapist should carefully question pa-tients on all measures they take to reduce anxiety no matter how peculiar, small, or embarrassing they may appear.

For example, halfway through treatment, the therapist realized that Allison performed a series of half-blinks whenever she had an im-age of Michael dying. Upon questioning, Allison revealed that she did so automatically in an effort to neutralize the obsessional image.

Reassurance Seeking. Reassurance seeking is yet another maneuver that many patients use to reduce anxiety or to diminish their sense of perceived responsibility. Reassurance seeking may be repetitive and ritualized, and patients can often drive others around them crazy with endless questions to make sure that things are as they should be. Are you sure the stove is off? Did I lock the door? Are you sure I didn't run over someone?

Subtle requests for reassurance should also be prevented. Patients may pose questions and examine the person's nonverbal expression for clues, and may also feel released from responsibility by just ask-ing questions, particularly if they are asking people whose expert opinion they trust such as doctors, therapists, and other relevant authorities. Hence, it is important that the therapist not be drawn into the patient's need for endless reassurance. However, it is important to distinguish between reasonable questions on potential dangers involved in performing one or another action and repetitive requests for reassurance.

Allison repeatedly questioned Michael to see if he was feeling okay, made calls to him at work and asked him questions about whether he thought the food was spoiled or the milk was too old. She also called her primary care physician and the Centers for Disease Control regularly with questions on issues of contamination and disease.

Preparing a List of Rituals

Once the hierarchies are completed, the therapist and patient now turn their attention toward planning for ritual prevention so that exposure and response prevention can be initiated at the same time. The therapist examines the list of rituals obtained from the patient during Session 2 and compares it to the information recorded by the patient on the Obsession-Compulsion Monitoring form over the past several weeks. The therapist determines which rituals are most salient, whether certain rituals thought to be troublesome are not, and if some rituals have declined through the monitoring process itself. All ritualized efforts to alleviate anxiety are noted, including any participation by family members. For example, Mike cooperated with Allison in washing his hands before he touched her, got into bed, left the house, and touched appliances.

Deciding on the Prevention Method: Abstinence Versus Graded Response Prevention

The therapist and patient now formulate a plan on how rituals will be blocked when exposure begins next week. Studies demonstrating the efficacy of behavioral therapy have utilized strategies requiring a complete cessation of ritual performance from the first session itself (Foa et al. 1992, Foa et al. 1984). However, these studies have been conducted on inpatient populations where the therapist has a greater degree of control over the patient's environment than does the outpatient therapist who can only oversee a weekly session. Hence, complete abstinence from ritual performance right from the start of treatment is not a realistic goal with many outpatients.

As a practical alternative, many graded response-prevention strategies have been proposed wherein a patient learns to block rituals selectively and gradually until he is finally able to refrain from performing all rituals (Steketee 1993). Like graded exposure, graded response prevention involves building in a hierarchy of manageable tasks for the patient until he is ready to handle more difficult tasks. However, it is important to note that the efficacy of graded ritual-prevention strategies has yet to be fully determined.

Whichever form of prevention is used, the ultimate goal of treatment is for patients to completely abstain from rituals that have no functional purpose (e.g., repeating "6, 6, 6, 6, 6, 6") and to reduce behaviors that serve a functional purpose to normal levels (briefly washing soiled hands once). In this regard, patients are given instructions on "normal" behaviors at the end of treatment (see Chapter 9).

Abstinence

The patient is asked to completely refrain from performing rituals as soon as the first exposure exercise begins. Often, patients are required to forego even "normal" behaviors during this time. For example, individuals with checking rituals are not permitted to check at all, with some exceptions (e.g., checking the front door once before leaving the house). Washers are asked to forego daily showers and are not permitted to wash their hands during treatment even though taking daily showers or washing hands periodically is the norm for most people. Patients are frequently alarmed by this news and will usually argue with the therapist about the true dangers inherent in not performing normal behaviors (washing hands is sanitary).

So why is it necessary for patients to refrain from doing what most of us do routinely, particularly when there are safety and health consequences (not washing your hands could possibly lead to salmonella poisoning) associated with these behaviors? Simply because the consequences, although real, are not as likely or as great as patients perceive them to be. Since persons with OCD have wasted so much time overestimating risk or harm and have used exaggerated caution as a way of coping with this perceived harm, teaching them to take minor risks restores the balance and restructures their fundamental beliefs about the inherent dangers involved. For example, not taking showers for a while may be unpleasant but it will not lead to their death. And, unless they are handling objective contaminants (like a mother who comes into contact with her baby's fecal matter), the most likely risk from not washing hands is that they may catch a cold. As patients take risks and the feared consequences do not occur, they learn that using exaggerated caution may not be necessary.

Graded Response Prevention

Near Abstinence. This strategy represents a slight variation of complete abstinence for patients who simply cannot tolerate the process. However, patients are still encouraged to abstain as much as they can. They are asked to refrain from ritualizing but are permitted to perform some normal behaviors. Individuals with washing rituals are permitted to take a brief shower daily or wash their hands briefly if they are objectively soiled. Patients with checking rituals are allowed to check once, especially for certain objects or situations (iron unplugged, front door locked).

Patients are also advised to avoid objects, people, or situations that are high on the exposure hierarchy until they have confronted lower-rung items, in order to prevent them from prematurely confronting them and then ritualizing.

Reducing Number of Repetitions per Ritual. Here, patients are asked to gradually reduce the number of repetitions per ritual until they are able to stop completely, or perform the behavior only once. This strategy is most effective for patients who perform exact numbers of repetitions (washing hands six times during each handwashing episode).

Reducing Number of Rituals per Day. This represents a slight variation for patients who find it easier to calculate the number of rituals per day rather than the number of repetitions per ritual (twelve handwashing episodes versus six repetitions per each of the twelve handwashing episodes). If the Obsession-Compulsion Monitoring form reveals that patients tend to ritualize similar amounts on a daily basis, then patients may be instructed to gradually reduce the number of rituals they perform each day (twelve, then ten handwashing episodes, etc.).

Reducing Length of Time per Ritual. Gradually reducing the time taken per ritualization episode is another form of grading response prevention (showering for fifteen minutes, then ten minutes, etc.). Using the Obsession-Compulsion Monitoring form as a guide, the therapist and patient examine the average time taken per ritual and then develop a hierarchy whereby patients gradually reduce the time taken until normal levels (those that do not create functional impairment) are reached.

Reducing Amount of Daily Time Spent Ritualizing. This strategy involves gradually reducing the time spent ritualizing per day (eight hours, then seven hours, etc.), and is yet another slight variation for patients who feel more comfortable monitoring the total amount of time taken per day rather than calculating the time taken per ritual. Both the OCM form and the Y-BOCS may be used to determine the average amount of time spent ritualizing every day. The disadvantage of this method is that it is more approximate than monitoring time per ritual. It also has the added disadvantage that patients can suddenly use up all the ritual time early on in the day and then discover they have six waking hours left during which they cannot ritualize, and be unable to keep to their regimen.

Reducing Frequency of Rituals. This strategy involves reducing the length of time between rituals (not ritualizing for half an hour, then not for forty-five minutes, etc.). Patient and therapist examine the Obsession-Compulsion Monitoring form to determine on average how frequently rituals occur. The patient is then instructed to gradually increase the length of time between each ritualization episode until his rituals are down to normal levels

Ritualizing to Selective Triggers. This strategy is often a simpler alternative to the graded strategies outlined above, which require constant monitoring and calculations. Here, patients are instructed to refrain from ritualizing to exposure items that have been addressed or are currently being addressed in treatment, but are permitted to ritualize to items that have not yet been the subject of exposure. For example, a patient is asked to refrain from washing his hands after he touches faucets since his obsessive fear of touching faucets has already been confronted via exposure. Similarly, he is not permitted to wash his hands if he comes into contact with doorknobs since that is currently the subject of exposure. However, he is allowed to wash his hands after entering a public restroom, after he comes into contact with dirt, or if he handles garbage, since these items are higher on the hierarchy and have yet to be addressed in treatment.

On occasion, ritualizing to items higher on the hierarchy will offer inadvertent relief to the anxiety created by exposure to items lower on the hierarchy—as in the example of an individual who is permitted to wash his hands after he touches garbage but not when he touches doorknobs. It may turn out that washing his hands after he touches garbage inadvertently alleviates anxiety from his earlier contact with doorknobs. To combat this problem, patients are asked to immediately reexpose themselves to items already addressed in the hierarchy if they perform rituals to any items not yet addressed in exposure. For example, a patient who is allowed to ritualize when he has an image of his son dying but not to an image of him getting injured is instructed to immediately reexpose himself to the injury image after he ritualizes to images of him dying. This way, any inadvertent relief associated with the image of his son's being injured is mitigated.

Outlining the Strategy

Once the strategy has been chosen, the therapist informs the patient that response prevention will be implemented during the next session along with direct exposure. The therapist now provides the patient with the specifics of the chosen strategy. Often, the patient is given a written list of guidelines outlining what mental acts or behaviors are not permitted and which rituals may continue until further discussion. This list should be as specific as possible so that patients do not have to wonder if a particular behavior is permitted or not. A written list is also helpful for the co-therapist, who then does not have to rely on the patient to tell him what he is permitted to do (see Riggs and Foa 1993, Steketee 1993 for a general list of rules for response prevention).

Clinical Vignette

A comprehensive list of Allison's rituals was constructed (Table 6–8) by asking her questions during the session, by examining the information gathered in Session 2 (see Table 2–3), and by reviewing her Obsession-Compulsion Monitoring forms. The following vignette describes the collaborative decision-making between therapist and patient as they decide how rituals will be prevented.

Table 6–8. Allison's Comprehensive List of Rituals

Behavioral Rituals: All rituals conducted in multiples of six (minimum six, maximum seventy-two times a day).

1. Washes hands (usual: thirty-six times a day)
2. Takes lengthy showers (twice a day)
3. Checks to see that knives are in place (usual: thirty-six times a day)
4. Checks to see if Michael is alive and well by calling him on the telephone if he is in the office or by going to him if he is in another room (usual: six times a day).
5. Performs a series of half-blinks with her eyes

Mental Rituals: All mental rituals conducted in multiples of six (minimum six, maximum twelve times each, up to eight to ten hours a day).

1. Prays in a ritualized way
   —God is mighty
2. Repeats phrases
   —mercy, mercy
   —how shall I fly
   —I challenge you not
   —safe Mike
3. Repeats numbers
   —"6, 6, 6, 6, 6, 6,"
   —"not 3, 3, 3"

Reassurance Seeking:

1. Asks Michael if it is okay to touch certain objects
2. Calls the CDC to ask about infectious disease transmission
3. Calls her internist to ask about infectious disease transmission

THERAPIST: Now that we have a list of rituals, let's talk about how best to go about preventing them. Our goal is for you to not ritualize at all and there are many different ways to go about doing that. Stopping all rituals from now on would clearly be the fastest way for us to accomplish that. How likely is it you could do that, with my help, and with Michael's assistance at home?

ALLISON: If pigs had wings . . . Are you kidding? I couldn't do that. That's why I'm here.

THERAPIST: I realize that would be difficult for you. Once we come up with the type of ritual prevention we will use, we'll discuss ways to make it easier for you to do.

ALLISON: What other types are there besides not doing it at all?

THERAPIST: There are many different ways. One way is to do fewer and fewer rituals. You can either do fewer rituals per day or you can do fewer repetitions each time you ritualize. For example, if you wash your hands twelve times a day, you could try washing them ten times, and then maybe eight times and so on. Or you could count another way. Let's say that for each of the twelve handwashing episodes, you now wash your hands six times each. You could focus on cutting the repetitions down. So in the beginning, you stick to your twelve episodes a day but you wash only five times each, then four times each. Once you get to the point of only washing your hands once each time, then you could begin cutting back the episodes.

ALLISON: Well, doing fewer at a time seems like a possibility—I've washed my hands less than thirty-six times before. Just two days ago I only did it twenty-four times. Okay, I can try and do that. But I don't know about doing twelve or ten—I would have to cut it down by multiples of six.

THERAPIST: We could begin with you cutting down some of your rituals in multiples of six. But since doing things in multiples of six is also part of your ritual, we will have to work on ultimately stopping that as well. This method could work for your handwashing rituals, checking the knives, and also for your mental rituals since they occur so many times a day.

ALLISON: You mean it may not work for all of them.

THERAPIST: It may, but let's see if anything else may be more appropriate. You could cut some of your rituals down in terms of time, or you could take less time doing them on each occa-

sion. For example, you could take a shower lasting ten minutes instead of twenty minutes.

ALLISON: I think that could work for the shower, but I can't see
that working for anything else. I don't look at the time a lot. I
know I've been monitoring in time blocks with your form here,
but that would be hard. What other ways are there?

THERAPIST: There are slight variations around counting and measuring time. You could measure how long it takes you per day
or you could space your rituals further out.

ALLISON: I think counting numbers is easier for me to do than
looking at the clock.

THERAPIST: Okay, that may not work for you. The only problem is
that counting may not work for your mental rituals because although you repeat them six times, you do that countless times
a day. So timing may work. But there's another way. Let's say
you begin confronting your fear of handling soiled laundry. We
have already discussed that you will not be permitted to wash
your hands during the exposure exercise. So when we sit together
and you handle dirty laundry, no washing at all. But with this
method of ritual prevention, you will not be able to ritualize to
dirty laundry even after the exercise. And that means if your
obsession gets triggered because of looking at soiled laundry,
seeing a commercial about dirty clothes, touching them, then
nothing, no washing at all, no showers or any other ritual to make
yourself "clean." You will still be permitted to ritualize to every
other item on your hierarchy that we have not worked on as yet.
But you will not be permitted to ritualize to items we have already worked on and the one we are currently working on.

ALLISON: That sounds more doable to me. Could we do a combination of that and doing fewer rituals? This could work for the
mental rituals too?

THERAPIST: Yes, it could. We could do a combination. Well, we
discussed three types, doing fewer, doing it selectively, and
the third one would be taking briefer showers. Let's keep to

this regimen for now and then we'll evaluate it if you have any problems next week. But since we haven't started exposure yet, could you see if you can cut down the amount of time you do your mental rituals this week? We'll see how difficult it is. Remember, you will be monitoring your rituals anyway on the Obsession-Compulsion Monitoring form. We estimated that you take up to eight hours a day. Last week (scans last week's forms) you did it for about eight hours. How about you try to keep it to six this week?

ALLISON: I can try. That's true, I'll be using the form. Okay, let me try and see if it works.

THERAPIST (begins writing down): So here's the plan. For the next week, you'll begin cutting down all your rituals—by six for now—your handwashing, checking knives, checking on Michael. We'll see how it goes. If it's tedious to keep counting, we can think of some other way to do it. And since you're not showering as frequently, we can cut those down by amount of time taken. How about you begin with taking a shower for ten minutes. You can still do it twice a day for this week. And then your mental rituals, no more than six repetitions each time, and you will cut the time down by two hours.

ALLISON: I hope I can stick to this.

THERAPIST: I would like you to give it your best try, with Michael's assistance. If you have difficulties, we will talk next week about things that you can do to make it easier. Is that a deal?

ALLISON: It's a deal.

THERAPIST: Now, I'm going to make three copies of this list, one for me, one for you, and one for Michael [see Table 6–9]. As we agreed, Michael will be supervising you if it's hard for you to do it by yourself. I will be speaking to him on the telephone tonight to let him know that we've begun and to again tell him how I would like him to supervise you. I would also like him to come in next week so we can go over it in some detail together.

Table 6–9. Allison's Graded Response Prevention Plan for Session 5

Graded Response Prevention

1. Washing hands (twenty-four times)
2. Showers (twice a day, for ten minutes only)
3. Checking to see that knives are in place (twenty-four times)
4. Checking on Michael on telephone or at home (six times)
5. Repeating the following things no more than 6 times:
   —God is mighty
   —mercy, mercy
   —how shall I fly
   —I challenge you not
   —safe Mike
   —"6, 6, 6, 6, 6, 6"
   —"not 3, 3, 3"

List of things to bring for exposure next week

1. Newspapers
2. Clothes that have been in the laundry bin for a day
3. Clothes that have been in the laundry bin for a week

ALLISON: Okay, but what if we get into a fight over it?

THERAPIST: That's the kind of thing I would like not to happen. It's important that he be firm but supportive. I would like him not to get angry with you, though. I would also like you to think about ways he can best help you do your homework. Think about it and we'll talk about it tonight and then again next week.

ALLISON: Okay.

THERAPIST: Now we will begin exposure next week as well. So you also have to remember to bring in some items next week. I will write it down at the end of this list before I make a copy. You will need to bring in some newspapers, clothes that have been in your laundry bin for a day, and some other clothes that have been in your laundry bin for a week. Michael can carry them in for you. Are you ready for that?

ALLISON: I don't think I'll ever be ready but I guess I'll have to try it anyway.

THERAPIST: That's a good way to look at it.

ALLISON: You really think I could do three things next week?

THERAPIST: I don't know if we can do all three. It depends on how quickly your anxiety goes down. If it does, we'll be prepared to go ahead. Now, any concerns before we end?

ALLISON: No—yes—just that I'll be very nervous.

THERAPIST: That's right, you'll be nervous this week, you'll be nervous next week, and you'll be nervous during the initial part of the exercise. But you will be able to handle it. And as you handle it, tolerate it, your anxiety will start to lessen during the session, and you'll feel less anxious for the first time.

ALLISON: But what if I really can't handle it?

THERAPIST: If you feel at any point that you can't handle it, we'll stop, of course. Remember, you will be guiding these sessions too. Your input will be very important in letting me know if the rung we have chosen is too high for you to climb at the moment. If it is, we'll just lower it a rung. And then you'll be able to handle it. Okay?

ALLISON: Okay, see you next week.

NEXT WEEK

The events of the current session are summarized and the patient's fears of initiating exposure and response prevention next week are also addressed. The importance of tolerating anxiety without escaping, avoiding, or ritualizing are again emphasized, and the patient is informed that the events of the next few sessions will be guided by the patient and not imposed on him. Emphasizing the patient's sense of control will help reduce his fears about initiating behavioral strategies.

The patient is also given assignments to be completed over the next week. He is instructed to continue recording and revising his thoughts using the Revised Thought Log, to use flash cards when anxiety is triggered, and to monitor his obsessions and compulsions using the OCM form. He is also given a written ritual-prevention plan for the week, specifically outlining which rituals he must prevent.

7

Session 6: Exposure and Response Prevention (Phase II)

CONDUCTING IN VIVO EXPOSURE
AND RESPONSE PREVENTION

Session Goals	*Check* *When Done*

1. Review (5–10 minutes) ☐
   - Obtain feedback on Session 5
   - Review homework
     —Revised Thought Log (RTL)
     —Obsession-Compulsion Monitoring form
       (OCM)
   - Briefly review events that occurred over past
     week

2. The Session (Exposure and Response Prevention ☐
   Phase II)
   - Conducting in vivo exposure
     ( ) Goals of in vivo exposure
     ( ) What is in vivo exposure
     ( ) Conducting in vivo exposure
   - Conducting response prevention
     ( ) Goals of response prevention
     ( ) What is response prevention
     ( ) Conducting response prevention

3. Next Week (5 minutes) ☐
   - Discuss homework to be completed
     ( ) Obsession-Compulsion Monitoring form
       (OCM) (see Table 3–3)
     ( ) Revised Thought Log (RTL) (see Table 5–1)
     ( ) Collect phobic paraphernalia
   - Anticipate potential stressors that may occur
     during the week

SESSION OVERVIEW

Following a discussion of the previous week's events, the second phase of exposure and response prevention begins and may be conducted in or outside the session. The therapist outlines the goals of *in vivo exposure* and *response prevention*, describes each procedure again with examples, discusses the response-prevention strategies that will be used to help patients refrain from ritualizing, and then finally initiates the exposure exercise. Patients are confronted with the obsessively feared stimulus for the majority of the session until their anxiety declines. Repeated presentations of the same stimulus may occur during the same session. Other items on the hierarchy may also be confronted if time permits. As in vivo exposure is occurring, patients refrain from avoiding, escaping, using distraction, or ritualizing. Although behavioral rituals (not permitting the patient to leave the office and wash his hands) are easier to observe and restrict than mental rituals (the patient silently repeats a phrase during the procedure), the therapist and patient discuss strategies beforehand to prevent mental rituals or subtle behavioral rituals during the session. After the exposure exercise is terminated, the therapist requests feedback from the patient and then assigns exposure and response-prevention exercises for the patient to conduct over the next week.

Although in vivo exposure and response prevention are jointly initiated in this session, they are described separately, one after the other, for ease of understanding. Another reason they are separated here is to facilitate the application of response prevention in conjunction with imaginal exposure during the next session (Chapter 8). However, the case vignette, described here at the end instead of being interspersed throughout the chapter, will demonstrate how the sequence of events would actually occur in this session. Thus, the goals and explanations for in vivo exposure and response prevention would first occur together, followed by the ritual prescription to be followed during the session. In vivo exposure would then be initiated and conducted for the remainder of the session. At the end, the therapist and patient would then plan out how to help the patient prevent rituals at home.

One final note: in vivo exposure and response prevention are described here as occurring during a single session. In reality, exposure and response prevention occur repeatedly until the patient's anxiety associated with all his obsessional items declines. Even after in vivo exposure and response prevention no longer occur within therapy sessions, the patient still conducts them on the outside.

REVIEW

After requesting feedback on the previous session, the therapist reiterates concepts to reinforce the patient's understanding of the previous week's session. The rationale for exposure and response prevention is outlined briefly, along with a general definition of the two concepts. The therapist reminds the patient of the work they did together in planning for the session today (developing exposure hierarchies and deciding how response prevention would be initiated), and checks to see that the obsessional items needed for today's exposure are present.

The therapist also discusses significant events that may have occurred over the past week and uses the patient's anxiety levels as a guide in deciding which events or episodes of anxiety were significant. The therapist checks to see if the patient did the assigned homework and resolves any problems that may have come up during homework assignments.

THE SESSION: EXPOSURE AND
RESPONSE PREVENTION PHASE II

The therapist informs the patient that in vivo exposure exercises along with response prevention will form the bulk of what occurs during the session, but that sufficient time will be allotted at the end so that patients can discuss how they felt during the exercise and so that homework may be assigned.

IN VIVO EXPOSURE

As stated earlier, in vivo exposure is usually more effective than imaginal exposure in alleviating anxiety associated with obsessional triggers, unless it is contraindicated. However, if patients are too fearful to confront tasks directly, then imaginal exposure to the same phobic stimulus is done first, so that patients are less anxious about directly confronting the phobic situation (see Chapter 8 for a description of imaginal exposure). Hence, in vivo exposure will be postponed until the anxiety associated with confronting the task in imagination has declined significantly and the patient is ready to confront the obsessively feared stimulus directly. Alternatively, if in vivo exposure is contraindicated (the patient does not have external triggers of anxiety), imaginal exposure alone will be conducted at this point.

The therapist outlines the specific goals to be accomplished, explains how in vivo exposure and response prevention will be conducted, and finally initiates exposure and response prevention. The exposure hierarchy is reviewed again in case any changes need to be made to the hierarchy before exposure proceeds with the selected task.

The process of exposure outlined below is discussed mostly with regard to patients who present with either contamination fears or fears about causing harm to self or others, because a majority of individuals with obsessive-compulsive disorder have one or both these fears. Further, the exposure process is described in general, and any deviations in its application to contamination versus fears of future harm are noted.

Goal of In Vivo Exposure

The goal of in vivo exposure is to diminish the anxiety associated with obsessions, thereby reducing the frequency and persistence of these thoughts, images, impulses, or urges. Specifically, the therapist attempts to break the association between obsessions and anxiety by directly confronting patients with the external or environmental phobic objects, situations, or people that trigger obsessional anxiety.

What Is In Vivo Exposure?

In vivo exposure, as mentioned earlier, involves direct, prolonged confrontation with anxiety-provoking stimuli in the patient's environment. The individual with obsessive-compulsive disorder is taught to directly confront external or environmental triggers of obsessional anxiety (e.g., contact with garbage) for a prolonged period of time until his anxiety reaction decreases. The confrontation is terminated when he habituates to the phobic stimulus and experiences a reduction in anxiety. Repeated exposure ultimately leads to a progressive reduction in anxiety associated with these stimuli as the patient learns that the consequences he fears do not occur when he confronts them. For example, a patient who avoids touching the garbage can because he is afraid of being contaminated with germs will be required to ultimately come into physical contact with a garbage can until his anxiety associated with it declines. With repeated exposure sessions, the patient gradually learns that he is not in danger of being contaminated, which facilitates his habituation to this stimulus, and his anxiety associated with it decreases.

Because exposure is done in a systematic, hierarchical fashion, patients learn to tolerate manageable levels of anxiety as they first confront low-grade phobic situations and then confront situations that create higher levels of anxiety. By tolerating the anxiety caused by the phobic stimulus rather than escaping it, the patient will experience increased efficacy in coping with higher-level phobic situations. Exposure provides a corrective experience, allowing the patient to disconfirm the threatening appraisal by facing progressively more threatening experiences, and enhances the patient's attention to the absence of the feared consequences.

Conducting In Vivo Exposure

Beginning

The location where exposure will occur depends on the nature of the phobic object, person, or situation that is to be confronted. Exposure sessions are often conducted in the therapist's office, due both to practical constraints (therapist's schedule) and because it provides a safe, contained environment in which to trigger anxiety. However, as treatment progresses, some fieldwork is essential to promote generalizability of treatment effects. Ideally, earlier exposure sessions may be scheduled in the office while later sessions may include field sessions as well.

Of course, the location of exposure depends greatly on whether the obsessively feared stimulus can easily be brought in, re-created, or simulated in the therapist's office. If not, the majority of in vivo exposure may have to be conducted outside the therapeutic environment. Tasks related to contamination fears are more easily conducted in the therapist's office, as they frequently involve objects (e.g., household cleaning fluids) that are easily transportable. Obsessive fears about future harm to self or others are less easily re-created in the office environment for purposes of in vivo exposure unless they involve external objects that trigger these fears. For example, Allison's fear of Michael's coming to harm was triggered by contact with knives, which were easily brought into the session. Of course, not all contaminating stimuli can be confronted in the therapist's office and not all stimuli involving future harm need be confronted outside the therapeutic environment. Hence, the therapist has to work closely with the particular patient in determining which location may be more appropriate for exposure.

Once the location is selected and exposure is about to begin, the therapist addresses any apprehension that the patient has, and restructures fears about the dangers inherent in the exercise. It is important to inform the patient that he will be uncomfortable (anxious) during the exercise but that the discomfort will decline as the exercise proceeds. In fact, patients often note that the anticipatory anxiety is often greater than the anxiety that occurs during the actual exercise. The patient's anxiety about the task and his reluctance to proceed are also normalized before the task begins.

The patient's baseline anxiety is recorded on the Exposure Monitoring Form (see Table 7–1), and he is asked to confront the first item on the hierarchy. If the patient is still reluctant to go ahead, the therapist can model the behavior first and then encourage the patient to proceed. The therapist reminds the patient that he must refrain from using distraction maneuvers or ritualizations during the exercise (see the section below on response prevention), and that he should inform the therapist if violations occur (if he distracts himself by focusing on a neutral object in the room).

Middle

The patient's anxiety is monitored periodically (about every five to ten minutes) throughout the exposure exercise and is recorded on the Exposure Monitoring Form. The therapist queries patients on how they feel and what they are thinking (e.g., What are you thinking or feeling now?), helps them confront the phobic stimulus without escaping, avoiding, or ritualizing, and helps patients attend to their catastrophic fears related to the task at hand (I am afraid that Michael will die if I touch this knife). Flash cards that encapsulate the patient's revised thoughts are also used to restructure the patient's catastrophic fears.

The therapist may also modify exposure as needed if he determines that sufficient anxiety is not being triggered during the exercise. For example, the therapist may suggest that the patient rub a feared object all over his body if he feels that merely touching it is not creating sufficient anxiety. Alternately, the decision may be made to move on to the next item on the hierarchy if anxiety is not being triggered. Of course, the therapist should first investigate if the lack of anxiety is a function of the task being less anxiety provoking than

Table 7–1. Exposure Monitoring Form (Sample)

Name:

Date:

Exposure task:

Number of times exposed to same task:

Baseline anxiety (1–100):

Anxiety levels during exposure (1–100):

5 min	10 min	15 min	20 min	25 min	30 min	35 min	40 min	45 min

50 min	55 min	60 min	65 min	70 min	75 min	80 min	85 min	90 min

Thoughts expressed during exposure (*note feared consequences in particular*):

_____

_____

_____

_____

Exposure Violations:

Violation	*No*	*Yes*	*If yes, specify*
Avoidance			
Escape			
Distraction			
Ritual			

Comments:

_____

_____

_____

the patient previously anticipated and *not* because the patient is using avoidance maneuvers to alleviate the anxiety.

The patient is encouraged to continue with the exercise despite his increasing anxiety, and is periodically reminded that he should concentrate on the exposure, rather than distract his attention from it. In addition, the therapist should be careful not to speak too much during exposure, as talking to the therapist may in and of itself be a form of avoidance. If the patient reports that he ritualized or used mental distraction during an aspect of the exercise, the therapist must reexpose the patient to the particular aspect of the exercise so that the avoidant or ritualistic act is undone.

The demeanor of the therapist is critical in ensuring a smooth session. The therapist must be empathic, understanding, and respectful of the patient's fears, but must be firm and encouraging—all at the same time. The therapist is supportive, and firmly encourages the patient to continue exposure and tolerate the anxiety. The patient is also praised for not avoiding or ritualizing, but is not reassured, since that may lessen the patient's anxiety prematurely. If the patient fails to complete the exercise, the therapist should praise the patient for getting as far as he did, and encourage the patient to try again next time ("Well, it's great that you got that far—next time will be even easier").

Ending

Because in vivo exercises usually do not run as long as imaginal sessions, patients may be exposed to the same item more than once, or be exposed to multiple items from the hierarchy during the same session. However, the length of the exposure exercise may vary from time to time and is determined both by the patient's self-reported level of anxiety and by the therapist's observations during the exercise.

Anxiety usually increases up to a certain point and then slowly declines as the patient continues to confront the feared stimuli. The session may only be terminated when anxiety levels decrease significantly. Ideally, the anxiety should go down to baseline or at least decline to 50 percent below the peak level experienced during the exercise. However, at a minimum, anxiety should go down below peak levels (even if the degree of reduction is less than 50 percent) before the exercise is terminated. If the exercise is terminated while the anxiety is still climbing or at the peak, the anxiety associated with the phobic stimulus will be heightened rather than diminished, and patients will more than likely (and understandably) refuse to participate in future exercises. If anxiety continues to spiral upward and shows no sign of abating despite increased session time, the therapist should check to see if the patient is inadvertently ritualizing (neutralizing, or performing mental rituals, etc.).

Prolonged exposure is easier to accomplish with contamination fears, because staying in the situation is what tends to generate anxiety. However, staying in the same situation is often contraindicated for patients who present with checking rituals, since by definition their fear involves an inability to move away from the situation without checking. For example, take the case of an individual who fears that a fire may break out unless he checks to see if the gas stove is off. If he is instructed to stand next to the gas range and is not permitted to check the knobs manually, he may continue to glance at the stove, thus reassuring himself that the stove is indeed off. Exposure for this individual would entail confronting the situation, leaving it when anxiety levels are high, and sitting in another room until anxiety declines naturally.

Future Sessions

The patient is exposed to the same item on the hierarchy until his anxiety associated with that item is minimal over two subsequent presentations and until the patient feels ready to move to the next item on the hierarchy. However, patients will rarely feel entirely comfortable with the phobic stimuli and will usually need some encouragement to move on to the next item. Hence, the therapist has to assess whether the patient is ready or if he is merely postponing the next task due to avoidance. Two or more in vivo presentations may occur during a single session, and so the next item on the hierarchy may be confronted during the same session.

Therapist-assisted exposure can be terminated when there is a significant reduction in the patient's anxiety associated with items higher up on the hierarchy. Since these are the most feared items, they may require many repeated presentations before there is a significant reduction in anxiety. Patients are then encouraged to continue daily scheduled exposure to all items, but particularly to the most feared ones, until they are able to confront these phobic stimuli routinely without fear.

RESPONSE PREVENTION

Goals of Response Prevention

The goal of response prevention is to break the association between performance of rituals and the reduction of anxiety, thereby enabling anxiety associated with obsessions, thoughts, images, and impulses to decline on its own. It is essential that the patient refrain from rituals.

What Is Response Prevention?

Response prevention is the blocking of behavioral and mental compulsions (e.g., leaving the kitchen without checking the stove), and is used in conjunction with exposure exercises designed to treat obsessions. Patients are taught ways to overcome their urge to ritualize, and to tolerate their anxiety associated with obsessions until the urge to ritualize subsides. As their anxiety declines naturally, the individual's urge to ritualize also decreases over time.

Conducting Response Prevention

How to Implement Response Prevention During Exposure

The patient is asked to refrain from performing rituals or avoiding or escaping the exposure situation. The patient is also encouraged to not use other means of reducing anxiety (by taking benzodiazepines, alcohol, or any such agent) if possible, because it is essential that during in vivo exposure anxiety be evoked and tolerated without escape, avoidance, or ritualization maneuvers.

Before the imaginal exercise begins, the therapist reminds the patient that he must focus on the task at hand and must refrain from using any means to reduce his anxiety. The therapist lists all the maneuvers that the patient has previously used with regard to the current phobic stimulus so that patients have a very specific idea of what they can or cannot do in the session. For example, the therapist may tell the patient that he cannot distract himself, silently repeat a "good" phrase, leave the situation during the task, and so on. He is also told that he cannot perform these or any other rituals, such as washing his hands when he returns home, in order to alleviate his anxiety associated with the exposure exercise.

Although it will be evident if the patient decides to leave the situation or begins to overtly check, it may not be clear if the patient is using subtle or mental rituals during the task. For example, the patient may silently repeat a phrase in his mind, distract himself, or seek reassurance from the therapist. Hence, the patient is told that he must notify the therapist if he inadvertently performs any of these anxiety-reducing maneuvers during the task so that the therapist can design means to "undo" the ritual (see the section below on reexposure). The therapist should also be vigilant to see if the patient is doing anything to reduce his anxiety during the exercise. For example, on one such occasion, the therapist noticed that Allison repeatedly put her hand in her purse during an exercise, as if to look for something. Upon questioning, Allison revealed that she was checking to make sure that her Xanax (a tranquilizer) was still in her purse. Once

this was identified as an anxiety-reducing maneuver that would artificially reduce her anxiety, Allison was encouraged to hand over the
Xanax to the therapist so that she would not gain comfort from knowing that she could use it if she wanted.

Strategies to Help Patients Engage in Response Prevention

Although much has been written on response prevention, therapeutic
strategies have rarely outlined ways to help patients accomplish this
goal. Traditionally, ritual prevention is usually accomplished by con-
trolling the patient's environment (e.g., tap water may be turned off
in inpatient settings), or by closely supervising the patient's moves
(a spouse is asked to monitor the patient's moves). Although the
patient is given rules about what he cannot do, the patient himself
is rarely given guidelines on how to prevent rituals and essentially is
asked to exert "willpower" in accomplishing this goal. Patients are
understandably frustrated by this dictum and often respond by com-
menting that if they could just stop ritualizing, they would have done
so already. As a result, we began compiling the different methods
we have used in helping our patients who have struggled in their
efforts to stop ritualizing and hope that they will come in handy for
other patients who have also struggled with the same situation. Many
of these strategies are derived from those used for habit prevention.
However, please note that these methods have not been empirically
tested on individuals with OCD and are based on clinical experience alone.

Building Motivation

Building motivation is the first step in engaging patients. The therapist refers to the behavioral rationale again as an attempt to build on
the patient's motivation for ritual prevention. Most patients are reluctant to stop ritualizing, and so the first task is to emphasize that
rituals are under their control even if it seems that they come from

without. The therapist also reiterates concepts such as why rituals are unnecessary, and how and why ritual prevention is critical to the success of treatment.

Therapists should be empathic and supportive when they build arguments to increase motivation, but should be careful not to come across as too demanding or critical of the patient's rituals.

Increasing Awareness of Ritual Performance

Many rituals become so routine that the patient is barely aware that he is getting ready to perform them. Although some rituals are consciously done in response to obsessions, many patients describe a sensation of being on autopilot when they perform rituals. This is particularly true for mental rituals. Hence, increasing the individual's awareness of those times when the urge to ritualize occurs helps them combat the automatic urge to ritualize. As stated in earlier chapters, the process of monitoring not only makes patients aware of the fact that they are ritualizing, but the self-awareness alone may lead to a reduction in rituals. Hence, the patient continues to fill out the Obsession-Compulsion Monitoring form both in an effort to determine if rituals are declining and also to continue awareness of ritual performance. Other creative ways to increase awareness may also be used. For example, patients with washing rituals may be asked to place a red dot or a Band-aid on their thumb to increase their awareness of what they are about to do when they automatically reach for the tap.

Assigning a Co-Therapist

As stated earlier, appointing a co-therapist to help monitor the patient's behavior is the method most frequently used to help outpatients refrain from rituals. The identified family member or friend is brought into the session and is given detailed guidelines for how he should supervise the patient. He is then advised to give the therapist regular updates on the patient's progress, either in person or by telephone. It is important that the family member chosen for this task be supportive, noncritical, and nonhostile. He is advised to be firm, to remind the patient that he is not to ritualize, but is cautioned not to use force of any kind.

Because studies show that in the long run self-controlled treatments lead to more improvement than therapist-assisted treatments (Emmelkamp and Kraanen 1977), supervision should gradually be phased out so the patients are able to engage in self-controlled ritual prevention before treatment ends.

Using Flash Cards

Rational arguments based on cognitive restructuring methods used in previous sessions can be encapsulated on index cards for patients to use when the urge to ritualize occurs. Logical arguments should contain the rationale for why it is important to experience and tolerate anxiety, why it is crucial to refrain from rituals, why rituals are unnecessary, and even rational arguments that address the likelihood of future consequences coming true. Flash cards should also focus on consequences of ritual performance (e.g., My OCD will not get better, I will feel bad about myself if I ritualize, etc.). Patients are then instructed to use these flash cards as a way to combat urges to ritualize at the time they occur.

One potential danger in using cognitive restructuring when the urge to ritualize occurs is that the rational dialogue can by itself become ritualized and lead to relief not because of the rational content embedded in it but because of the process of repeating certain sentences in a ritualistic, stereotypical manner. The therapist should be alert to such uses and should attempt to vary the content and presentation sufficiently to prevent particular statements from becoming ritualized. For example, statements can be reworded, or can be presented by the patient's spouse or co-therapist.

Distraction

Some experts have suggested a limited use of distraction in helping patients overcome the urge to ritualize. This is particularly useful for mental rituals that may be performed automatically and without being observed by others. Patients are asked to use distraction maneuvers that are personally meaningful, enjoyable, and unlikely to become ritualized. However, distraction maneuvers should be used with caution and should be used sparingly. In addition, it is vital that patients not be allowed to use distraction when confronting obsessions. Since exposure and response prevention are used in conjunction, it is vital that the therapist specify that distraction maneuvers may be used to combat the urge to ritualize and not to enable patients to distract themselves from the anxiety associated with the obsession. For example, after the patient has confronted and tolerated the anxiety associated with touching the contaminants in the session, he may be permitted to read a book on his return home to prevent himself from washing his hands. However, no distraction is allowed during the moments that he confronts the phobic stimuli.

Rewards for Ritual Prevention

Patients may also be rewarded for engaging in ritual prevention both by therapist praise and encouragement and by building in personally rewarding items for patients when certain milestones are accomplished. Personally rewarding items may be outlined during this session (e.g., eating frozen yogurt if rituals are successfully overcome for a day). Rewards may also be varied based on the milestone reached. For example, the patient may purchase a desired piece of sports equipment if he does not perform the specified rituals for a month, or may plan a Caribbean vacation if he refrains as planned for a year.

Punishments for Ritual Performance

Building in punishments for engaging in ritual performance is another way of reducing performance of rituals. The type of punishment is creatively tailored to meet the individual's needs, since what may be punitive for one person may not be so for another. The therapist and patient frankly discuss what measures would be punitive for the patient and outline how and when to use the punishment. For example, Allison's punishment was sending $5 to a politician she disliked. Allison was instructed to send the politician a $5 bill each time she ritualized against instruction.

Reexposure

Despite the many strategies used to help them combat the urge to ritualize, it is inevitable that patients will occasionally slip. Hence, the therapist must devise other strategies to help patients cope when they inadvertently or consciously perform rituals. Reexposing patients to the obsessively feared stimulus if they ritualize the first time around is a way of undoing the ritual. Reexposure may be used for both mental and behavioral rituals. For example, if the patient has a "bad" thought (obsession) and then instinctively follows it up with a "good" thought (ritual), he will be required to think the "bad" thought again until his anxiety naturally decreases. A patient with washing rituals will be asked to "contaminate" himself again if he washes his hands or performs any other decontaminating ritual when he is exposed to a feared object.

Preventing Self-Criticism If Rituals Are Performed

Although corrective measures are taken if the patient slips and performs a ritual, the therapist should caution the patient against being critical or harsh on himself. Potential negative effects of self-disparaging statements, such as feelings of guilt, shame, or behavioral passivity, are outlined, and the patient is given more constructive ways of talking to himself when a slip occurs. For example, a patient might be encouraged to say something like, "It would have been better if I had not performed this ritual, but now that I have, let me try and do something constructive about it instead of criticizing myself. When I criticize myself, I feel worse and it doesn't help me prevent my rituals. Instead, it would be more helpful if I reexpose myself and work harder to abstain next time."

Future Sessions

If abstinence is the prescribed form of ritual prevention, future sessions merely involve monitoring patients in their ability to refrain, praising patients when they succeed, or trying alternate strategies to help patients stop ritualizing if they have difficulties abstaining. If the patient has difficulty abstaining despite trying the different strategies outlined above, graded forms of response prevention may need to be considered. If graded-response prevention is being used, then future sessions involve gradually decreasing the number of rituals until the patient is no longer permitted to ritualize at all (e.g., you can check for two minutes, then one minute, then thirty seconds).

The therapist also has regular conversations with the family member assigned as a co-therapist to make sure that the patient is abstaining from rituals at home. This provides the opportunity to resolve conflict areas that may come up periodically between the patient and the co-therapist. For example, Allison complained that Michael was often extremely critical of her when she did not abstain. During one of her conversations with Michael, the therapist suggested a variety of noncritical statements that he could make when Allison performed her rituals. And finally, the therapist also takes the opportunity to update the co-therapist on any new rituals the patient has developed or any ritual he is no longer permitted to do.

Future sessions also involve discussion of problems and pitfalls that come up from time to time, the realistic danger of obsessions, and so on. For example, Allison developed strep throat during the course of treatment and became extremely panic stricken. She began questioning the validity of the treatment, convinced that had she been performing her rituals and avoiding "contaminated" areas, this would not have occurred. The therapist empathized with her concern, agreed that what she was saying had some validity, but also helped Allison examine the actual harm in getting strep throat (uncomfortable but not catastrophic) versus continuing with avoidance behaviors and rituals for the rest of her life on the small chance that she might get treatable infections from time to time (extremely debilitating and not worth it).

Patients are also presented with guidelines for normal behavior at the end of treatment, since their idea of normalcy has been disrupted with their illness. For example, Allison was told that she could wash her hands for a maximum of thirty seconds if she objectively soiled or stained her hands, and no more than four to five times a day. She was also told that she could take only one ten-minute shower a day unless she exercised in the evening, in which case another five-minute shower was permissible.

Clinical Vignette

THERAPIST: Let me tell you exactly what we will be doing today. After that, we will outline what you can and cannot do, and then we will begin exposure. At the end, I will help you with ways to prevent rituals over the next week. I see you have all the paraphernalia we need today (the therapist points to a stack of newspapers and soiled laundry brought in by Michael). I'm glad to see that. Michael will come back toward the end of the session and then we'll all sit together to discuss how he can help you stay away from your rituals at home.

ALLISON: I'm feeling quite nervous, I feel a little sick to my stomach.

THERAPIST: I can imagine you are. You're being brave and although it's necessary for you to get better, it's understandable that you're anxious today. (Pause). So let's go over the goals for this exercise. Our goal is to help you have fewer obsessions and compulsions, and in order to do that, we first have to make you less nervous about your obsessions. That's where exposure comes in. In order to make you less nervous about your obsessions, you have to confront all the things that bring them on, such as these newspapers. For example, I am asking you to touch and hold newspapers today to help you realize that touching them will not give you germs that make you sick. As you repeatedly do this, you will be less afraid to touch them, and, as a result, your obsessions about getting infected with germs will gradually decrease over time, because the consequences you fear will not occur.

To reduce your obsessions, we also have to stop you from doing your rituals. I want you to see that the things you are afraid will happen will not happen, even if you do not ritualize. For example, today you will not be permitted to wash your hands after you touch the newspaper. You may get black ink on your hands, but you won't fall sick or get germs. As you realize that you don't need to wash your hands so much, and as you realize that your anxiety will subside naturally, your urge to do the rituals will get weaker and weaker over time.

ALLISON: But any person would wash their hands if they got black ink on them.

THERAPIST: You're right, but they wouldn't be doing it to prevent themselves from getting contaminated with ticks, or germs. They would just be doing it to take off the ink. They also wouldn't do it over and over again. They would do it once.

ALLISON: So I'm going to sit here with newspaper ink all over my hands and I won't be able to wash my hands.

THERAPIST: That's right. At the end of the session, I'll give you some lotion to take the ink off—and that's it for the rest of the evening.

ALLISON: Wow.

THERAPIST: Okay, so today you will first touch the newspapers. Depending on how anxious you get, I will tell you to rub them over different parts of your body. As you do this, your anxiety will probably start to climb. I want you to focus on nothing else but how contaminated you feel. I don't want you to distract yourself by looking elsewhere, blinking your eyes, saying any of your mental rituals, leaving the room, or washing your hands. If you start to do any ritual that I can't see, let me know at once. Your anxiety will climb for a while, maybe five or ten minutes, perhaps a bit more, but then it will slowly start to come down. We will stop the exercise when you feel significantly less anxious. I will be asking you to tell me how anxious you feel every now and then, and I would like you to rate it for me on our usual scale of 1 to 100. If an urge to ritualize is very strong, let me know at once so I can try to help you make it subside.

ALLISON: Okay.

THERAPIST: Any questions before we start?

ALLISON: No.

THERAPIST: Okay, here goes. How anxious do you feel now? On a scale of 1 to 100.

ALLISON: About 40.

THERAPIST (records it on the Exposure Monitoring Form [see Table 7–2]): Now, I want you to pick up the first newspaper from the pile. I want you to hold it with both hands and feel it.

ALLISON: (touches it gingerly).

THERAPIST: That's it, you're doing well. Now place it firmly in both hands and begin turning pages. Feel it with your hands, not just your fingers.

Table 7–2. Allison's Exposure Monitoring Form (In Vivo)

Name: Allison

Date: 5/5/96

Exposure task: Touching newspapers

Number of times exposed to same task: Once

Baseline anxiety (1–100): 40

Anxiety levels during exposure (1–100):

5 min	10 min	15 min	20 min	25	30 min	35 min	40 min	45 min
100	100	80	100	80	40			

50 min	55 min	60 min	65 min	70 min	75 min	80 min	85 min	90 min

Thoughts expressed during exposure (*note feared consequences in particular*):

Why did I agree to this? I will get contaminated, I can't believe I am doing it. I can't wait to ritualize.

Exposure violations:

Violation	*No*	*Yes*	*If yes, specify*
Avoidance	✓		
Escape	✓		
Distraction		✓	focused on performing future rituals
Ritual		✓	said "mercy, mercy" six times.

Comments:

Was able to do more than initially planned. Managed to rub it all over body.

Successfully tolerated anxiety. Anxiety levels declined within 30 minutes.

ALLISON (complies): Oh, this is disgusting. I can't stand it.

THERAPIST: I know it's hard for you, but keep in mind that you *can* stand it. Go on. That's it. Now turn your hands over and rub the newspaper on the back of your hands.

ALLISON: This is awful. I'm feeling very sick to my stomach.

THERAPIST: How anxious do you feel?

ALLISON: 100.

THERAPIST: Good, try and stay at it. You're doing very well. Any rituals?

ALLISON: I'm trying, I'm really trying. No, not yet.

THERAPIST: Good, I'm so pleased. You're winning the battle. Now can you take the newspaper and rub it across your hand, right up to your shirt sleeve?

ALLISON: What? No!

THERAPIST: Try it. Come on, you can do it. Remember, you're doing it for a good cause.

ALLISON (laughs): Who, me? I'm the good cause?

THERAPIST: You are a pretty good cause. I'm glad to see you can find your sense of humor in this.

ALLISON: Wait till I tell my friends what I do in therapy.

THERAPIST: They'll never believe it. Now rub it over your arms.

ALLISON: (complies).

THERAPIST: Now over your legs.

ALLISON: (complies, starts breathing quickly).

THERAPIST: How anxious do you feel now?

ALLISON: Still 100. My heart is racing.

(Pause)

THERAPIST: What are you thinking?

ALLISON: I'm thinking I can't wait to wash this off. I'm plotting ways to do it.

THERAPIST: But you won't, because otherwise this whole session would have been for nothing.

ALLISON: I won't—can't I plot though?

THERAPIST: Not if it's making you feel better. Is it?

ALLISON: It is.

THERAPIST: Okay, come back, focus on how the newspaper smells and feels. If you find yourself distracting again let me know.

ALLISON: All right.

(Pause)

ALLISON: Oops, I just slipped.

THERAPIST: What did you do?

ALLISON: I just said "mercy, mercy." It just happened.

THERAPIST: I'm glad you told me. How do you feel?

ALLISON: 80.

THERAPIST: Now take the newspaper and rub it all over your hands, arms, and legs again so that we can undo the ritual. Place this newspaper under the soles of your feet now. Good, now fold the newspaper over your legs and your arms so that it can touch every part of your body.

ALLISON (agrees): Uh huh.

(Pause)

THERAPIST: How do you feel now?

ALLISON: 100.

(Pause)

THERAPIST: How is your anxiety now?

ALLISON: Still 100.

THERAPIST: Stay with it. You're tolerating it well. Focus on how the anxiety feels and don't allow yourself to distract from it.

(Pause)

ALLISON: I'm trying very hard not to distract. It's hard.

THERAPIST: I know it is, but you're tolerating it well. Just remember that the anxiety will come down naturally, without any rituals.

(Pause)

ALLISON: It just went down. It's at 80 now.

THERAPIST: Good. Stay with it. Focus on how it feels to have the newspaper all over you.

ALLISON: Not great, but not that bad anymore. I'm feeling better.

THERAPIST: How much better?

ALLISON: It's going down. I really don't feel very anxious anymore.

THERAPIST: How anxious do you feel?

ALLISON: About 35?

(Pause)

THERAPIST: Good. Open your eyes now. How do you feel?

ALLISON: Okay. Not bad.

THERAPIST: Anxiety still down?

ALLISON: Yes.

THERAPIST: You can remove the newspaper now. Fold it up and put it in your bag so you can use it later.

ALLISON: Wow! That was hard to do!

THERAPIST: I know, but you did very well. I know how hard it is for you—you have to be very brave to face such intense fears. I admire what you did. Now, I would like you to do the same exercise at home under Michael's supervision three times this week. And from now on, you cannot ritualize to newspapers or paper of any sort. Let's plan what days you will do it now.

ALLISON: Remember, I told you earlier, I had some difficulty sticking to the checking this week. What if the same thing happens?

THERAPIST: Let's discuss that, and let me write everything down for you to take home [see Table 7–3 for Allison's homework assignment]. If you inadvertently wash your hands after you touch newspapers, think about them, get reminded of it, whatever, recontaminate yourself the way we did today. That will undo the ritual. After the exercise is over, if the urge to wash your hands is strong, use your flash cards and do some thought revising, or tell Michael so he can help you. I am going to write these down so you remember. I also have to give you a new ritual-prevention plan.

ALLISON: Recontaminate myself, use flash cards, and tell Michael. Got it.

Table 7–3. Allison's Session 6 Homework Sheet

Homework for the Week:
1. Expose to newspapers without ritualizing three times
2. Stick to ritual-prevention plan
3. Use flash cards as and when needed
4. Follow through with consequence if I stick to the plans
5. Follow through with consequence if I don't stick to the plan

Ritual-Prevention Plan for the Week:
1. Washing hands (twelve times)
2. Showers (once a day for ten minutes only)
3. Checking to see that knives are in place (twenty-four times)
4. Checking on Michael on telephone or at home (six times)
5. Repeating the following things no more than six times (no more than seven hours)
   —God is mighty
   —mercy, mercy
   —how shall I fly
   —I challenge you not
   —safe Mike
   —"6, 6, 6, 6, 6, 6"
   —"not 3, 3, 3"

Things to do if I ritualize against prescription
   —Send money to the governor
   —Do not flagellate myself

Things to do if I ritualize according to prescription
   —Buy myself a massager from Hammacher Schlemmer

Things to do if I ritualize during exposure
   —Recontaminate myself
   —Tell Michael

List of things to bring for exposure next week
1. Newspapers
2. Clothes that have been in the laundry bin for a day
3. Clothes that have been in the laundry bin for a week

THERAPIST: Let's write them down so you remember when you're anxious [see Table 7–2]. As far as the general rituals, if you do slip, I would like to give you a consequence for it. We need a punishment.

ALLISON: Punishment! Are you kidding? Who will give me the punishment?

THERAPIST: I'm dead serious. You will give yourself the punishment or a negative consequence for slipping. What I find very useful is to think of a politician you absolutely cannot stand, someone who makes your stomach turn. Then, each time you don't stick to the ritual prevention plan, you will have to mail this person some money.

ALLISON (starts laughing): This is so funny. Actually, I do have someone I'm against. The governor. I don't agree with any of her policies. I don't know how she was ever elected.

THERAPIST: Perfect. How much money do you want to send her?

ALLISON: Fifty cents?

THERAPIST: Will that hurt?

ALLISON: No, not really. How about $5?

THERAPIST: Sounds good.

ALLISON: How will I give it to her?

THERAPIST: Find out where she accepts campaign donations, get her address, take some envelopes and write out her name and address. If at the end of every week you don't keep to your plan, her reelection chest gets rich.

ALLISON: Over my dead body.

THERAPIST: That's the attitude, I don't want her to get rich either. Now one more thing before we end. I would like you to reward yourself, too, if you are able to keep to the plan. How about planning something nice for yourself as a reward if you do keep to it this week?

ALLISON: Like what?

THERAPIST: You tell me.

ALLISON: This could get expensive.

THERAPIST: It doesn't have to be. Are there any inexpensive things you could buy, an activity you could do, any treat you could give yourself?

ALLISON: Well, I could get myself this massage thing from Hammacher Schlemmer. It's about $20. I've always wanted it.

THERAPIST: Sounds good. Now one more thing before you leave. If you slip, I want you to send the money to the governor, but I don't want you to start flagellating yourself. You can be very good at that. If you find that you're criticizing yourself, I would like you to do some cognitive restructuring. Take one of the Revised Thought Logs and begin filling it out. Okay?

ALLISON: See you next week.

NEXT WEEK

Although exposure and response prevention first occur during therapy sessions, practice sessions are prescribed and patients are encouraged to confront anxiety-provoking situations between sessions as well. The therapist and patient discuss the homework to be completed prior to the next formal exposure session. Specifically, the therapist instructs the patient on which item or items of the hierarchy should be confronted and how exposure is to occur. The therapist also reminds the patient that he cannot perform rituals during exposure exercises, and discusses how the assigned co-therapist may assist in the tasks. The patient is asked to complete the Exposure Monitoring form for each exposure task.

At the end of each exposure session, the patient is also given a list of stimuli that he must no longer avoid and rituals he can no longer perform in general. To facilitate the process, homework assignments can be written down. Finally, the patient is also instructed to continue monitoring and revising automatic thoughts, obsessions, and rituals, using the appropriate forms.

Session 7:
Exposure and Response
Prevention (Phase III)

CONDUCTING IMAGINAL EXPOSURE
AND RESPONSE PREVENTION

Session Goals	*Check When Done*

1. Review (5–10 minutes) ☐
    * Obtain feedback on Session 7
    * Review homework
        ( ) Exposure and Ritual Prevention Tasks
        ( ) Exposure Monitoring Form
        ( ) Revised Thought Log (RTL)
        ( ) Obsession-Compulsion Monitoring form
        (OCM)
    * Briefly review events that occurred over past
    week

2. The Session ☐
    * Conducting imaginal exposure and response
    prevention
        ( ) Goals of imaginal exposure
        ( ) What is imaginal exposure
        ( ) Conducting imaginal exposure
    * Response prevention
    * Cautionary notes for beginning cognitive
    behavior therapists

3. Next Week (5 minutes) ☐
    * Discuss homework to be completed
        ( ) In vivo exposure tasks
        ( ) Ritual prevention tasks
        ( ) Completing Exposure Monitoring Form,
        Rational Thought Logs, Obsession-Compulsion
        Monitoring forms as and when needed.
    * Anticipate potential stressors that may occur
    during the week

SESSION OVERVIEW

The third and final phase of behavioral therapy involves imaginal exposure and response prevention. The therapist quickly reviews the previous session and any significant events that may have occurred over the past week, and then spends time discussing homework assignments. However, since imaginal sessions are usually longer than other sessions, it is better to begin the tasks of the current session as soon as possible. If there is time left over at the end, the discussion on homework assignments and the week's events may be elaborated. If not, the discussion may need to be postponed until the next session or discussed over the telephone.

The therapist outlines the goals of imaginal exposure, describes what imaginal exposure is, why it is being conducted today, explains that the patient cannot ritualize during the session, and discusses how rituals will be prevented. The therapist also addresses the patient's fear about the current session in some detail. The therapist starts the tape recorder (with the patient's permission) and then begins the imaginal exercise. As the session proceeds, the therapist monitors the patient's anxiety levels, is vigilant to see that rituals are not performed, and ends the exercise when anxiety levels are safely down. Time is left at the end in order to debrief the patient and receive feedback from him about the exercise. Homework assignments are given out and the patient is instructed to complete all tasks and forms by the next session.

REVIEW

The therapist reviews the previous session and events of the last week. Homework assignments are reviewed to ensure that they were done correctly, and the therapist praises the patient on his progress made over the last week. Problem areas are identified and troubleshooting strategies are discussed. Did the in vivo exposure tasks go

as planned? Was the patient able to confront the situation successfully? Was he able to refrain from ritualizing during the exercise and
at other times during the week? Was the co-therapist supportive and
helpful?

THE SESSION: EXPOSURE AND
RESPONSE PREVENTION PHASE III

Imaginal Exposure

Once it is determined that the patient will benefit from confronting
the phobic stimuli in imagination, the tasks of conducting imaginal
exposure begin. The therapist outlines the specific goals to be accomplished, explains in detail how imaginal exposure will be conducted, develops anxiety-provoking scenes to be used, and finally
initiates exposure.

The following discussion pertains mostly to phobic stimuli that
may only be accessed via imaginal exposure. However, when imaginal exposure is used in conjunction with in vivo exposure for the same
phobic stimulus, the same principles apply.

Goal of Imaginal Exposure

The goal of imaginal exposure is to diminish the anxiety associated
with the obsession, thereby reducing the frequency and persistence
of these thoughts, images, impulses, or urges. Specifically, the therapist attempts to break the association between obsessions and anxiety by imaginally confronting patients with the catastrophic fears
inherent in the obsessions.

What Is Imaginal Exposure?

In imaginal exposure, the individual with obsessive-compulsive disorder is confronted in imagination with his anxiety-provoking stimuli

as well as the feared disasters he believes will occur if he does confront these stimuli. As his anxiety increases, the individual is encouraged to stay with the exercise until he habituates to the image and experiences a reduction in anxiety. Repeated exposure ultimately leads to a reduction in anxiety associated with these stimuli as the patient learns that the consequences he fears do not occur when he confronts them. During the exercise, the patient does not try to avoid or escape from the anxiety experienced by detaching from the image or by performing rituals. For example, let us take the case of a patient who believes that he will kill his mother if he has an obsession about her dying. Through imaginal exposure, the individual is helped to visualize the obsession about his mother dying. Although initially this scene creates tremendous anxiety, the patient is encouraged to continue visualizing the image of his mother dying until he habituates to the image. The exercise is terminated when his anxiety has reduced significantly. With repeated exposure sessions, where this scene is visualized in greater and greater detail, the patient gradually learns that imagining his mother dead will not lead to her death. He habituates to this image, and the anxiety associated with it decreases.

For imaginal exposure to be successful, it is essential that anxiety be evoked during imaginal exposure and that the patient tolerate this anxiety without escaping, avoiding, or ritualizing. Hence, exposure works best when conducted with response prevention (see below) and when the patient does not use other means of reducing anxiety (by taking benzodiazepines, alcohol, or any such agent).

A word of caution: if imaginal exposure is being conducted to internal images, thoughts, and obsessions, particularly those of causing future harm to others, anxiety levels may be excessive and fears regarding the exercise may need to be countered more than once. For example, a patient may be overwhelmed at the notion of spending the entire session visualizing his wife coming to harm. He may have a hard time understanding why his anxiety about her coming to harm is being alleviated, and feel that it is normal to feel anxious if you think about your wife getting hurt. The therapist can once again explain that the purpose of the exercise is not to make him callous or unfeeling about his wife dying, but to allow him to see that thinking about or imagining such a scene (without ritualizing) will not lead to her getting injured in reality.

Conducting Imaginal Exposure

Beginning

The patient is seated comfortably, the office lights are dimmed if possible, and all external distractions are minimized (phone ringer is off, windows are shut). The therapist informs the patient that the imaginal exposure exercise is about to begin, and again warns the patient that his anxiety will increase as the session continues, but also restates that his anxiety will ultimately go down. Bracing patients for what is about to happen helps them stay with the anxiety when it spirals upward, seemingly uncontrollably.

The therapist asks that the patient close his eyes, then records the patient's baseline anxiety. The patient is reminded that he must refrain from using distraction maneuvers or ritualizations during the exercise (see the section below on response prevention). Guidelines about how the patient should communicate to the therapist (raise his hand) if he does ritualize during the exercise (imagines a neutralizing image during exposure) should also be communicated at this point so the image will not be disrupted. The therapist then begins the narration, but rarely reads it out verbatim as there is a possibility that a rote narrative will not induce the intended anxiety. In fact, the therapist is as expressive as the narrative demands, so that relevant themes are communicated to the patient not just by the content of the narrative but by the therapist's manner of speaking (tone, volume, rate). Although written scripts are usually narrated by the therapist, some exceptions do exist. For example, patients with mental rituals may find it easier to refrain from ritualizing if they read out the scene themselves, at least in earlier exposure sessions.

The therapist narrates the image in the present tense to enhance the sense that the image is occurring right then, and requests that the patient also imagine the scene in the immediate moment. Just as the patient is asked not to use distraction maneuvers or ritualizations during the exercise, he is also requested to refrain from using any methods to distance himself from the image. For example, the patient is asked that he make every effort to "be" in the image and not observe it from afar.

Middle

During the exercise, the therapist monitors associated thoughts, feelings, and actions (e.g., What are you thinking or feeling now?), helps the patient attend to the feared scene (stay with the portion of the scene that is most anxiety provoking by reiterating the description), and may also modify the image as necessary (the script may be lengthened in areas where it is more anxiety provoking or details may be added if sufficient anxiety is not being triggered). The therapist also monitors the level of anxiety (How are you feeling now?) either at regular time intervals (every five to ten minutes or so), or upon completion of certain tasks (after each written script is read out). However, the therapist must be careful not to speak through the entire exposure exercise, as this may interfere with the patient's ability to effectively visualize the image. Periodically requesting feedback from the patient is a good way to ensure that the exercise is proceeding as it should and is having the intended effect on the patient.

As the anxiety rises, the patient is encouraged to stay with the scene and to continue visualizing it as vividly as possible. If the patient reports that he ritualized during an aspect of the scene, the therapist must repeat the section of the narrative that triggered the need to ritualize so that the ritualistic act is undone. The written narrative or other medium may be presented again during the session if it helps the patient visualize the scene more effectively. The therapist is supportive, provides encouragement to the patient for not ritualizing, but does not try to reassure the patient, as that may lessen the patient's anxiety prematurely. Anxiety is allowed to spiral upward naturally and the therapist must have the confidence to be able to observe the progression of anxiety without fearing that the patient may "flip out." The therapist's confident, supportive stance goes a long way in making the session successful.

Ending

As with in vivo exposure, the level of anxiety experienced by the patient during imaginal exposure is used as a guide in deciding when to terminate the session. Studies indicate that anxiety is observed to increase for up to thirty minutes, but it may continue up to ninety minutes in imaginal sessions. In addition, therapists should allow a few minutes after the exercise is terminated to obtain the patient's feedback and assign the next week's homework. Hence, exposure sessions are usually longer than other sessions. Ideally, the therapist should book a double session when exposure is initiated. The session is terminated when anxiety levels go down to baseline, or decline to 50 percent below peak levels, or at the very least reduce significantly below peak levels even if the degree of reduction is less than 50 percent. The session should not be terminated while the anxiety is still climbing or at its peak to prevent the possibility of fear sensitization. If anxiety continues to spiral upward and shows no sign of abating despite increased session time, the therapist should check to see if the patient is inadvertently ritualizing (neutralizing the image, or performing mental rituals).

Feedback

Once the exercise is terminated, the therapist requests feedback on the patient's subjective experience of the exercise. Was it as bad as he anticipated? What were the most difficult portions of the exercise? Was the patient surprised to find that his anxiety declined as predicted? The therapist praises the patient for tolerating the exercise and emphasizes to the patient the fact that his anxiety declined despite the fact that he did not ritualize. Any fears that patients may express about catastrophic fears coming true (e.g., maybe my mother is dead and I don't even know it) may now be restructured. As an aside, when feared consequences do not eventually come true (the patient goes home and sees that the parent is alive and well), that fact is collected as evidence in the cognitive restructuring of such fears in the future.

Future Imaginal Exposure Sessions

As patients habituate to the first image, more details are added, until the patient visualizes the scene in as much detail as possible. The next scene on the hierarchy is only introduced if there is minimal anxiety to the current scene on at least two consecutive presentations. If the patient reports minimal anxiety to the scene in between sessions, the therapist should still continue exposure to the same scene during the therapy session to ensure that the exposure was conducted appropriately at home. Usually, two or three exercises are sufficient to reduce the anxiety associated with a particular scene. Scenes lower on the hierarchy usually require fewer exposure exercises, but more anxiety-provoking scenes may require multiple exercises before anxiety levels dissipate.

CONDUCTING RESPONSE PREVENTION
WITH IMAGINAL EXPOSURE

The strategies outlined in Chapter 7 to help patients conduct response prevention are also used here in conjunction with imaginal exposure. Before imaginal exposure begins, the patient is reminded that he cannot use any means to artificially reduce his anxiety. If needed, the specific rules for response prevention are outlined again. Strategies that will be used to prevent rituals during the session are discussed and implemented during the session.

Washing and checking rituals are the easiest to prevent during the session itself, because the patient would either have to leave the room during the exercise in order to perform them or do something overt enough for the therapist to see. However, the patient must agree not to wash or check after the session is over. Mental rituals, on the other hand, are not as easy to observe or reduce during the imaginal session. To combat this, the patient can be instructed to raise his hand if he inadvertently performs a mental ritual during the task. The patient is then asked to revisualize or reimagine the particular aspect of the image that was being visualized when the ritual occurred. This way, the "benefits" of the ritual are undone.

Tackling Complications in Exposure and Response Prevention

Lack of Compliance

Although some patients may have an easier time confronting phobic stimuli than others, confronting situations that have been avoided for many years is a difficult process for all patients. It is important to remember that patients' reluctance to proceed, or their continued avoidance at home, is not usually a sign of resistance, passive aggressiveness, or hostility toward the therapist, but is more often than not a reflection of the degree to which they are afraid of facing what they fear. However, if some patients refuse to move ahead with exposure, or continue to avoid homework assignments, the therapist must come up with constructive ways to address this stalemate so that therapy sessions do not turn into a battleground involving endless attempts at persuasion.

One way to reduce this impasse is to prepare patients beforehand that this may occur during therapy. Not only are patients prepared for the fact that they will experience anxiety, but they should be prepared for the fact that they may fight the therapist, and refuse to proceed or comply at different stages of treatment. The therapist and patient then collaboratively discuss ways that the therapist can help the patient become unstuck if and when this occurs in the future. If it does occur, the therapist can remind the patient of their earlier conversation and refer to the different strategies that they had mutually agreed on in the beginning.

Other strategies that can be used to deal with lack of compliance include breaking down exposure tasks into even smaller steps, adding serotonergic medication if patients are not already on it, and, as the last resort, temporarily adding anxiolytic medications for the first few exposure attempts. However, it is strongly advised that tranquilizers be discontinued as soon as possible because they are believed to reduce the efficacy of exposure. Hence, using anxiolytic medications should be perceived as adding a few lower rungs on the hierarchy and not as a permanent way of coping with exposure tasks. If none of the above strategies work to increase compliance, patients may have to be referred out for alternative treatments (inpatient treatments, medications).

Difficulty Habituating

If anxiety does not decrease during exposure, the therapist should quickly investigate the reasons why this may be occurring. If exposure sessions regularly end when anxiety levels are high, the relationship between the exposure task and obsessional anxiety will be strengthened rather than weakened, leading to a poorer outcome in the long run. Fear may not habituate during exposure for several reasons. In most cases, the exposure sessions may be of insufficient duration, or patients may be intermittently using subtle avoidance during exposure tasks (mentally distracting from the exposure task, or performing mental rituals). To facilitate habituation, the therapist can try to increase session length and uncover and prevent avoidance of any type.

In some cases, habituation may not occur if patients become highly overaroused during exposure or if they are severely depressed. If this occurs, patients may be referred for medication before exposure sessions can proceed.

Clinical Vignette

THERAPIST: If you remember, Allison, in this session I am going to help you confront your fears about Michael in your imagination. I know you're very nervous today because these are your biggest fears. But you've been doing very well with your other exposure tasks so there is every reason to think that you will do just as well with confronting these in your imagination.

ALLISON: But I wasn't able to do any of the knife exposures.

THERAPIST: Yes, I know. That's fine—remember we decided that the rung was too high for you to climb and that we would get to it after we had begun confronting your fears in your imagination? That still doesn't take away from your success at all the other exposure tasks.

ALLISON: Yes, you're right.

THERAPIST: So let's again go over the goals for the session today before we begin exposure. Now that you have some experience with how exposure works, you can see that the more you confront things, the less anxious you feel, and the fewer obsessions you have. Our goal is to make your obsessions and compulsions continue on their downward trend. And as you can see, now you are able to pick up a garbage can, and touch it. As a result, your obsessions about being infected are significantly less. You have begun learning that you don't need to wash your hands over and over again in order to feel safe. Did you ever think that would happen?

ALLISON: No, not really. I really didn't. I'm surprised and quite relieved. It hasn't been easy, though. And I still haven't completely stopped washing my hands.

THERAPIST: There you go again, not giving yourself enough credit. How many times were you washing your hands before?

ALLISON: Usually about thirty-six, but it could be more.

THERAPIST: And now?

ALLISON: I'm down to seven.

THERAPIST: I think the progress speaks for itself.

ALLISON: I know I'm hard on myself.

THERAPIST: And you have been a real trooper for sticking through this. When I spoke to Michael the other day, he told me how proud he was of your ability to keep going.

ALLISON (face flushes): He did? That's nice to hear, it's been a while since I've given him an opportunity to say something nice about me.

THERAPIST (smiles): Now we're switching gears a little bit. We are going to begin working on your fears about Michael. I will help you confront these fears in your imagination today. To make you less nervous about these obsessions, I have to help you confront the obsessional images that run through your mind time and time again. Usually, when you have an obsessional thought, you force yourself to stop thinking about it, you distract yourself, and then you start ritualizing because you feel sure in your heart that you will save Michael from imminent disaster if you do it.

ALLISON: That's exactly what I do. Sometimes I know that I'm going to have an image, and I haven't even had one yet, and I will just start saying "safe Mike" or something like that to ward it off.

THERAPIST: Right, and that doesn't give you the opportunity to let your anxiety about the image go down naturally. Today, I'm going to have you imagine the first scene in the hierarchy, the scene where Michael gets into an accident and is injured. I am going to have you imagine the scene for a prolonged period of time until your anxiety reduces. It will reduce, because that's how anxiety is. It goes down after prolonged exposure if there is no real danger. And as we said before, I want you to habituate to the image, not because I want you to be cold and heartless and not care if something happens to him, but because I don't want you to spend your whole life thinking about things that may never happen. You are trying to get used to the *image* of Michael getting hurt, not to him getting hurt in real life. There is a big difference. And Michael told you before that he understands why you will be spending sessions discussing bad things happening to him.

ALLISON: Yes, he does understand. He knows I love him, I just can't think like this anymore.

THERAPIST: That's right. You'll see that as your fear reduces naturally, you will obsess less and less about Michael just the way you're now obsessing less about getting infected with germs. But, as with the other exposure tasks, it's very important that you don't distract yourself or perform any of your rituals during the scene. For example, during the exposure exercise you will not be permitted to repeat any of your ritualistic phrases or numbers, so you can learn that having the image will not kill him, even if you don't say anything "good." You will also not be permitted to check up on him in any way. As you realize that you don't need to ritualize in order to save Michael from getting hurt, you will see that your anxiety will decline naturally, and your need to do it will also get less and less.

(Pause)

THERAPIST: I am going to read out the accident scene [see Table 8–1] and help you imagine it as if it were happening right now. You will get anxious, and your anxiety will probably start to climb. It will probably climb for a while, too, so I want you to

Table 8–1. Narrative Guide for Imaginal Scene 1, Car Accident Scene

Michael is leaving his office now. It is about 6:30 P.M., it's getting dark. It is misty and damp outside. He is in the parking garage and he is walking toward his car. He is wearing his London Fog coat in case it starts to rain. He has an umbrella in one hand and his briefcase in the other. It starts to drizzle slightly as he gets into his silver Honda. You wish that he would have taken the Jeep which is much safer. The car smells new, he has always wanted to buy this car. But he is tired, preoccupied, and can't even enjoy the newness of the car. He thinks to himself, "I hope Allison is not too bad today, I can't deal with her obsessions today, I just want to relax and unwind in front of the TV." He has a heavy heart as he drives out of the garage. He drives out of the garage and soon he is getting onto the Long Island Expressway. He is maneuvering his car and trying to open his bottle of water. He takes a gulp, and as he begins to put the bottle down, suddenly, out of nowhere, a tractor trailer comes and hits him. He is so shocked, he doesn't know what hit him. He tries to swerve but he can't, and he knows there is nothing he can do about it. The Honda smashes against the trailer and his head goes straight through the windshield. The trailer still goes, but the driver is trying to stop, there is a sound of screeching brakes as both car and trailer screech to a halt. There is blood everywhere, shattered glass everywhere. The driver is unharmed, he gets out to see how Michael is. Michael is unconscious. The driver starts running and flagging down oncoming traffic. After a while, someone stops. They call 911 and try to help Michael out. He is not moving, you are sure he is dead, you are feeling very anxious. The ambulance takes a long time to come, and they finally come. They take him out, put him on a stretcher and drive to the nearest hospital. He looks very pale and weak just lying there. His eyes are now open so you know he isn't dead but he looks like he is in a lot of pain. He is still bleeding profusely, and he looks all alone. His leg is broken for sure, and you are not sure what else is broken. You wish you could comfort him but he can't hear you. The ambulance speeds up and they disappear into the night. You are overwhelmed with your feelings of guilt, sadness, and anxiety.

be prepared. That's why we have booked a double session today, because anxiety can continue to climb up to thirty minutes or so before it starts to come down in this type of exposure. And it could go on for much longer, up to ninety minutes before it completely goes away.

ALLISON (smiles nervously): Wow. This is going to be a fun session, I can see that.

THERAPIST: I want you to focus on the scene completely. I don't want you to distract yourself, escape in your mind, blink, do any mental rituals. If you start to say your phrases or numbers or anything else to reduce your anxiety, let me know at once, just as you've been telling me during the other exercises. We will stop the exercise when you feel significantly less anxious. I will be asking you how you feel every now and then but I will also be keeping quiet for periods at a time because I don't want my voice to become a distraction. Again, if an urge to ritualize is very strong, let me know at once so I can try to help you make it subside.

ALLISON: Okay.

THERAPIST: Any questions before we start?

ALLISON: No.

THERAPIST: Here goes. How anxious do you feel now?

ALLISON: About 50.

THERAPIST: (records it on the Exposure Monitoring Form [See Table 8–2].

The therapist dims the lights in the room, turns on a white noise machine to block outside noise, turns down the ringer on the phone, turns on the tape recorder, and asks the patient to recline on the couch.

THERAPIST: Now I want you to close your eyes, Allison. I am going to read out the scene and fill in some things to make the image come more to life. I want you to imagine it in the present tense as if it's happening right now, and I want you to try very hard not to observe the scene from a distance. I want you to be right there. If any of the details are incorrect, let me know.

ALLISON: (closes her eyes).

THERAPIST: Michael is leaving his office now. It's about 6:30 P.M. It's getting dark. It's misty and damp outside. He's in the parking garage and is walking toward his car. He's tired so he's

Table 8–2. Allison's Exposure Monitoring Form (Imaginal)

Name: Allison

Date: 8/12/96

Exposure task: Car accident scene

Number of times exposed to same task: Several times to different sections, full narrative read only once

Baseline anxiety (1–100): 50

Anxiety levels during exposure (1–100):

5 min	10 min	15 min	20 min	25 min	30 min	35 min	40 min	45 min
80	100	100	100	80	65	65	50	30

50 min	55 min	60 min	65 min	70 min	75 min	80 min	85 min	90 min

Thoughts expressed during exposure (*note feared consequences in particular*):

I wish I could stop him. I know he is going to die or get badly hurt. I wish I could help.

Exposure violations:

Violation	*No*	*Yes*	*If yes, specify*
Avoidance	√		
Escape	√		
Distraction	√		
Ritual		√	safe Mike, God is mighty

Comments:

walking slowly. He's wearing his London Fog coat because he knows it will probably start to rain. You hear his umbrella tap on the ground as he walks and you hear his footsteps. He reaches the car, and you begin to feel anxious, you know exactly what's going to happen. Your palms are getting sweaty in anticipation. It starts to drizzle slightly as he gets into his new car. You wish you could warn him, you wish he had taken the Jeep. The car smells new. He has always wanted to buy this car. But he's tired, preoccupied, and he can't even enjoy the newness of the car. He thinks to himself, "I hope Allison isn't too bad today, I can't deal with her obsessions today. I just want to relax and unwind in front of the TV."

ALLISON (starts crying): Oh, God!

THERAPIST: How do you feel, Allison?

ALLISON: Very bad, I feel so nervous, so sad for him. About 80 for anxiety.

THERAPIST: Good, you're doing well. You're feeling guilty that he's not looking forward to coming home, sad because it's making him preoccupied. He has a heavy heart as he drives out of the garage. You are filled with dread now. He is driving unthinking, knowing nothing of the danger that faces him. The rain is whipping on the windshield and you can hear the wipers swish back and forth, back and forth. He turns down the windows a little bit because the car is fogging up and he can't see too well. He is almost at the Long Island Expressway. He reaches over to pick up his bottle of water and you wish that he wouldn't. "Stop! Stop, Michael," you scream—but he can't hear you. He is maneuvering his car and trying to open his bottle of water. He takes a gulp, and as he begins to put the bottle down, suddenly, out of nowhere, a tractor trailer comes and hits him. He is so shocked, he doesn't know what hit him. You see his eyes widen as he tries to swerve but he can't, and he knows there is nothing he can do about it.

ALLISON: Stop. I just ritualized.

THERAPIST: What did you say?

ALLISON: I said "safe Mike."

THERAPIST: Do you remember at what point?

ALLISON: Right when you said "his eyes widen."

THERAPIST: What was your anxiety at that point?

ALLISON: 100.

THERAPIST: Let me read that section again. I would like you to imagine that scene once more.

(Reads section again).

ALLISON: Oops, I did it again. I'm sorry.

THERAPIST: (reads it again).

(Pause)

THERAPIST: How are you doing?

ALLISON: Good. I managed not to ritualize.

THERAPIST: Good. Shall I go on?

ALLISON: All right.

THERAPIST: The car smashes against the trailer and his head goes straight through the windshield. There is the sound of glass shattering everywhere. You see pieces of glass on his head. The trailer is still going, but the driver is trying to stop. There is a sound of screeching brakes as both car and trailer come to a halt. There is blood everywhere, shattered glass everywhere. There is a smell of gas, burnt rubber in the air. You are shaking now, you are so scared you can't think. Your heart is pounding. You want to run over to him. The driver is unharmed. He is running over to Michael now, screaming "Oh my God, I didn't see him coming."

ALLISON (agitated, restless): I'm feeling pretty bad, about 100 still.

THERAPIST: Continue imagining the scene. You're doing very well. I'm very proud of you.

ALLISON (starts weeping): I can't do this, I can't.

THERAPIST: Yes, you can, you've already done it. And you will continue with it until your anxiety goes down.

ALLISON (shaking): What if it doesn't?

THERAPIST: It will, you know it will. Continue with the scene, take it slowly. Picture Michael. He's unconscious.

ALLISON (closes her eyes again): I just said "God is mighty."

THERAPIST: Can you imagine the portion of the scene again? Exactly when you ritualized?

ALLISON: Yes, I imagined him going through the windshield.

(Long pause)

THERAPIST: How anxious do you feel now?

ALLISON: Still 100. My heart is racing.

THERAPIST: Any thoughts?

ALLISON: I just want to stop him and I can't.

THERAPIST: Let me go ahead with the scene some more (pause). The truck driver is hysterical. He's running and trying to flag down oncoming traffic. The rain is pouring now, down on his face. And the cars keep whizzing by, "Stop! Stop," you scream, "Someone please stop and help my husband." After a while, someone stops. They call 911 and try to help Michael out. He's not moving, you're sure he is dead, you're feeling very anxious. Sick at heart, you wait and wait.

(Pause)

ALLISON: I'm at 90. I feel a little better. I'm not sure why but I do.

THERAPIST: Good. Continue at the same scene. You keep waiting for the ambulance, sick at heart. The rain is pouring down everywhere.

(Pause)

THERAPIST: The ambulance takes a long time to come, and they finally come. They take him out, put him on a stretcher and drive to the nearest hospital. He looks very pale and weak just lying there. His eyes are now open so you know he isn't dead but he looks like he's in a lot of pain. He is still bleeding profusely. He looks all alone and you want to hug him. His leg is broken for sure, and you're not sure what else is broken. You wish you could comfort him but he can't hear you. The ambulance speeds up and they disappear into the night. You feel sick with guilt, and you're so tired.

ALLISON: About 80.

THERAPIST: Good. Continue imagining it. Now go back to the point where the impact first occurs and his eyes widen.

ALLISON: Okay.

(Pause)

THERAPIST: How do you feel?

ALLISON: Okay—about 65.

(Pause)

THERAPIST: Now proceed with the scene. Where are you now?

ALLISON (eyes closed): There's broken glass everywhere.

THERAPIST: You can smell the rubber, the smell of singed metal.

ALLISON: I see him with his eyes closed.

(Pause)

THERAPIST: You're now waiting for help again. The truck driver is running around trying to get everyone to stop.

ALLISON: I'm down to 50.

(Pause)

THERAPIST: Good. Let's continue. Imagine the ambulance coming. Hear the sirens. They get out. They gently lift Michael out.

(Pause)

THERAPIST: Are you able to focus on the scene?

ALLISON: Yes. It was getting harder there for a while. It's better now.

THERAPIST: Good. Any rituals?

ALLISON: No.

THERAPIST: Good.

(Pause)

ALLISON: I really don't feel very anxious anymore. It's about 30 now.

THERAPIST: Good. You did very well. How do you think you did?

ALLISON: I feel worn out. I feel like I went through a battle.

THERAPIST: But you won the battle even though you're exhausted.

ALLISON: I can't believe that at the end I was getting a little bored with the scene. I had to work hard to focus on it.

THERAPIST: That's good. It's hard to stop thinking about it when you try to stop, but when you force yourself to think about it, it goes away.

ALLISON: Isn't that amazing?

THERAPIST: Yes, I agree. Now, I would like you to take this tape home and listen to it, daily if you can, but at least three times a week. And remember, you cannot ritualize to this scene during exposure, or to any spontaneous obsessions about the car accident. You can continue ritualizing to the other scenes but not to this one. And I want you to continue lessening your other rituals according to our plan [see Table 8–3]. I see that the governor has only received $10 so far. I thought she would have gotten rich by now.

ALLISON: No chance of that happening. Even the $10 burns me up.

THERAPIST: Good. How will you reward yourself this week if you keep to the plan?

ALLISON: Michael is taking me to a movie I want to see.

THERAPIST: Good, I'll see you next week.

NEXT WEEK

Imaginal exposure sessions conducted during the session are usually taped on a continuous loop tape so that patients may continue exposure at home. This is particularly useful for patients who have mental thoughts or ideas, because it leaves them no time to perform the ritual. The patient is instructed to continue imaginal exposure to the same scene between sessions. Daily exposure is ideal, but a minimum of three times a week is essential to maintain gains made during the therapy session. Patients are requested to refrain from all prescribed rituals, but in particular are asked to refrain from ritualizing during

Table 8–3. Allison's Session 7 Homework Sheet

Homework for the Week:
1. Expose to accident scene without ritualizing.
2. Stick to ritual-prevention plan.
3. Use flash cards as and when needed.
4. Follow through with consequence if I stick to the plans.
5. Follow through with consequence if I don't stick to the plan.

Ritual-Prevention Plan for the Week
1. Washing hands (five times)
2. Showers (once a day for ten minutes only)
3. Checking to see that knives are in place (twelve times)
4. Checking up on Michael on the telephone or at home (five times)
5. Repeating the following things no more than six times (five hours only)
   —God is mighty
   —mercy, mercy
   —how shall I fly
   —I challenge you not
   —safe Mike
   —"6, 6, 6, 6, 6, 6"
   —"not 3, 3, 3"

Things to do if I ritualize against prescription
   —Send money to the governor
   —Do not flagellate myself

Things to do if I ritualize according to prescription
   —Go to a movie

Things to do if I ritualize during exposure
   —Recontaminate myself
   —Tell Michael
   —Distract from rituals (read a book) (Important: do not distract during exposure)

the homework exercise or if the obsessive image appears spontaneously. Potential times when their urge to ritualize will be strong are anticipated and alternate coping strategies are discussed.

As noted earlier, although imaginal exposure is described as occurring over one session, it may actually go on for several weeks until the patient has been exposed to the most feared scenes. In Allison's case, these were images of Mike getting stabbed. However, it is not essential that each step on the hierarchy be confronted. Hierarchies are periodically rated by the patient and it is not uncommon to see fear levels decline for scenes that were not used for exposure. Further, as treatment continues, patients are encouraged to begin conducting more and more exposure sessions on their own.

Patients are also instructed to continue monitoring and revising dysfunctional automatic thoughts associated with their obsessions. In particular, they are encouraged to use flash cards during potential periods of stress during the coming week.

Session 8:
Maintaining Gains
and Preventing Relapse

	Check
Session Goals	*When Done*

1. Review (5–10 minutes)   ☐
   - Obtain feedback on Session 7
     ( ) Imaginal exposure and response prevention
   - Review homework
     ( ) Taped imaginal sessions
     ( ) Response prevention tasks
   - Briefly review events that occurred over past week

2. The Session   ☐
   - Discontinuing active treatment
   - Maintaining gains
     ( ) Promoting self-controlled treatment
     ( ) Generalizing effects of treatment
     ( ) Planning lifestyle changes
     ( ) Treatment as a continuing process
     ( ) Tapering treatment
   - Preventing relapse
     ( ) Understanding symptom recurrence
     ( ) Identifying and coping with stressors
     ( ) Overcoming setbacks
     ( ) Joining a support group

3. Next Sessions (5 minutes)   ☐
   - Taper sessions as needed
   - Discuss homework to be completed

SESSION OVERVIEW

Once all the treatment components have been introduced and the patient has reached the desired treatment goals, the focus of therapy becomes one of maintaining gains and preventing relapse. This last session (1) outlines when it is appropriate to discontinue active treatment, (2) details the strategies to help patients preserve what they have learned in treatment, and (3) outlines ways to cope if symptoms recur.

The therapist first reviews the previous week and addresses any problems related to homework assignments. The next phase is spent assessing whether the patient is ready to terminate active treatment. Although this decision process begins well before this last session, the patient is usually given relevant assessment forms before this specific session in order to objectively assess therapy gains and help the decision-making process.

The rest of the session is spent discussing ways to maintain or continue to increase therapeutic gains, and to prevent relapse. The therapist discusses how sessions will be tapered, and encourages patients to continue treatment on their own and to view using the strategies as a process that will continue throughout their lives. The therapist also facilitates the application of treatment to the patient's environment. Specific strategies are then outlined to help patients cope if there is a resurgence of symptoms. The patient is also helped to understand the distinction between a worsening of symptoms and a true relapse, and is taught ways to identify and overcome high-risk moments and setbacks. Homework is assigned at the end of treatment, and sessions are gradually tapered over time.

REVIEW

The therapist inquires about events of the previous week and the previous session. When appropriate, events are tied to any increases in anxiety so that patients are able to link relevant stressors with a worsening of symptoms. Homework assignments are also reviewed. Did the patient use an audiotape loop to conduct imaginal exposure? Did he take any measures to cope with the anxiety generated? Problem areas are discussed and troubleshooting strategies are generated.

THE SESSION: DISCONTINUING ACTIVE TREATMENT

Active treatment is defined as the period when patients learn the required techniques, exhibit a reduction of presenting symptoms and distress associated with symptoms, and display a general improvement in functioning. Specifically, the decision to terminate active treatment is made when patients are experiencing fewer clinically significant obsessions and compulsions, are significantly less distressed about their obsessions and compulsions, are less anxious in general, and are able to function more effectively in their social milieu. Questionnaires such as the Y-BOCS, the BAI, the BDI, and Sheehan Disability Scale, which were used to assess symptom severity prior to treatment, may now be administered again to assess therapy gains. As a general rule of thumb, patients should be experiencing no functional impairment before active treatment is terminated.

Although symptom improvement is an important goal in deciding when to discontinue active treatment, the decision should also be based on patients' readiness to continue therapy on their own. Patient's readiness to guide their own treatment may be determined in many ways, including the following: (1) ability to comply with treatment; (2) ability to tolerate the anxiety associated with treatment, particularly around situations they fear most; (3) ability to recognize the role their avoidance plays in maintaining symptoms; (4) ability to evaluate and direct their own progress; and (5) ability to creatively problem solve when obstacles arise.

Once it is determined that active treatment must be discontinued, the therapist uses the rest of the session (and future sessions) maintaining treatment gains and preventing relapse.

At the end of her active treatment, Allison's symptoms and level of functioning had improved substantially. She scored 10 on the Beck Depression Inventory, 15 on her Beck Anxiety Inventory, and 14 on her Y-BOCS, suggesting that her symptoms were in the mild to minimal range. She expressed minimal anxiety about her obsessions and unwaveringly maintained insight into the senselessness of her symptoms. Her rituals had also drastically reduced, but were still higher than normal. She enrolled in college during active treatment and, after a rocky start, began doing well in her courses. Allison had also begun limited social contact with close friends and—much to her relief—had been able to renew her relationship with her sister-in-law. However, she still experienced anxiety being around strangers. Marital relations were vastly improved as well. Although conflicts still arose periodically between Michael and Allison, they were usually not centered on her symptoms, as they had previously been. Allison stayed compliant with treatment for the most part, but she didn't always succeed in sticking with her ritual-prevention plan the first time it was prescribed. After a few tries, she was usually able to lessen her rituals as prescribed. At the time the decision was made to taper treatment, Allison was still struggling hard with her avoidance but making steady gains. She did all her homework conscientiously and showed tremendous creativity in coming up with new ways to confront her obsessions.

MAINTAINING GAINS AND PREVENTING RELAPSE

Since obsessive-compulsive disorder, like the other anxiety disorders, is usually a chronic condition that often waxes and wanes in severity, individuals suffering from this disorder require techniques to address and manage these symptoms over their lifetime. Research studies show that between two-thirds and three-quarters of patients with obsessive-compulsive disorder respond to behavior therapy, and that many stay better for an extended period of time. However, relapse occurs in a significant number of patients, and thus its prevention should be a focus of attention so that recurrence may be avoided.

The current session focuses on giving the patient tools to maintain therapeutic gains and prevent symptom relapse. Studies show that patients who receive specific maintenance and prevention techniques, such as home sessions, telephone calls, cognitive restructuring, training in self-exposure, and a specific plan to change their lifestyles, maintain greater improvement than patients who do not (Foa 1994).

Maintaining Gains

Promoting Self-Controlled Treatment

Research studies indicate that patients who have some control over their treatment are more likely to maintain gains even after treatment is discontinued than patients whose treatment is directed completely by the therapist (Emmelkamp and Kraanen 1977). There is also evidence that patients who attribute the gains made in treatment to themselves are more likely to do better than patients who attribute their gains to external factors.

Hence, patients should be encouraged to make independent treatment decisions and conduct tasks on their own as soon as they are able. For example, therapist- or family-assisted exposure and response prevention must be tapered as soon as patients are able to tolerate the anxiety associated with these tasks. Patients are praised on their accomplishments and their movement toward independent functioning. Fostering a sense of independence gives patients the confidence and skills they need to continue treatment on their own.

Allison made greater strides in exposure once she decided that it was time to throw out her "safe zones" from her purse. These included an old Xanax (which she never used but carried around), a list of emergency telephone numbers, and a bottle of water. As she began taking risks on her own, and began attributing the success of exposure to herself rather than her "safe zones," Allison's avoidant behaviors declined at a much faster rate.

Generalizing Effects of Treatment

One way to maintain therapy gains is to apply the treatment directly to the patient's environment. Although homework assignments are already built in on an ongoing basis to facilitate generalization, the therapist also utilizes other measures to enhance this process. For example, the therapist may schedule home sessions to see that treatment is being administered correctly and to resolve any areas of difficulty in applying treatments at home.

Although home sessions were occasionally scheduled if warranted by the exposure hierarchy (garbage exposure), the therapist began scheduling regular home sessions toward the end of active treatment to ensure continuity of care. She observed how Allison conducted her self-exposure at home, and in fact sat in on one entire home exposure session without intervening to determine if it was being administered appropriately. The home visit also enabled the therapist to see where and how Allison performed her rituals and how Michael supervised her when she failed to do response prevention. By offering feedback to both, the therapist ensured that Allison and Michael would conduct treatment as intended in the future.

Planning Lifestyle Changes

As active treatment comes to an end, the therapist should also plan for all the lifestyle changes that the patient faces now that his symptoms have subsided. Patients are given detailed guidelines for "normal" behaviors, as many of them have no way of knowing what "appropriate" levels of washing or checking may be. For example, Allison's guidelines did not permit her to say any of her mental rituals or to check her knives. She was allowed to wash her hands once if they were objectively soiled or stained, but no more than four or five times a day. It was also permissible for her to call Michael every now and then if she had something specific to address, but she was not to call him every single day, especially if her anxiety was high.

Patients may also need help in managing the time that was previously spent on obsessive-compulsive symptoms. The therapist can help identify lost hobbies and kindle new interests. As patients are able to perform and enjoy such activities, the therapist can gradually help them to reach other goals as well. For example, a patient may have lost ties with friends, been unable to complete his education, or lost his job. However, these goals should be reached slowly and must be based on an accurate assessment of the patient's capabilities. It is important that the therapist's enthusiasm over the patient's progress not blind them to the patient's true capability. For example, Allison returned to school, something that had long been a goal for her. Although she was ready and had been adequately prepared to face the challenge of academic work, she was ill prepared for the social aspects of college and found it hard to make friends. She felt extremely stressed, experienced a slight worsening of symptoms, and could not concentrate on her classes. In hindsight, the therapist could have helped her mend or develop social contacts on a less intimidating scale before she returned to college. As it was, she was seen more frequently for a few sessions, during which a hierarchy of social exposure was initiated and conducted. Once she felt comfortable being around people, her academic work improved and her symptoms subsided (see Sanderson and McGinn [1997] for a discussion addressing comorbid conditions in patients with anxiety disorders).

Treatment as a Continuing Process

Patients are encouraged to view strategies utilized in treatment as a permanent way of approaching the symptoms for the rest of their lives, and not something they can stop doing when they feel better (just as people who lose weight through dieting must continue dieting to maintain the loss). Toward that goal, the therapist should be sure to spend enough time coaching patients on how to restructure dysfunctional cognitions, particularly when they have obsessional "attacks." The importance of modifying these anxiety-maintaining cognitions each time they occur is also emphasized. Patients are encouraged to see that it is not enough to "know" that their thoughts may be dysfunctional or that there may be other ways to look at the same situation, but that, in order to promote more lasting change, they must actively replace these thoughts with more functional ways of thinking.

Patients are also encouraged to see that avoidance is something they must strive against for the rest of their lives, whether it takes the form of passive maneuvers such as escaping or evading situations, distracting from them, or actually performing rituals. The relationship between avoidance, anxiety, and impairment in functioning is emphasized again, and patients are encouraged to see that confronting feared situations (particularly those related to obsessional triggers) and preventing rituals is a permanent lifetime strategy.

Tapering Treatment

Although some individuals with obsessive-compulsive disorder may terminate therapy and do fine for the rest of their lives, most individuals typically need to be followed in treatment for an extended period of time. Once active treatment is over, sessions are gradually tapered until patients need only come in for booster sessions.

We rarely go from having weekly sessions to discontinuing treatment altogether. Although it varies from patient to patient, we recommend that patients go from weekly to biweekly to once-a-month sessions and so on. Patients may ultimately come in once every three months, six months, or even once a year as they are able to maintain gains on their own for longer and longer periods of time.

Tapering treatment helps reduce relapse for several reasons. First of all, it gives patients the confidence needed to manage on their own while being secure in the knowledge that they are still in treatment. Second, it allows treatment effects to generalize to all aspects of patients' lives, as they directly apply what they learn in therapy to their home environment. Third, since relapse often occurs when patients fail to continue therapeutic work, staying in treatment, however intermittent, serves as a periodic reminder to practice homework in between sessions. And finally, it allows them to resume intensive treatment immediately in the case of relapse or a significant return of symptoms.

Clinical Vignette

THERAPIST: Now that we're going to be seeing each other less frequently, it's very important that you continue to do the therapy work by yourself. Remember, these are healthy habits that have to be incorporated into your life. It's like dieting to lose weight. It never works. People with a weight problem have to change and maintain their new eating habits for the rest of their lives if they want to keep the weight off. That's how it is with you and anxiety—you will always have a tendency toward it. Your OCD may fluctuate up and down, just as weight does for people with a weight problem. The question is, how best to manage it?

ALLISON: So it's something I will always have to do.

THERAPIST: Yes, your symptoms are controlled now. It's as if you're getting closer to normal weight right now, so you will not need to do the treatment at the same intensity that you and I have been doing, but you will still need to do it regularly. For example, because of your OCD, you will always have a tendency to avoid things and ritualize. Just like someone with an eating problem may crave foods. That is something you will have to resist, because you may say, "Why don't I just not go today, I'll do it tomorrow?" Or "Let me just wash my hands this time, I won't do it again." And then before you know it, you're avoiding newspapers, garbage, frequently calling Michael, and checking and checking. We don't want that. The subtle changes here and there can add to a considerable problem, so we will both need to be alert for any patterns.

ALLISON: How do I know that I'm not avoiding something because I don't feel like doing it?

THERAPIST: You'll know. Just ask yourself, am I nervous? If you are, chances are that it's your OCD talking.

ALLISON: Let me write that down.

THERAPIST: And finally, the thoughts. You've come a long way and have become an expert in restructuring all the thoughts that make you feel guilty, sad, and anxious. You are very conscientious about doing that. I would like to see you continue doing that even if it becomes routine and you think, "I know that, I don't have to do it." It will stay routine only if you practice it. But remember not to use the rational dialogue in a ritualized fashion—remember when that happened a few weeks ago?

ALLISON: I know, I have to be careful about that. I have to vary the words if it does become ritualized.

Preventing Relapse

Studies show that patients who exhibit significant improvement (approximately 70 percent) at the end of treatment are less likely to relapse than those who only partially improved (Foa et al. 1983a,b, O'Sullivan et al. 1991). Hence, ensuring that symptoms have decreased significantly at the end of active treatment is perhaps the best way to reduce the risk of relapse. However, several other factors have been implicated in occurrence of relapse, and are reviewed with the patient.

Understanding Symptom Recurrence

Patients' expectancies of cures are once again discussed at the end of active treatment. Patients are informed that obsessive-compulsive disorder is a chronic condition that waxes and wanes in severity over a person's lifetime, usually as a function of stress, so that symptoms may return at different points. However, if symptoms do worsen or recur, it does not mean that patients are now back to where they started, because they have now learned the tools to manage and reduce their symptoms. Patients are also encouraged by the fact that if techniques are applied again, recurring symptoms will probably subside more quickly, since they already have learned the tools to bring about change.

The definition of relapse is further clarified by encouraging patients to differentiate between an actual return to pretreatment symptoms (relapse) versus a worsening of post-treatment symptom levels. To help them decide if they have relapsed or are merely experiencing some symptom worsening, patients are asked to compare their symptoms and functioning to a time six months ago rather than a few days or a week ago. This way, patients learn not to become unduly worried about day-to-day changes and can examine their progress from a more realistic, long-range perspective. Their fears about going back to square one are further addressed by informing them that relapse does not occur suddenly but is a gradual process that occurs if patients slip back into a pattern of avoidance.

Identifying and Coping with Stressors
That Trigger Symptoms

By the end of treatment, the therapist should have gathered sufficient data on what specific life stressors tend to exacerbate the patient's obsessive-compulsive symptoms. Stressors may range from having conflict with family or friends, anxiety about social situations, and occupational stress, to the death of a loved one, and more. Using these data as a guide, the therapist and patient try to identify potential stressors that may come up until they meet again. The therapist reviews with the patient how he would cope with these potential stressors, particularly if the triggers lead to obsessive-compulsive symptoms. The therapist first reinforces the patient's adaptive coping methods, and then may suggest other coping methods that may be used to manage stressful situations (exercise, meditation, cognitive restructuring, not avoiding the stressful situation). The therapist can then help the patient rehearse these coping strategies to facilitate their effectiveness in the event that the stressors occur.

Overcoming Setbacks

If patients experience a resurgence of anxiety during exposure, or a negative outcome (one that occurs directly as a result of exposure or that they associate with exposure), they may decide not to enter the phobic situation again, thereby increasing their risk of eventual relapse. For example, if an individual with contamination fears develops salmonella poisoning, he may decide that he was right all along and that being overly cautious is far better than taking risks.

The best way to minimize relapse is by forewarning patients that negative events will occur in their lives, and that they may also have negative consequences to exposure on occasion. The therapist should then help patients restructure their cognitions regarding the significance of setbacks when they do occur. Depending upon the nature of the setback, patients are helped to see that negative events happen to everyone. Patients are also helped to dissociate the negative event from the exposure task if the two are not objectively related, and to weigh the pros and cons of being cautious versus taking risks. The actual event is itself decatastrophized if it is indeed not objectively catastrophic. If the event is truly catastrophic (e.g., death of brother), patients are helped to cope with it, and are helped to dissociate it from obsessive-compulsive disorder and the treatment process (he died because I have not been checking). Ultimately, patients are helped to confront the exposure situation again while refraining from rituals until they are back to their pre-setback levels of anxiety. If the patient is no longer in active treatment when a setback occurs, the therapist may decide to see the patient more regularly for a few sessions until the patient is back to his post-treatment baseline.

Joining a Support Group

Although support groups are not for everyone, they serve a useful function for many patients and may be a useful bridge between active and maintenance treatment. Patients can share their symptoms with people who know exactly what it is to suffer from obsessive-compulsive disorder, learn coping strategies from other members, and feel empowered by offering support and help to others in the group. A potential downside is that patients may feel depressed at hearing about the misery of others and may feel more hopeless if they learn about more severe cases of OCD. In addition, unless the support group has a cognitive-behavioral focus, the goals of the group may differ from those of your patient. For example, patients who primarily receive medication for their OCD may not be able to provide your patient with the needed support in overcoming avoidance or restructuring cognitions.

If patients appear interested, the pros and cons of support groups are reviewed with them, and the therapist helps them locate support groups or online support networks. A listing of organizations and online links is provided in Chapter 3.

Clinical Vignette

THERAPIST: I know that you worry sometimes that your symptoms will come back. Am I right?

ALLISON: Yes, that's why I'm nervous about cutting down the treatment. I know it's the right thing to do, and I feel ready, but there is a niggling part of me . . .

THERAPIST: And what does the niggling part of you say?

ALLISON: What if I get worse?

THERAPIST: Well, what if? What does worse mean?

ALLISON: What if the symptoms come back and I'm back to square one?

THERAPIST: Your symptoms will go up and down as we discussed. They will usually go up when you're stressed out about something or a major change occurs in your life. It doesn't mean that they will go back to square one, though, and fortunately that doesn't happen overnight. Relapsing to where you were before you began treatment is quite a different matter from the usual ups and downs of obsessive-compulsive disorder. And you will know when it's a true relapse, because it will gradually happen if you don't stick to your treatment. It will not be a surprise.

The ups and downs are an entirely different matter, and you will have to be prepared not to be thrown off by them if your symptoms get worse. And they will, especially if you're under stress. But now you've learned ways to reduce your symptoms on your own, so if your symptoms do increase, they will be back down in no time.

ALLISON: You were saying that we would be writing down a list of things that could stress me out.

THERAPIST: Well, from what I've noted, fights with Michael are a big one, and we know college is another big one right now, particularly around exam time. Being around strangers is also stressful.

ALLISON: (begins writing down).

THERAPIST: Can you think of anything stressful that might come up before we meet in two weeks?

ALLISON: Well, I have an exam.

THERAPIST: And how would you cope with this stress?

ALLISON: I'll study hard, not stay up too late, make sure I don't compare myself to the other students, and try and not be too hard on myself.

THERAPIST: Very good, I'm impressed. You sound very prepared. Perhaps you can also prepare yourself for the fact that you may have a resurgence of symptoms around those few days, but if they recur, it will be temporary and you'll be able to handle them.

ALLISON (writes down): I'll try my best. See you in two weeks.

NEXT SESSION

Sessions may now be tapered as needed, going from once a week to once every other week, and so on. Future sessions involve strengthening patients' prowess in managing their symptoms, and reducing the risk of relapse. Strategies learned in this session will help patients normalize day-to-day changes in symptoms and identify and combat the times when they are vulnerable to a worsening of obsessive-compulsive symptoms. Patients are encouraged to utilize techniques of cognitive restructuring, and exposure and response prevention on a daily basis, whenever anxiety is triggered. Specific homework assignments are given and the next session is scheduled.

✢ References ✢

Abramowitz, J. S. (1997). Effectiveness of psychological and pharmacological treatments for obsessive-compulsive disorder: a quantitative review. *Journal of Consulting and Clinical Psychology* 65(1): 44–52.

American Psychiatric Association (1987). *Diagnostic and Statistical Manual of Mental Disorders* (3rd ed. rev.). Washington, DC: Author.

——— (1994). *Diagnostic and Statistical Manual of Mental Disorders* (4th ed.). Washington, DC: Author.

Baxter, L., Schwartz, J., Guse, B., et al. (1990). Neuroimaging in obsessive-compulsive disorder: seeking the mediating anatomy. In *Obsessive-Compulsive Disorder: Theory and Management*, ed. M. A., Jenike, L. Baer, and W. B. Minichiello, pp. 167–188. Chicago: Year Book Medical Publishers.

Beck, A. T. (1969). Thinking and depression: II. Theory and therapy. *Archives of General Psychiatry* 10:561–571.

——— (1976). *Cognitive Therapy and the Emotional Disorders*. New York: International Universities Press.

Beck, A. T., Epstein, N., and Bron, G. (1988a). An inventory for measuring clinical anxiety. *Journal of Consulting and Clinical Psychology* 56:893–897.

Beck, A. T., Steer, R. A., and Garbin, M. G. (1988b). Psychometric properties of the Beck depression inventory: twenty-five years later. *Clinical Psychology Review* 8:77–100.

Beck, J. S. (1995). *Cognitive Therapy: Basics and Beyond*. New York: Guilford.

Beech, H. R., and Liddell, A. (1974). Decision making, mood states, and ritualistic behavior among obsessional patients. In *Obsessional States*, ed. H. R. Beech, pp. 143–160. London: Methuen.

Billett, E., Richter, M. A., and Kennedy, J. L. (1998). Genetics of obsessive-compulsive disorder. In *Obsessive-Compulsive Disorder: Theory, Research and Treatment*, ed. R. P. Swinson, M. Antony, S. Rachman, and M. A. Richter, pp. 181–206. New York: Guilford.

Black, A. (1974). The natural history of obsessional neurosis. In *Obsessional States*, ed. H. R. Beech, pp. 19–54. London: Methuen.

Boersma, K., Den Hengst, S., Dekker, J., and Emmelkamp, P. M. G. (1976). Exposure and response prevention: a comparison with obsessive compulsive patients. *Behaviour Research and Therapy* 14:19–24.

Boulougouris, J. C., and Bassiakos, L. (1973). Prolonged flooding in cases with obsessive-compulsive neurosis. *Behaviour Research and Therapy* 11:227–231.

Boulougouris, J. C., Rabavilas, A. D., and Stefanis, C. (1977). Psychophysiological responses in obsessive-compulsive patients. *Behaviour Research and Therapy* 15:221–230.

Burns, D. D. (1989). *The Feeling Good Handbook: Using the New Mood Therapy in Everyday Life*. New York: Morrow.

Carr, A. I. (1974). Compulsive neurosis. a review of the literature. *Psychological Bulletin* 8:311–318.

Catts, S., and McConaghy, N. (1975). Ritual prevention in the treatment of obsessive-compulsive neurosis. *Australian and New Zealand Journal of Psychiatry* 9:37–41.

Chambless, D. L., Sanderson, W. C., Shoham, V., et al. (1997). Empirically validated therapies: a project of the division of clinical psychology. American Psychological Association, Task Force on Psychological Interventions. *The Clinical Psychologist* 49(2):5–15.

Charney, D. S., Goodman, W. K., Price, L. H., et al. (1988). Serotonin function in obsessive-compulsive disorder. *Archives of General Psychiatry* 45:177–185.

Chouinard, G., Goodman, W. K., Greist, J., et al. (1990). Results of a double-blind placebo controlled trial of a new serotonin reuptake inhibitor, sertraline, in the treatment of obsessive-compulsive disorder. *Psychopharmacology Bulletin* 26:279–284.

Cobb, J. P., McDonald, R., Marks, I. M., and Stern, R. (1980). Marital versus exposure therapy: psychological treatments of co-existing marital and phobic obsessive problems. *Behavioural Analysis and Modification* 4:3–16.

Crino, R. D., and Andrews, G. (1996). Obsessive-compulsive disorder and Axis I comorbidity. *Journal of Anxiety Disorders* 10:37–46.

Crits-Christoph, P., Frank, E., Chambless, D. L., et al. (1996). Training in empirically validated therapies: What are clinical psychology students learning? *Professional Psychology: Research and Practice* 26(5):514–522.

DeVeaugh-Geiss, J., Katz, R., Landau, P., et al. (1990). Clinical predictors of treatment response in obsessive-compulsive disorder: exploratory analyses from multicenter trials of clomipramine. *Psychopharmacology Bulletin* 26:54–59.

DeVeaugh-Geiss, J., Landau, P., and Katz R. (1989). Treatment of OCD with clomipramine. *Psychiatric Annals* 19:97–101.

Dollard J., and Miller, N. E. (1950). *Personality and Psychotherapy: An Analysis in Terms of Learning, Thinking, and Culture.* New York: McGraw-Hill.

Emmelkamp, P. M. G, and Beens, H. (1991). Cognitive therapy and obsessive-compulsive disorder. a comparative evaluation. *Behaviour Research and Therapy* 29:293–300.

Emmelkamp, P. M. G., deHaan, E., and Hoogduin, C. A. L. (1990). Marital adjustment and obsessive-compulsive disorder. *British Journal of Psychiatry* 156:55–60.

Emmelkamp, P. M. G., Hoekstra, R. J., and Visser, S. (1985). The behavioral treatment of OCD: prediction of outcome at 3.5 years follow-up. In *Psychiatry: The State of the Art*, ed. P. Pichot, P. Berner, R. Wolf, and K. Thau. New York: Plenum.

Emmelkamp, P. M. G., and Kraanen, J. (1977). Therapist-controlled exposure in vivo versus self-controlled exposure in vivo: a comparison with obsessive-compulsive patients. *Behaviour Research and Therapy* 21:341–346.

Emmelkamp, P. M. G., and Kwee, K. G. (1977). Obsessional ruminations: a comparison between thought stopping and prolonged exposure in imagination. *Behaviour Research and Therapy* 15:441–444.

Emmelkamp, P. M., van den Heuvell, C. V. L., Ruphan, M., and Sanderman, R. (1989). Home-based treatment of obsessive-compulsive patients: intersession interval and therapist involvement. *Behaviour Research and Therapy* 27:89–93.

Emmelkamp, P. M., van der Helm, M., van Zanten, B. L., and Plochg, I. (1980). Contributions of self-instructional training to the effectiveness of exposure in vivo: a comparison with obsessive-compulsive patients. *Behaviour Research and Therapy* 18:61–66.

Emmelkamp, P. M., Visser, S., and Hoekstra, R. J. (1988). Cognitive therapy vs. exposure in vivo in the treatment of obsessive-compulsives. *Cognitive Therapy and Research* 12:103–114.

Fals-Stewart, W., Marks, A. P., and Schafer, J. (1993). A comparison of behavioral group therapy and individual behavior therapy in treating obsessive-compulsive disorder. *Journal of Nervous and Mental Disease* 181:345–350.

Foa, E. B. (1994). *Recent findings on the efficacy of behavior therapy and clomipramine for obsessive-compulsive disorder.* Paper presented at the annual meeting of the Anxiety Disorders Association of America, Santa Monica, CA, March.

Foa, E. B., Franklin, E. B., and Kozak, M. J. (1998). Psychosocial treatments for obsessive-compulsive disorder: literature review. In *Obsessive-Compulsive Disorder: Theory, Research and Treatment*, ed. R. P. Swinson, M. Antony, S. Rachman, and M. A. Richter, pp. 258–276. New York: Guilford.

Foa, E. B., and Goldstein, A. (1978). Continuous exposure and response prevention of obsessive-compulsive disorder. *Behavior Therapy* 9:821–829.

Foa, E. B., Grayson, J. B., and Steketee, G. S. (1982). Depression, habituation and treatment outcome in obsessive-compulsives. In *Practical Applications of Learning Theories in Psychiatry*, ed. J. C. Boulougouris, pp. 129–142. New York: Wiley.

Foa, E. B., Grayson, J. B., Steketee, G. S., et al. (1983a). Success and failure in the behavioral treatment of obsessive-compulsives. *Journal of Consulting and Clinical Psychology* 51:287–297.

Foa, E. B., Grayson, J. B., Steketee, G. S., and Doppelt, H. G. (1983b). Treatment of obsessive-compulsives: When do we fail? In *Failures in Behavior Therapy*, ed., E. Foa and P. M. G. Emmelkamp, pp. 10–34. New York: Wiley.

Foa, E. B., and Kozak, M. J. (1985). Treatment of anxiety disorders: implications for psychopathology. In *Anxiety and the Anxiety Disorders*, ed. A. H. Tuma and J. D. Maser, pp. 421–452. Hillsdale, NJ: Lawrence Erlbaum.

——— (1986). Emotional processing of fear: exposure to corrective information. *Psychological Bulletin* 44:20–35.

Foa, E. B., Kozak, M. J., Steketee, G. S., and McCarthy, P. R. (1992). Imipramine and behavior therapy in the treatment of obsessive-compulsive symptoms: immediate and long-term effects. *British Journal of Clinical Psychology* 31:279–292.

Foa, E. B., McNally, R., Steketee, G. S., and McCarthy, P. R. (1991). A test of preparedness theory in anxiety-disordered patients using an avoidance paradigm. *Journal of Psychophysiology* 5:159–163.

Foa, E. B., Steketee, G. S., Grayson, J. B., et al. (1984). Deliberate exposure and blocking of obsessive-compulsive rituals: immediate and long-term effects. *Behavior Therapy* 15:450–472.

Foa, E. B., Steketee, G. S., and Milby, J. B. (1980a). Differential effects of exposure and response prevention in obsessive-compulsive washers. *Journal of Consulting and Clinical Psychology* 48:71–79.

Foa, E. B., Steketee, G. S., and Ozarow, B. (1985). Behavior therapy with obsessive-compulsives: from theory to treatment. In *Obsessive-Compulsive Disorder: Psychological and Pharmacological Treatment*, ed. M. Mavissakalian, pp. 49–129. New York: Plenum.

Foa, E. B., Steketee, G. S., Turner, R. M., and Fischer, S. C. (1980b). Effects of imaginal exposure to feared disasters in obsessive-compulsive checkers. *Behaviour Research and Therapy* 18:449–455.

Foa, E. B., and Tillmans, A. (1980). The treatment of obsessive-compulsive neurosis. In *Handbook of Behavioral Interventions: A Clinical Guide*, ed. A. Goldstein and E. B. Foa, pp. 416–500. New York: Wiley.

Foa, E. B., and Wilson, R. (1991). *Stop Obsessing! How to Overcome Your Obsessions and Compulsions.* New York: Bantam.

Fontaine R., and Chouinard, G. (1985). Fluoxetine in the treatment of obsessive-compulsive disorder. *Progress in Neuropsychopharmacology and Biological Psychiatry* 9:605–608.

Freeston, M. (1994). Characteristiques et traitement de l'obsession sans compulsion manifeste. Unpublished thesis. Université Laval, Quebec.

Goodman, W. K., Price, L. H., Delgado, P. L., et al. (1990). Specificity of serotonin reuptake inhibitors in the treatment of obsessive-compulsive disorder: comparison of fluvoxamine and desipramine. *Archives of General Psychiatry* 47:577–585.

Goodman, W. K., Price, L. H., Rasmussen, S. A., et al. (1989a). Efficacy of fluvoxamine in obsessive-compulsive disorder: a double-blind comparison with placebo. *Archives of General Psychiatry* 46:36–44.

Goodman, W. K., Price, L. H., Rasmussen, S. A., et al. (1989b). The Yale-Brown Obsessive-Compulsive Scale. I. Development, use and reliability. *Archives of General Psychiatry* 46:1006–1011.

Goodman, W. K., Price, L. H., Rasmussen, S. A., et al. (1989c). The Yale-Brown Obsessive-Compulsive Scale. II. Validity. *Archives of General Psychiatry* 46:1012–1016.

Greist, J. H. (1990). Treatment of obsessive-compulsive disorder:

psychotherapies, drugs, and other somatic treatments. *Journal of Clinical Psychiatry* 51:44–50.

———— (1994). *Update on the treatment of obsessive-compulsive disorder: pharmacotherapy.* Paper presented at the annual meeting of the Anxiety Disorders Association of America, Santa Monica, CA, March.

Greist, J. H., Chouinard, G., Duboff, E., et al. (1995). Double-blind comparison of three dosages of sertraline and placebo in the treatment of outpatients with obsessive-compulsive disorder. *Archives of General Psychiatry* 52:289–295.

Greist, J. H., Jefferson, J. W., Rosenfeld, R., et al. (1990). Clomipramine and obsessive-compulsive disorder: a placebo-controlled double-blind study of 32 patients. *Journal of Clinical Psychiatry* 51:292–297.

Guidano, V. L., and Liotti, G. (1983). *Cognitive Processing and the Emotional Disorders.* New York: Guilford.

Headland, K., and McDonald, R. (1987). Rapid audio-tape treatment of obsessional ruminations: a case report. *Behavioural Psychotherapy* 15:188–192.

Hodgson, R. J., and Rachman, S. (1972). The effects of contamination and washing in obsessional patients. *Behaviour Research and Therapy* 10:111–117.

Hodgson, R. J., Rachman, S., and Marks, I. (1972). The treatment of chronic obsessive-compulsive neurosis: follow-up and further findings. *Behaviour Research and Therapy* 10:181–189.

Hoogduin, C. A. L., and Hoogduin, W. A. (1984). The outpatient treatment of patients with an obsessional-compulsive disorder. *Behaviour Research and Therapy* 22:455–459.

Hornsveld, R. H. J., Kraaimaat, F. W., and van Dam-Baggen, R. M. J. (1979). Anxiety/discomfort and handwashing in obsessive-compulsive and psychiatric control patients. *Behaviour Research and Therapy* 17:223–228.

Ingram, I. M. (1961). Obsessional illness in mental hospital patients. *Journal of Mental Science* 107:382–402.

Insel, T. R., Murphy, D. L., Cohen, R. M., et al. (1983). Obsessive-compulsive disorder: a double-blind trial of clomipramine and clorgyline. *Archives of General Psychiatry* 40:605–612.

Jakes, I. (1996). Theoretical approaches to obsessive-compulsive disorder (problems in the behavioral sciences). Cambridge, England: Cambridge University Press.

Jenike, M. A., Baer, L., Summergrad, P., et al. (1989a). Obsessive-compulsive disorder: a double-blind placebo-controlled trial of clomipramine in 27 patients. *American Journal of Psychiatry* 147: 923–928.

———— (1990b). Sertraline in obsessive-compulsive disorder: a double-blind comparison with placebo. *American Journal of Psychiatry* 147:923–928.

Jenike, M. A., Buttolph, L., Baer, L., et al. (1989b). Open trial of fluoxetine in obsessive-compulsive disorder. *American Journal of Psychiatry* 146:909–911.

Jenike, M. A., Hyman, S., Baer, L., et al. (1990a). A controlled trial of fluvoxamine in obsessive-compulsive disorder: implications for a serotonergic theory. *American Journal of Psychiatry* 147:1209–1215.

Julien, R. A., Riviere, B., and Note, I. D. (1980). Traitement comportemental et cognitif des obsessions et compulsions: resultats et discussion. *Seance du Lundi* 27:1123–1133.

Karno, M., Golding, J. M., Sorenson, S. B., and Burnam, M. A., (1988). The epidemiology of obsessive-compulsive disorder in five US communities. *Archives of General Psychiatry* 45:1094–1099.

Kasvikis, Y., and Marks, I. M. (1988). Clomipramine, self-exposure, and therapist-accompanied exposure in obsessive-compulsive ritualizers: two year follow-up. *Journal of Anxiety Disorders* 2:291–298.

Katz, R. J., DeVeaugh-Geiss, J., and Landau, P. (1990). Clomipramine in obsessive-compulsive disorder. *Biological Psychiatry* 28: 401–414.

Kearney, C. A., and Silverman, W. K. (1990). Treatment of an adolescent with obsessive-compulsive disorder by alternating response prevention and cognitive therapy: an empirical analysis. *Journal of Behavior Therapy and Experimental Psychiatry* 21:39–47.

Khanna, S., Kaliaperumal, V. G., and Channabasavanna, S. M. (1986). Reactive factors in obsessional compulsive neurosis. *Indian Journal of Psychological Medicine* 9:68–73.

Knight, R. P. (1949). Evaluation of results of psychoanalytic therapy. *American Journal of Psychiatry* 98:434–446.

Kozak, M. J., Foa, E. B., and McCarthy, P. R. (1987). Assessment of obsessive-compulsive disorder. In *Handbook of Anxiety Disorders*, ed. C. Last and M. Hersen. Elmsford, NY: Pergamon.

Kringlen, E. (1965). Obsessional neurotics: a long-term follow-up. *British Journal of Psychiatry* 111:709–722.

Lang P. J. (1979). A bio-informational theory of emotional imagery. *Psychophysiology* 6:495–511.

Leon, A. C., Shear, M. K., Portera, L., and Klerman, G. L. (1992). Assessing impairment in patients with panic disorder: the Sheehan Disability Scale. *Social Psychiatry and Psychiatric Epidemiology* 27:78–82.

Lo, W. H. (1967). A follow-up study of obsessional neurotics in Hong Kong Chinese. *British Journal of Psychiatry* 113:823–832.

Malan, D. (1979). *Individual Psychotherapy and the Science of Psychodynamics*. London: Butterworth.

Mallya, G. K., White, K., Waternaux, C., and Quay, S. (1992). Short- and long-term treatment of obsessive-compulsive disorder with fluvoxamine. *Annals of Clinical Psychiatry* 4: 77–80.

Marks, I. M. (1977). Recent results of behavioral treatment of phobias and obsessions. *Journal of Internal Medicine Research* 5:16–21.

Marks, I. M., Hodgson, R., and Rachman, S. (1975). Treatment of chronic obsessive-compulsive neurosis in vivo exposure: a 2-year follow-up and issues in treatment. *British Journal of Psychiatry* 127:349–364.

Marks, I. M., Lelliott, P., Basoglu, M., et al. (1988). Clomipramine, self-exposure and therapist-aided exposure for obsessive compulsive rituals. *British Journal of Psychiatry* 152:522–534.

Marks, I. M., Stern, R. S., Mawson, D., et al. (1980). Clomipramine and exposure for obsessive-compulsive rituals—I. *British Journal of Psychiatry* 136:1–25.

Mavissakalian, M., Jones, B., Olson, S., and Perel, J. M. (1990). Clomipramine in obsessive-compulsive disorder: clinical response and plasma levels. *Journal of Clinical Psychopharmacology* 10:261–268.

McCarthy, P., and Foa, E. B. (1990). Treatment interventions for obsessive-compulsive disorder. In *Handbook of Outpatient Treatment for Adults*, ed. M. Thase, B. Edelstein, and M. Hersen, pp. 209–234. New York: Plenum.

McFall, M. E., and Wollersheim, J. P. (1979). Obsessive-compulsive neurosis: a cognitive behavioral formulation and approach to treatment. *Cognitive Therapy and Research* 3:333–348.

Meyer, V. (1966). Modification of expectation in cases with obsessional rituals. *Behaviour Research and Therapy* 4:273–280.

Meyer, V., and Levy, R. (1973). Modification of behavior in obsessive-compulsive disorders. In *Issues and Trends in Behavior Therapy*, ed. H. E. Adams and P. Unikel, pp. 77–138. Springfield, IL: Charles C Thomas.

Meyer, V., Levy, R., and Schnurer, A. (1974). The behavioural treatment of obsessive-compulsive disorders. In *Obsessional States*, ed. H. R. Beech, pp. 233–258. London: Methuen.

Mills, H. L., Agras, W. S., Barlow, D. H., and Mills, J. R. (1973). Compulsive rituals treated by response prevention. *Archives of General Psychiatry* 28:524–527.

Montgomery, S. A., McIntyre, A., Osterheider, M., et al. (1993). A double-blind, placebo-controlled study of fluoxetine in patients with *DSM-III-R* obsessive-compulsive disorder. *European Neuropsychopharmacology* 3:142–152.

Moras, K., DiNardo, P. A., Brown, T. A., and Barlow, D. H. (1994). *Comorbidity, functional impairment, and depression among the DSM-III-R anxiety disorders.* Unpublished manuscript.

Mowrer, O. A. (1939). A stimulus-response analysis of anxiety and its role as a reinforcing agent. *Psychological Review* 46:553–565.

———— (1960). *Learning Theory and Behavior.* New York: Wiley.

O'Sullivan, G., Noshirvani, H., Marks, I., et al. (1991). Six-year follow-up after exposure and clomipramine therapy for obsessive-compulsive disorder. *Journal of Clinical Psychiatry* 52:150–155.

Pato, M. T., Zohar-Kadouch, R. Zohar, J., and Murphy, D. L. (1988). Return of symptoms after discontinuation of clomipramine in patients with obsessive-compulsive disorder. *American Journal of Psychiatry* 145:1521–1525.

Perse, T. L. (1988). Obsessive-compulsive disorder: a treatment review. *Journal of Clinical Psychiatry* 49:48–55.

Perse, T. L., Greist, J. H., Jefferson, J. W., et al. (1987). Fluvoxamine treatment of obsessive-compulsive disorder. *American Journal of Psychiatry* 144:1543–1548.

Pitman, R. K. (1987). A cybernetic model of obsessive-compulsive psychopathology. *Comprehensive Psychiatry* 28:334–343.

Price, L. H., Goodman, W. K., Charney, D. S., et al. (1987). Treatment of severe obsessive-compulsive disorder with fluvoxamine. *American Journal of Psychiatry* 144:1050–1061.

Rabavilas, A. D., and Boulougouris, J. C. (1974). Physiological accompaniments of ruminations, flooding and thought stopping in obsessive patients. *Behaviour Research and Therapy* 12:239–243.

Rabavilas, A. D., Boulougouris, J. C., and Stefanis, C. (1976). Duration of flooding sessions in the treatment of obsessive-compulsive patients. *Behaviour Research and Therapy* 14:349–355.

Rachman S. (1993). Obsessions, responsibility and guilt. *Behaviour Research and Therapy* 31:149–154.

Rachman, S. and DeSilva, P. (1978). Abnormal and normal obsessions. *Behaviour Research and Therapy* 31:149–154.

Rachman, S. J., and Hodgson, R. (1980) *Obsessions and Compulsions.* Englewood, NJ: Prentice Hall.

Rachman, S. J., Hodgson, R., and Marks, I. M. (1971). The treatment of chronic obsessive-compulsive neurosis. *Behaviour Research and Therapy* 9:237–247.

Rachman, S. J., Marks, I. M., and Hodgson, R. (1973). The treatment of obsessive-compulsive neurotics by modelling and flooding in vivo. *Behaviour Research and Therapy* 9:237–247.

Rachman, S., and Wilson, G. T. (1980). *The Effects of Psychological Therapy.* Oxford, England: Pergamon.

Rasmussen, S. A., and Eisen, J. L. (1990). Epidemiology of obsessive-compulsive disorder. *Journal of Clinical Psychiatry* 51(2 suppl):10–13.

———— (1992). The epidemiology and differential diagnosis of obsessive-compulsive disorder. *Journal of Clinical Psychiatry* 53 (4 Suppl):4–10.

Rasmussen, S. A., and Tsuang, M. T. (1986). Clinical characteristics and family history in *DSM-III* obsessive-compulsive disorder. *American Journal of Psychiatry* 143(3):317–322.

Reed, G. E. (1985). *Obsessional Experience and Compulsive Behavior: A Cognitive Structural Approach.* Orlando, FL: Academic Press.

Riggs, D. S., and Foa, E. B. (1993). Obsessive-compulsive disorder. In *Clinical Handbook of Psychological Disorders,* ed. D. H. Barlow, pp. 189–239. New York: Guilford.

Riggs, D. S., Hiss, H., and Foa, E. B. (1992). Marital distress and the treatment of obsessive-compulsive disorder. *Behavior Therapy* 23:585–597.

Robins, L. N., Helzer, J. E., Weissman, M. M., et al. (1984). Lifetime prevalence of specific disorders in three sites. *Archives of General Psychiatry* 41:949–958.

Roper, G., and Rachman, S. (1976). Obsessional-compulsive checking: experimental replication and development. *Behaviour Research and Therapy* 14:25–32.

Roper, G., Rachman S., and Hodgson, R. (1973). An experiment on obsessional checking. *Behaviour Research and Therapy* 11:271–277.

Roper, G., Rachman, S., and Marks, I. M. (1975). Passive and participant modelling in exposure treatment of obsessive-compulsive neurotics. *Behaviour Research and Therapy* 13:271–279.

Roth, A. D., and Church, J. A. (1994). The use of revised habituation in the treatment of obsessive-compulsive disorders. *British Journal of Clinical Psychology* 33:201–204.

Rudin, E. (1953). Ein beitrag zur frage der zwangskranheit insebesondere ihrere hereditaren beziehungen. *Archiv fur Psychiatrie und Nervenkrankheiten* 191:14–54.

Salkovskis, P. M. (1983). Treatment of an obsessional patient using habituation to audiotaped ruminations. *British Journal of Clinical Psychology* 22:311–313.

——— (1985). Obsessional compulsive problems: *Behaviour Research and Therapy* 23:571–583.

——— (1989). Cognitive-behavioral factors and the persistence of intrusive thoughts in obsessive-compulsive problems. *Behaviour Research and Therapy* 23:571–583.

Salkovskis P. M., and Kirk, J. (1997). Obsessive-compulsive disorder. In *Science and Practice of Cognitive Behaviour Therapy,* ed. D. M. Clark and C. G. Fairburn, pp. 179–208. Oxford, England: Oxford University Press.

Salkovskis, P. M., and Warwick, H. M. C. (1985). Cognitive therapy of obsessive-compulsive disorder: treating treatment failures. *Behavioral Psychotherapy* 13:243–255.

——— (1986). Morbid preoccupations, health anxiety, and reassurance: a cognitive-behavioral approach to hypochondriasis. *Behavior Research and Therapy* 24: 597–602.

Salkovskis, P. M., and Westbrook, D. (1989). Behaviour therapy and obsessional ruminations: Can failure be turned into success? *Behaviour Research and Therapy* 27:149–160.

Sanderson, W. C., DiNardo, P. A., Rapee, R. M., and Barlow, D. H. (1990). Syndrome comorbidity in patients diagnosed with a *DSM-III-R* anxiety disorder. *Journal of Abnormal Psychology* 99(3):308–312.

Sanderson, W. C., and McGinn, L. K. (1997). Psychological treatments of anxiety disorder patients with comorbidity. In *Treatment Strategies for Patients with Psychiatric Comorbidity*, ed. S. Wetzler and W. C. Sanderson, pp. 75–104. New York: Wiley.

Sasson, Y., Zohar, J., Chopra, M., Lustig, M., et al. (1997). Epidemiology of obsessive-compulsive disorder: a world view. *Journal of Clinical Psychiatry* 58(12):7–10.

Spitzer, R. L., Williams, J. B. W., Gibbons, M., and First, M. B. (1992). *The Structured Clinical Interview for the* DSM-III-R–*Patient Edition* (SCID-P Version 1.0). Washington, DC: American Psychiatric Press.

Stein, D. J., Hollander, E., Mullen, L. S., et al. (1992). Comparison of clomipramine, alprazolam, and placebo in the treatment of obsessive-compulsive disorder. *Human Psychopharmacology* 7: 389–395.

Stein, M. B., Forde, D. R., Anderson, G., and Walker, J. R. (1997). Obsessive-compulsive disorder in the community: an epidemiologic survey with clinical reappraisal. *American Journal of Psychiatry* 154(8):1120–1126.

Steiner, J. (1972). A questionnaire study of risk-taking in psychiatric patients. *British Journal of Medical Psychology* 45:365–374.

Steketee G. S. (1993). *Treatment of Obsessive-compulsive disorder*. New York: Guilford.

Steketee, G. S., Foa, E. B., and Grayson, J. B. (1982). Recent advances in the behavioral treatment of obsessive-compulsives. *Archives of General Psychiatry* 39:1365–1371.

Steketee, G. S., Quay, S., and White, K. (1991). Religion and guilt in OCD patients. *Journal of Anxiety Disorders* 5:359–367.

Stern, R. S. (1978). Obsessive thoughts: the problem of therapy. *British Journal of Psychiatry* 133:200–205.

Thoren, P., Asberg, M., Cronholm, B., et al. (1980). Clomipramine treatment of obsessive-compulsive disorder: a controlled clinical trial. *Archives of General Psychiatry* 37:1282–1285.

Tollefson, G. D., Rampey, A. H., Potvin, J. H., et al. (1994). A multicenter investigation of fixed-dose fluoxetine in the treatment of obsessive-compulsive disorder. *Archives of General Psychiatry* 51:559–567.

Turner, S. M., Hersen, M., Bellack, A. S., et al. (1980). Behavioral and pharmacological treatment of obsessive-compulsive disorders. *Journal of Nervous and Mental Disease* 168:651–657.

Tynes, L. I., White, K., and Steketee, G. S. (1990). Toward a new nosology of OCD. *Comprehensive Psychiatry* 31: 465–480.

van Oppen, P., de Haan, E., van Balkom, A. J., et al. (1995). Cognitive therapy and exposure in vivo in the treatment of obsessive-compulsive disorder. *Behaviour Research and Therapy* 33:379–390.

Warren, R., and Zgourides, G. D. (1991). *Anxiety Disorders: A Rational-Emotive Perspective*. Elmsford, NY: Pergamon.

Wegner, D. M. (1989). *White Bears and Unwanted Thoughts*. New York: Viking Penguin.

Weissman, M. M., Bland, R. C., Canino, G. J., et al. (1994). The cross-national epidemiology of obsessive-compulsive disorder. *Journal of Clinical Psychiatry* 53(3):5–10.

Wetzler, S. and Sanderson, W. C. (1997). *Treatment Strategies for Patients with Psychiatric Comorbidity*. New York: Wiley.

Yaryura-Tobias, J., Todaro, J., Grunes, M. S., et al. (1996). *Comorbidity versus continuum of Axis I disorders in OCD*. Paper presented at the annual meeting of the Association for the Advancement of Behavior Therapy, New York, NY, November.

Zohar, J., and Insel, T. R. (1987). Drug treatment of obsessive-compulsive disorder. *Journal of Affective Disorders* 13:193–202.

Zohar, J., and Judge, R. (1996). Paroxetine versus clomipramine in the treatment of obsessive-compulsive disorder. *British Journal of Psychiatry* 169:468–474.

✂ Index ✂

Abramowitz, J. S., 64, 66
Abstinence, prevention method, exposure and response prevention (phase I), 191–192
American Psychiatric Association (APA), 3, 57
Anxiety Disorders Association of America, 59
Anxiety-provoking scenes, construction of, exposure and response prevention (phase I), 183–185
Anxiety triggers, information collection, 28–34
Assessment, 15–45
  case example, 17–18
  diagnosis, 20–27
    comorbidity, 25–27
    principal diagnosis, 20–25
  information collection, 28–44. *See also* Information collection
  presentation of findings, 44
  session goals, 16
  session overview, 18
  therapeutic alliance, 19–20
Associations, psychoeducation, 59

Assumptions, beliefs and, automatic thoughts, cognitive restructuring (phase II), 115–119
Automatic thoughts
  assumptions and beliefs, cognitive restructuring (phase II), 115–119
  cognitive restructuring (phase I), 91–107. *See also* Cognitive restructuring
  identification of, 78
  linking feelings and behaviors to, cognitive restructuring (phase II), 113–115
  revision of, cognitive restructuring (phase II), 110, 139–146
  validity of, cognitive restructuring (phase II), 121–135
Avoidance, rituals and, information collection, 36–38

Bassiakos, L., 64
Baxter, L., 58
Beck, A. T., xi, 8, 11, 24, 80, 135

Beck, J., 11, 93, 115, 117, 118, 122, 135
Beck Anxiety Inventory, 24
Beck Depression Inventory, 24
Beech, H. R., 8, 80, 82
Beens, H., 65
Behavioral models, obsessive-compulsive disorder, 6–7
Behaviors, linking automatic thoughts and feelings to, cognitive restructuring (phase II), 113–115
Behavior therapy, psychoeducation, 64–65
Belief system
  assumptions and, automatic thoughts, cognitive restructuring (phase II), 115–119
  cognitive restructuring rationale, 80–84
  linking automatic thoughts, feelings, and behaviors, 113–115
Bibliography, psychoeducation, 59
Billett, E., 58
Biology, psychoeducation, 58
Black, A., 60
Boersma, K., 64
Boulougouris, J. C., 5, 7, 64
Burns, D. D., 79, 135

Carr, A. I., 8, 80, 81
Catastrophic fears
  hierarchy of, exposure and response prevention (phase I), 176–178, 183–185
  information collection, 34–36

Catts, S., 64
Charney, D. S., 58
Chronic condition, psychoeducation, 57
Church, J. A., 65
Classical conditioning model, obsessive-compulsive disorder, 6–7
Clomipramine, 61
Cobb, J. P., 64
Cognitive-behavioral model, 5–13
  DSM-IV, 3–4
  obsessive-compulsive disorder, 5–13
  treatment rationale, 11–13
Cognitive-behavior therapy. *See also* Cognitive restructuring
  psychoeducation, 64–68
  treatment components, 68–70
  treatment expectations and goals, 71
Cognitive restructuring
  described, 11–12
  treatment components, 69
Cognitive restructuring (phase I), 77–108
  automatic thoughts, 91–107
    clinical vignette, 94–97, 99–107
    defined, 91–93
    monitoring of, 97–99
    obsessive-compulsive disorder and, 93–94
  automatic thoughts identification, 78
  clinical vignette, 84–91
  complications, 107–108
  rationale, 80–84

review of previous session, 79–80
session overview, 79
Cognitive restructuring (phase II), 109–151
automatic thought modification and revision, 139–146
clinical vignette, 143–146
guidelines for, 141–143
automatic thoughts in larger framework, 115–119
automatic thoughts revision, 110
clinical vignette, 119–120
complications, 150–151
distortions identification, 135–139
linking automatic thoughts, feelings, and behaviors, 113–115
review of previous session, 111, 113
revised thought assessment, 149
session overview, 111
validity of automatic thoughts, 121–135
clinical vignette, 126–135
guidelines for, 122–126
Cognitive theories, obsessive-compulsive disorder, 8–10
Cognitive therapy, psychoeducation, 65–66
Comorbidity, diagnosis, 25–27
Compliance, response prevention, imaginal exposure, 242–243
Co-therapist
response prevention, 217–218
selection of, 72

Course of disorder, psychoeducation, 55–59
Daily functioning level
information collection, 40–41
psychoeducation, 59
DeSilva, P., 56, 81
DeVeaugh-Geiss, J., 61
Diagnosis, 20–27
comorbidity, 25–27
principal diagnosis, 20–25
Distortions identification, cognitive restructuring (phase II), 135–139
Distraction, response prevention, 219
DSM-IV
insight degree, 38
obsessive-compulsive disorder, 3–4, 13
principal diagnosis, 20–25
psychoeducation, 51–53
Eisen, J. L., 55, 57
Emmelkamp, P. M. G., 59, 64, 65, 218, 262
Epidemiology, psychoeducation, 55–59
Ethnicity, psychoeducation, 56
Etiology, psychoeducation, 59–60
Exposure and response prevention (phase I), 153–202
anxiety-provoking scenes construction, 183–185
clinical vignette, 161–164, 170–173, 178–183, 185–187, 195–201
hierarchy of catastrophic fears, 176–178

Exposure and response prevention
    (phase I) (*continued*)
  imaginal exposure preparation,
    173, 175–176
  imaginal or in vivo exposure,
    164–167
  prevention method, 190–195
    abstinence, 191–192
    graded response prevention,
      192–195
    strategy outline, 195
  rationale, 157–161
  rationale and preparation, 154
  response prevention
    preparation, 187–190
  review of previous session,
    155–156
  ritual list preparation, 190
  session overview, 155
  in vivo exposure preparation,
    168–173, 174–175
Exposure and response prevention
    (phase II), 203–231
  clinical vignette, 222–231
  future sessions, 221–222
  response prevention, 214–222
    conducting of, 215–221
    defined, 214
    goals of, 214
  review of previous session, 206
  session overview, 205–206
  in vivo exposure, 204, 207–214
    conducting of, 209–214
    defined, 208
    goal of, 207–208
Exposure and response prevention
    (phase III), 233–256
  clinical vignette, 244–254
  future sessions, 241

imaginal exposure, 236–241
  conducting of, 234, 238–241
  defined, 236–238
  goal of, 236
response prevention with
  imaginal exposure, 241–
  244
review of previous session,
  235–236
session overview, 235
Exposure techniques
  described, 12
  psychoeducation, 65
  treatment components, 69–70
External anxiety triggers,
  information collection, 32–33

Fals-Stewart, W., 64
Feelings, linking automatic
  thoughts and behaviors to,
  cognitive restructuring
  (phase II), 113–115
Flash cards, response prevention,
  218
Fluoxetine, 63
Fluvoxamine, 63
Foa, E. B., xi, 3, 7, 8, 9, 12, 13,
  25, 32, 33, 34, 38, 41, 57,
  61, 64, 65, 80, 81, 156, 165,
  191, 195, 262, 267
Freeston, M., 65
Functional impairment. *See* Daily
  functioning level

Gains maintenance. *See*
  Maintenance and relapse
  prevention
Gender differences,
  psychoeducation, 56

Generalization, gains
maintenance, 263
Genetics, psychoeducation,
58
Goldstein, A., 64, 165
Goodman, W. K., 19, 20, 54
Graded response prevention,
prevention method, exposure
and response prevention
(phase I), 192–195
Greist, J. H., 61
Guidano, V. L., 8, 80, 82

Habituation, response prevention,
imaginal exposure, 243–244
Headland, K., 65
Hierarchy of catastrophic fears,
exposure and response
prevention (phase I), 176–
178, 183–185
Hierarchy of obsessive fears, in
vivo exposure preparation,
exposure and response
prevention (phase I), 168–
169, 183–185
Hodgson, R. J., 5, 7, 41, 57, 64
Homework, psychoeducation,
71–73
Hoogduin, C. A. L., 64
Hoogduin, W. A., 64
Hornsveld, R. H. J., 5, 7

Imaginal exposure
conducting of, 234, 238–241
defined, 236–238
goal of, 236
preparation for, exposure and
response prevention
(phase I), 173, 175–176

in vivo exposure or, exposure
and response prevention
(phase I), 164–167
Information collection, 28–44
anxiety triggers, 28–34
avoidance and rituals, 36–38
catastrophic fears, 34–36
daily functioning level, 40–41
insight degree, 38–40
mood state, 41
onset and course of disorder,
41–42
patient motivation and
expectation, 43
prior treatments, 42–43
treatment eligibility, 44, 45
Information processing model,
obsessive-compulsive
disorder, 8–9
Ingram, I. M., 59
Insel, T. R., 61
Insight, degree of, information
collection, 38–40
Internal anxiety triggers,
information collection, 33–34
In vivo exposure
conducting of, 209–214
defined, 208
goal of, 207–208
imaginal exposure or, exposure
and response prevention
(phase I), 164–167
preparation for, exposure and
response prevention (phase
I), 168–173, 174–175

Jakes, I., 8, 10
Jenike, M. A., 61
Julien, R. A., 64

Karno, M., 41, 55, 56
Kasvikis, Y., 65
Katz, R. J., 61
Kearney, C. A., 65
Khanna, S., 59
Kirk, J., 11, 65, 66
Knight, R. P., 60
Kozak, M. J., 7, 8, 9, 80, 81, 82
Kraanen, J., 64, 218, 262
Kringlen, E., 59
Kwee, K. G., 65

Lang, P. J., 8
Leon, A. C., 25, 40
Levy, R., 64
Liddell, A., 8, 80, 82
Lifestyle changes, gains
    maintenance, 263–264
Liotti, G., 8, 80, 82
Lo, W. H., 59

Maintenance and relapse
    prevention, 257–272
  active treatment discontinued,
    260–261
  clinical vignette, 266–267,
    270–272
  gains maintenance, 262–266
  relapse prevention, 267–270
  review of previous session,
    259–260
  session goals, 258
  session overview, 259
Maintenance of symptoms,
    psychoeducation, 59–60
Malan, D., 60
Marks, I. M., 41, 61, 64, 65
Mavissakalian, M., 61
McCarthy, P., 61

McConaghy, N., 64
McDonald, R., 65
McFall, M. E., 8, 80, 82
McGinn, L. K., 264
Medication, psychoeducation,
    61–64
Meyer, V., 64
Mills, H. L., 65
Minorities, psychoeducation, 56
Mood state, information
    collection, 41
Motivation
  of patient, information
    collection, 43
  response prevention, 216–217
Mowrer, O. A., 6, 7

Obsessive-compulsive disorder
  assessment, 15–45. *See also*
    Assessment
  behavioral models of, 6–7
  cognitive theories, 8–10
  DSM-IV definition, 3–4
  treatment rationale, 11–13
Obsessive fears, hierarchy of, in
  vivo exposure preparation,
  exposure and response
  prevention (phase I), 168–
  169, 183–185
Onset, psychoeducation, 56–57
Organizations, psychoeducation, 59
O'Sullivan, G., 267

Paroxetine, 63
Past suffering, psychoeducation,
    58–59
Patient motivation, information
    collection, 43
Pato, M. T., 61

Perse, T. L., 60
Phobic stimuli, in vivo exposure
    preparation, exposure and
    response prevention (phase
    I), 168
Pitman, R. K., 8, 80
Prevalence, psychoeducation, 55–
    56
Principal diagnosis, 20–25
Prior treatments, information
    collection, 42–43
Psychoeducation, 47–75
    bibliography and organizations,
        59
    DSM-IV definition, 51–55
    epidemiology and course of
        disorder, 55–59
    etiology and maintenance of
        symptoms, 59–60
    evidence-based treatments, 60–
        68
        cognitive-behavior therapy,
            64–68
        medication, 61–64
    facts presentation, 50–51
    review of previous session, 49–
        50
    session goals, 48
    session overview, 49
    summary table, 74–75
    treatment components, 68–70
    treatment expectations and
        goals, 71
Punishments, response
    prevention, 220

Rabavilas, A. D., 5, 7, 64
Rachman, S. J., 5, 7, 41, 56, 57,
    64, 81, 83

Rasmussen, S. A., 55, 56, 57
Reed, G. E., 8, 80, 82, 119
Re-exposure, response prevention,
    220
Relapse prevention, 267–270. *See
    also* Maintenance and
    relapse prevention
Response prevention, 214–222.
    See also Exposure and
    response prevention
    conducting of, 215–221
    defined, 214
    described, 12–13
    goals of, 214
    imaginal exposure, 241–244
    preparation for, exposure and
        response prevention
        (phase I), 187–190
    treatment components, 70
Revised thought log, 112
Rewards, response prevention, 219
Riggs, D. S., 3, 8, 9, 12, 13, 32,
    33, 34, 38, 57, 59, 156, 195
Rituals
    avoidance and, information
        collection, 36–38
    list preparation of, exposure
        and response prevention
        (phase I), 190
    prevention methods, 190–195
    response prevention, 217
    response prevention
        preparation, exposure and
        response prevention
        (phase I), 187–190
Robins, L. N., 55
Roper, G., 5, 7, 64
Roth, A. D., 65
Rudin, E., 56

Salkovskis, P. M., xi, 8, 9–10, 11,
    65, 66, 80, 81, 82, 118
Sanderson, W. C., 25, 264
Selective serotonin reuptake
    inhibitors, psychoeducation,
    63
Self-controlled treatment, gains
    maintenance, 262–263
Self-criticism, prevention of,
    response prevention, 220–
    221
Serotonergic medication,
    psychoeducation, 61–64
Sertraline, 63
Sheehan Disability Scale, 25, 40,
    44
Silverman, W. K., 65
Spitzer, R. L., 20
Stein, D. J., 61
Stein, M. B., 56
Steiner, J., 81
Steketee, G. S., xi, 8, 9, 12, 58,
    64, 65, 81, 82, 156, 164,
    166, 191, 195
Stern, R. S., 65
Support groups, relapse
    prevention, 270

Tapering treatment, gains
    maintenance, 265–266
Thoren, P., 61

Tillmans, A., 3
Time of occurrence,
    psychoeducation, 56–57
Treatment eligibility, information
    collection, 44, 45
Tricyclic antidepressants,
    psychoeducation, 61
Tsuang, M. T., 56, 57
Turner, S. M., 65
Twin studies, psychoeducation, 58
Tynes, L. I., 25

Validity, of automatic thoughts,
    cognitive restructuring
    (phase II), 121–125
van Oppen, P., 65

Warren, R., 8, 80
Warwick, H. M. C., 65, 66
Wegner, D. M., 80
Weissman, M. M., 56
Westbrook, D., 65
Wetzler, S., 25
Wilson, G. T., 7
Wollershein, J. P., 8, 80, 82

Yale-Brown Obsessive-Compulsive
    Scale, 19

Zgourides, G. D., 8, 80
Zohar, J., 61